Carola Trips
English Syntax in Three Dimensions

Carola Trips

English Syntax in Three Dimensions

History – Synchrony – Diachrony

ISBN 978-3-11-028984-8
e-ISBN (PDF) 978-3-11-029009-7
e-ISBN (EPUB) 978-3-11-039514-3

Library of Congress Cataloging-in-Publication Data
A CIP catalog record for this book has been applied for at the Library of Congress.

Bibliographic information published by the Deutsche Nationalbibliothek
The Deutsche Nationalbibliothek lists this publication in the Deutsche Nationalbibliografie;
detailed bibliographic data are available on the Internet at http://dnb.dnb.de.

© 2015 Walter de Gruyter GmbH, Berlin/Boston
Cover image: Silvio Verrecchia/iStock/thinkstock
Printing and binding: CPI books GmbH, Leck
♾ Printed on acid-free paper
Printed in Germany

www.degruyter.com

To Ian and Sten, two great teachers

Preface

To be honest, I have always liked grammar, even in school. But the first time I was confronted with a syntactic tree at university I thought: 'Oh no, what's this?' and: 'Do they really represent sentences?' 'And why should we bother to draw them anyway?' The more I got into generative syntax, the more I understood why we should have these trees and linguistic theory. Today, as a teacher of linguistics I am often confronted with similar reactions by my students, and this is why I felt the need to write this book. I know exactly how you feel! And I also know that grammar, syntax and abstract theoretical models are hard to understand at first. At the same time they are fascinating and intriguing, especially—in my opinion—Chomsky's philosophy of language. The more I read about his ideas the more I realised that some of them had been there before and could be found way back in the history of philosophy and language, sometimes of course in a different shape. So I became interested in the history of grammatical theory which then not only helped me to better understand his theory but also, more generally, the development of other theories. The result of all this dealing with and brooding over syntax is this book.

The title and the structure of this book reflects what I have said above: I decided to call it *Syntax in three dimensions: history–synchrony–diachrony* because part I deals with the history of grammatical theory, part II with synchronic phenomena of Present-Day English, and part III with diachronic phenomena of the history of English. Of course, there's a lot to talk about so I had to make a choice. I chose the terms and phenomena which I thought have been most prominent in studying language, so for example in part I of the book you will learn that the terms 'subject' and 'predicate' have already been used by the Greeks and Romans. In part II you will then learn more about these terms and how they are applied today in an analysis of Present-Day English (PDE). In part III of the book these terms will be applied again, but this time by looking at older stages of English. So the most prominent phenomena introduced in part I will be discussed again in parts II and III of the book from different perspectives. This means that you can read the book either in a 'vertical' or 'horizontal' fashion (for example, if you're only interested in the development of English, you can read part III, although, of course, you'll miss a lot!). At the end of each chapter you will find a summary and recommendations for further reading, and in parts II and III you will also find exercises. The data presented in the exercises are all from text corpora so you can work with authentic data. There is also a webpage for this book with more material, a glossary, and model answers of the exercises (see my homepage for the link).

The aims of the book are then: 1) to provide an introduction to the history of grammatical theory in order to show how and why generative grammar evolved (alongside other theories); in this way, generative grammar is presented in its historical context, and the motivation for the ideas and assumptions of this theory becomes clear; 2) to show that the terms and phenomena discussed are still applicable and interesting today; 3) to investigate phenomena of PDE and their development in the history of English by means of authentic data, and to find explanations for the developmental paths they took by applying theory.

Throughout the book, and especially in parts II and III, English is often contrasted with German. This has to do with the fact that (most of) my students are native speakers of German and L2 learners of English. Since these languages are genetically related it is interesting to see that they developed quite differently. For example Old English (OE) had a grammatical system similar to New High German (NHG) which was lost in the course of time. As a result, PDE and NHG differ in many respects and we can investigate why that is. By contrasting the two languages we will gain insights we would not have gained if we had looked at them separately. Although English is contrasted with German in this book I am sure readers with another linguistic background will equally profit from reading it.

This book primarily aims at undergraduate students of English or linguistics who have already acquired some knowledge of syntax and generative syntactic theory. It is also well suited for students specialising in syntax, syntactic theory, and language change. It can further be used as a study aid for final exams.

This book owes a lot to my students and colleagues and could not have been written without their support. The students in my syntax classes, who were the testing ground, read versions of the book and gave me invaluable feedback. I would especially like to thank Valentina Wolf and Kevin Ehmann for reading the entire book and providing me with lists of comments which where extremely helpful in the revision process. Also thanks for your encouraging remarks! Further, I would like to thank Jonas Stork for correcting the bibliography and for working on the glossary of the website. And then, a big big thanks to you, Kirsten Alexander, for proofreading several versions of the book and for telling me that you like it a lot!

Many thanks also go to the following friends and colleagues who have generously put in their time and energy: Kristín Bjarnadóttir, Susann Fischer, Mareike Keller, Nicolas Mazziotta, Tom Rainsford and Swantje Westpfahl. Thanks for your critical comments and discussions, you helped improving the book a lot! A huuuge thanks to

Achim Stein for his everlasting support on all levels (of life)! Finally, I must not forget to thank the two people who inspired me to write this book in the first place: Ian Roberts and Sten Vikner, my great teachers in the good old Stuttgart times! Thanks, guys, for your interesting and enlightening classes, talks, discussions, and your support! I'm really grateful! And now let the journey back in time begin...

Before I forget, Syn and Tax will travel with you (yes, that's what they look like!). They will appear when something is especially noteworthy (summary of chapters) and when there is a special task for you to do (in parts II and III). Ok, now let's go!

Contents

Preface —— VII

List of abbreviations —— XIII

Part I: The history of grammar

1 Introduction —— 3

2 The Greeks and Romans and the first grammatical theory —— 6
2.1 Philosophical foundations of grammatical theory —— 6
2.2 The first Greek and Roman grammars —— 9

3 The Middle Ages —— 15
3.1 Language and the Christian Church —— 15
3.2 Scholasticism —— 19

4 Grammar in the Renaissance and the first grammars of English —— 25
4.1 Grammar in the Renaissance —— 25
4.2 The first grammars of English —— 27

5 Modern linguistics and structuralism —— 35
5.1 The nineteenth century —— 35
5.2 Structuralism —— 41

6 Chomsky and constituency grammars —— 49
6.1 The early Chomsky —— 49
6.2 The Theory of Principles and Parameters —— 55

Part II: Synchronic analysis of English syntax

7 Introduction —— 67

8 Sentence structure of Present-Day English —— 68
8.1 Constituents and constituency tests —— 68
8.2 Subjects, verbs, and negation —— 76

9 Dependency relations and linguistic universals —— 81

| 9.1 | Agreement and government in Present-Day English and New High German —— 81 |
| 9.2 | Universals revisited —— 89 |

10 Syntactic variation —— 95
| 10.1 | Standard and non-standard varieties —— 95 |
| 10.2 | Variation and parameters —— 98 |

11 Comparative syntax from a synchronic perspective —— 102
| 11.1 | Verb Second in the Germanic languages —— 102 |
| 11.2 | Verb Second in subordinate clauses —— 106 |

12 Movement and its application to the syntax of English —— 112
| 12.1 | Properties of I(nfl) —— 112 |
| 12.2 | Movement as an explanation for cross-linguistic differences —— 116 |

Part III: Diachronic analysis of English syntax

13 Introduction —— 127

14 Sentence structure of Early English —— 129
| 14.1 | Subjects, verbs, and word order in main sentences and subordinate clauses —— 129 |
| 14.2 | Negated sentences —— 142 |

15 Dependency relations in Early English —— 150
| 15.1 | Agreement and government in Early English —— 150 |
| 15.2 | Word order within the NP —— 163 |

16 Syntactic variation in Early English —— 170
| 16.1 | Variation within the verb phrase: OV and VO —— 170 |
| 16.2 | Syntactic variation and grammars in competition —— 178 |

17 Comparative syntax from a diachronic perspective —— 188
| 17.1 | Verb Second in Early English —— 188 |
| 17.2 | Loss of Verb Second in English —— 199 |

18 Syntactic movement in the history of English —— 207
| 18.1 | Loss of verb movement —— 207 |
| 18.2 | The rise of modals and *do*-support —— 216 |

Epilogue —— 225

Bibliography —— 227

Index —— 235

List of abbreviations

1-SG	First Person Singular	NEG	Negation
2-SG	Second Person Singular	NEUT	Neuter
3-SG	Third Person Singular	NHG	New High German
1-PL	First Person Plural	NOM	Nominative
2-PL	Second Person Plural	NP	Noun Phrase
3-PL	Third Person Plural	O	Object
ACC	Accusative	OE	Old English
ADJ	Adjective	OHG	Old High German
ADV	Adverb	OV	Object Verb
AUX	Auxiliary	OSV	Object Subject Verb
CP	Complementiser Phrase	OVS	Object Verb Subject
C	Complementiser	P&P	Principles and Parameters
D	Determiner	PART	Participle
DAN	Danish	PDE	Present-Day English
DAT	Dative	PF	Phonetic Form
DP	Determiner Phrase	PIE	Proto Indo-European
DUT	Dutch	PL	Plural
EModE	Early Modern English	PLD	Primary Linguistic Data
FEM	Feminine	PP	Prepositional Phrase
FRE	French	S	Sentence
G	Germanic	SG	Singular
GEN	Genitive	SOV	Subject Object Verb
ICE	Icelandic	SVO	Subject Verb Object
IND	Indicative	SWE	Swedish
I(nfl)	Inflection	UG	Universal Grammar
IP	Inflectional Phrase	V	Verb
ITA	Italian	V_{fin}	finite Verb
LAD	Language Acquisition Device	VO	Verb Object
LAT	Latin	VOS	Verb Object Subject
LF	Logical Form	VP	Verb Phrase
L2	Second Language	VSO	Verb Subject Object
MASC	Masculine	XP	any maximal projection
ME	Middle English		

Part I: **The history of grammar**

1 Introduction

This part of the book aims at providing students of linguistics with the background of the history of grammatical theory needed to understand the terminology and models of contemporary linguistics, or more precisely, grammar. These insights into former ideas about language help show things from different points of view and raise the reader's consciousness of the fact that the many ideas and models around all justify their existence, and that one's one-sidedness should be replaced by objectiveness which is essential to do science properly. This aim is pursued not only in this part of the book but also in the combination of parts one to three: only by taking a look at grammar from different perspectives—the history of grammar, synchronic and diachronic phenomena—do we get the broad perspective we need to fully understand what grammar really is.

Students of linguistics or a philology like English or German are generally introduced to the topic in their first year of study. Regardless of the definition of linguistics adopted in these classes (and textbooks used), language description, of course, always plays a prominent role. In the best case scenario, students come with some background knowledge of grammar from school and are able to apply grammatical terminology to language in an adequate way. So they will talk about nouns, verbs, adjectives, subjects and objects in a text. What most of them are not aware of is that by doing so they use terms and ideas from times when linguistics as a scientific discipline did not exist. Thus, there must have been times when people felt the need to deal with language but they had other reasons or aims to do so. Why should we, for example, divide a sentence into a subject and a predicate? What is the motivation behind it? The answer to these and similar questions can only be gained if we delve into the history of grammatical theory, which we will shortly do. It is an intriguing enterprise with 'wow' effects guaranteed!

Before we do so, however, we should at least briefly deal with the terms **grammar** and **grammatical theory**. Try to think of the meaning(s) that come to your mind without looking up the terms in a dictionary of linguistics. Most of you probably think of grammar as a formal system of a language's rules which may have the shape of a book. Quirk and Greenbaum's *A comprehensive Grammar of the English Language* would be one example. In a grammar book we find the systematic description of the rules of a (natural) language, and depending on the aim a grammarian pursues, the method can be either **descriptive** or **prescriptive**. The term descriptive refers to objectively elucidating observed properties of a language, whereas the term prescriptive refers to teaching 'proper', i.e. standardised, language. We will see that in the course of time the nature of grammars changed from being prescriptive to becoming descriptive. If you have heard of Noam Chomsky's ideas you might define grammar as the speaker's knowledge of his/her language which implies that grammar is a rather abstract notion, an internalised system in the brain of human beings. Here grammar is seen as a language theory representing the competence of a native speaker. To get to an understanding of this system, its abstract structure and form of organisation must be described and analysed.

The term grammar as such is very old and derives from Old Greek *grámma(ta)* which at that time referred to 'letter(s) of the alphabet or script', whereas *tekhnē grammatiké* referred to 'the study of the letter of the alphabet' in a very general sense. Since grammar was tightly linked to **rhetoric**, it comprised aspects of style as well as the interpretation of literary texts. Therefore, the term grammar had its broadest meaning in Classical Antiquity: it referred to the entirety of language, stylistics and rhetoric. During the Late Antiquity and the European Middle Ages the denotation of the term was narrowed and grammar was defined as a system of rules (compendium). It then acquired the status of only one part of the three verbal arts (grammar, rhetoric, dialectic), influenced by logic.

With the rise of linguistics as a scientific discipline in its own right in the nineteenth and twentieth centuries, grammar became one branch of this field. Grammatical theory subsumes many different ways of dealing with grammar, depending on the aims and purposes that its proponents think it should serve, and on the theoretical background and opinions they have about the workings of language. We have already come across the difference between prescriptive and descriptive grammars, but a further difference which will feature here prominently is the difference between **synchronic** and **diachronic** grammars. As we will see, this dichotomy, postulated by **Ferdinand de Saussure**, refers to two different ways to deal with language. Synchrony refers to the state of language existing at one point in time, whereas diachrony refers to the development of language throughout time. As already mentioned in the introduction of the book, in part II we will deal with grammar from a synchronic point of view, i.e. investigate the grammar of Present-Day English, and in part III of the book we will investigate the development of the most prominent grammatical features of English in the course of time.

Coming back to the term grammar, depending on the types of contemporary theories, we can make a distinction between **dependency grammar**, **valency grammar**, **functional grammar**, and **Generative Grammar**, just to name some of them. We will come back to these types of grammars or grammatical theories in the following sections.

Looking at the title of the book you might wonder why we have been talking about the term grammar without referring to the term **syntax**. After all the title of this textbook is *Syntax in three dimensions*. So we need to clarify that on the one hand, these terms are tightly linked, but on the other hand, they are used to refer to different aspects of language. As mentioned above, grammar refers to the study of the morphological and syntactic regularities of a language. In this traditional sense grammar deals with the formal aspects of language which can be studied independently of phonology and semantics. But since this book focuses on the investigation of phenomena in the framework of generative grammar, the definition of grammar is different: it is understood as the entire system of structural relationships, subsuming phonology, semantics, and syntax. In these terms, syntax is a subsystem of grammar which studies the interrelationships between elements of sentence structure and the rules which govern it. Thus, in the following when we talk about theoretical aspects concerning the entire system, we will use the term grammatical theory. In parts II and III of the book we will concentrate on a number of syntactic phenomena which will be predominantly explained in the framework of generative grammar. Shortly you will also see that syntax as a subdiscipline did not exist for a long time, so we will deal with grammar first and only later talk about syntax.

2 The Greeks and Romans and the first grammatical theory

2.1 Philosophical foundations of grammatical theory

As with many other things, it was the Greeks of the fifth and fourth centuries BC who started studying language in a systematic way and who set the agenda for discussing the most fundamental questions of linguistics in the western world (which is to say that this book focusses on Europe leaving out the development of linguistics in countries like India or China). They dealt with the nature of the linguistic sign, including the relationship between sound and meaning, in more general terms the relationship between language, thought, and reality, the origin of language, the nature of language change, and the analysis of linguistic structure. As you can clearly see, these are all red-hot issues that keep linguists occupied (until) today.

But why, may you ask, were the Greeks the first Europeans who started to think about language? Well, it has something to do with the way they viewed the world, which again was new. Before the Greeks, for people of the ancient Near East the world was not inherently intelligible, all things happening depended on the will of capricious gods and deities. Under such circumstances, intellectual inquiry does not arise. Of course, the Greeks also had numerous gods, and would explain a natural phenomenon such as thunder in terms of the moods of Zeus ('Zeus must be really angry today, he is thundering!'), but for them gods were not all-powerful, as opposed to the world view of the Persians or Egyptians, for example. So humans did have a free will; a nice piece of evidence can be found in the Iliad (eighth century BC) when Athena announces to Achilles 'I have come down from heaven to put a stop to your wrath - *if you consent* [emphasis inserted, CT]' (in Law (2003, 15)).

This gradual withdrawal from divine guidance led to more freedom and consequently to the development of the intellect. If gods are no longer responsible for everything then how do things happen? At that time people began to ask questions about the world, and the most general questions they sought answers to were: What is reality? Is there an absolute reality or is everything arbitrary, random and subject to change? Since the gods were no longer an authority in determining the world, people started to debate about these issues and arrived at different conclusions: intellectual disagreement was born.

During these debates and discussions a new philosophical question arose, namely, how can people claim to know about reality in the first place? And what does it mean to know something, and how is this knowledge acquired? That language plays a crucial role in answering these questions can be found directly and indirectly by pre-Socratic philosophers, the **Sophists**, **Socrates**, **Plato**, and **Aristotle**, although it should be kept in mind that only at the time of the Stoics did linguistic studies gain recognition independent of the vast field of philosophy (see below).

One of the groups that was particularly important at this time were the Sophists (fifth century BC) who taught men how to speak and which arguments to use in public debates. They showed an interest in language as an object of investigation and attributed meaning to grammatical structure. The background for their interest in language was the **naturalist-conventionalist debate** which actually affected all spheres of life, not just language. According to the naturalists (one proponent of which was Heraclitus), the shape of words and their meanings are based on natural affinity, whereas the conventionalists (one proponent of which was Democritus) claimed that this relation is based on convention and agreement. The most compelling pieces of linguistic evidence put forward by the naturalists were the etymology of words, onomatopoeia (e.g. *cock-a-doodle-doo*), and sound symbolism. The conventionalists' arguments, on the other hand, were based on the assumption that words (vocabulary) can be changed at will (e.g. if speakers decided to refer to the concept of *table* by using the word form of *chair*), and that this change does not affect the efficiency of language.

It is surprising, that Socrates (c. 470–399 BC), one of the most famous Greek philosophers, did not write anything himself during his life time. However, his arguments and viewpoints are reported by Plato (429–347 BC), one of Socrates's followers, in his famous *Dialogues of Plato*. In the *Cratylus* the naturalist-conventionalist debate is taken up again and Socrates, Plato's *alter ego*, argues in favour of a viewpoint between the two extremes: although words were created via conventions, there is an objective basis between the actual relation that exists between words and things.

It was Plato who explicitly tried to answer the questions raised above and who saw language as a route to reality as we have just seen with the example from *Cratylus*. He linked the problem of knowledge to language and assigned words a high importance, acting as a bridge between human beings, and as a means to access knowledge. Nevertheless, neither he nor his contemporaries would come to a satisfying conclusion as to whether words were a proper tool in the search for knowledge.

Apart from these invaluable insights, in his work *The Sophist* Plato develops a new model of sentence structure that was to have an enormous impact on syntactic theory. He used the terms **lógos**, **ónoma**, and **rhéma** that were translated in logic as 'proposition', 'subject', and 'predication'. He divided *lógos* into *ónoma* and *rhéma* thus assuming two parts of a sentence which are not interchangeable. This model of a sentence is tightly linked to the theory of predication in logic, where each substance has certain properties. Plato also determined the first syntactic rules: only the combination of *ónoma* and *rhéma*, i.e. the *lógos*, is meaningful, the parts of such a complete statement are not. So in this model of a sentence consisting of subject and predication we find a bidirectional relation: a thing is named (by *ónoma*), and something is said about the thing (by *rhéma*). In the context of grammar these terms were translated differently: *lógos* was the sentence, *ónoma* the noun, and *rhéma* the verb. It was not until the twelfth century that grammarians used these terms as we would use them today.

Aristotle (384–322 BC) who was Plato's pupil is certainly one of the most remarkable intellects of his time. You probably know that he worked in practically all fields of human knowledge (ethics, politics, logic, physics, biology, natural history). As with Plato, his theory of language did not come to us in one piece of work but rather in several writings. The works *De interpretatione* and the *Poetics* deal especially with ideas about language. Keep in mind, however, that his comments on the nature of language were always linked with philosophical questions. Aristotle's central question was: What constitutes real knowledge? For him, the answer lies immanently in the things themselves, and it can be induced rather than deduced. Language is seen as an instrument to think and feel, and it can only be used as tool in our search for the truth. More precisely, language is arbitrary and conventional (so it does not have truth values), but because of its functioning as a tool to search for truth, it is important to know how it works. This is why he wrote a number of treatises on the use of language.

In these treatises, Aristotle defines spoken signs as representations of impressions in the soul, and written signs as representations of the spoken ones. Just as letters are not the same for all men, so the sounds are not the same either. However, what these signs stand for—the impressions of the soul—are the same for everyone, and the real-world things of which they are the likeness are also the same.

Further, Aristotle developed formal logic to formulate the laws of thought in a way that was absolute and universally valid. Based on Plato's system, he suggested a system of propositions consisting of the following three components:
- ónoma, 'name': an utterance which has meaning by convention and lacks tense/time; no part of it has meaning by itself
- rhéma, 'predication': it signifies time, no part of it has meaning by itself, it is always a sign of something said about something else
- lógos = ónoma + rhéma

Whereas parts of sentences (words) have meaning, parts of words lack meaning (letters, sounds). Words are thus the smallest meaningful units which differ in part of speech: the verb, the noun, the adjective which is part of the class of nouns. New classes added are the indeclinable conjunction (sýndesmos) and the article (árthron).

A further step towards a discipline of grammar was taken by the **Stoics**. They were the most famous philosophical school in the ancient world, founded by **Zeno of Citium** (third century BC). In line with Plato and Aristotle, for them language was a tool to search for truth rather than a subject in its own right. Nevertheless, they dealt with language, i.e. speech, in surprising detail and understood grammar as being part of logic.

In Hellenistic times, philosophy was subdivided into **logic**, ethics and physics. Logic was further subdivided into dialectic and rhetoric. The Stoics adopted this structure but now defined logic as the central part of philosophy. They recognised the fundamental importance of language for thinking and assumed a close connection

between logic and grammar. Based on these insights, the Stoics constructed their theory of speech around the following key terms:
- **phōnē** = 'noise, sound, voice, vocal utterance'. It is a natural phenomenon and belongs to the domain of physics. Sounds can be written down and then have the status of a *lexis*.
- **lexis** = 'writeable sound'. It does not necessarily convey meaning (e.g. an onomatopoetic entity) and because it is a written utterance, it consists of smaller units, letters of the (Greek) alphabet.
- **lógos** = 'meaningful sound or utterance'. It is a meaningful word, or a sentence or part-sentence. Five parts of *lógos* can be identified: the proper noun, the common noun, the verb/predicate, the linking-word, the article.

Clearly in this theory each successive entity is a subset of the following one.

Another aspect of language that the Stoics were interested in were mental representations. They made a distinction between *sēmainon* 'that which signifies', *sēmainómenon* 'that which is signified' (quite similar to Saussure's *signifiant* and *signifié*, see chapter 5 below), and *lektón* 'that which may be put into words'. The latter term denotes something that we would describe today as speech act. The Stoics differentiated between different types of speech acts and thus actually developed a syntactic theory which was based on predicates. Surprisingly, in the years to come this quite progressive idea was not pursued any further.

2.2 The first Greek and Roman grammars

The era of Socrates, Plato, and Aristotle could be described as a period of rapid intellectual change. What followed was a period of consolidation in the Hellenistic age (323–30 BC). Greek scholarship became the centre of the written word, manuscripts were copied and spread (although still passed on by word or mouth); Alexandria was the cultural centre famed for the study of literary texts and for famous scholars like Aristophanes of Byzantium or Aristarchus. Throughout that time the term 'grammar' referred to literary and textual criticism (compare Greek **tekhnē grammatikē**, Latin **ars grammatica**). **Dionysius Thrax** (170–90 BC), a pupil of Aristarchus, is said to have written the first grammar of Greek although today a number of scholars raise doubts about the authenticity of parts of the work. Be that as it may, the work called the *tekhnē grammatikē* is still closely connected with the name Dionysius Thrax. The work contains twenty sections and begins with an exposition of the context of studies: 'Grammar is the practical knowledge of the general usages of poets and prose writers' (Robins, 1994, 31). Obviously, for the author aspects like the interpretation of texts were part of grammar. Other aspects discussed are accurate reading, phraseology, etymology, and analogical regularities. In the strictly grammatical section, Thrax distinguishes eight word classes: the noun, the verb, the participle, the article, the pronoun, the preposition, the adverb and the conjunction. This system will remain valid until modern times.

Interestingly, Thrax distinguishes between inflecting parts of speech (the first five) and non-inflecting parts of speech (the last three). Moreover, two main categories, noun and verb, are subject to a formal distinction: nouns inflect for case, verbs do not. Further he provides a differentiated classification of nouns (into categories like case, number, gender, derived, underived, etc.) and verbs (into categories like tense, person, mode, etc.). One shortcoming of this otherwise very impressive work is that the central aspect of syntax is not mentioned at all.

During the Golden Age of Greece (400 BC) and the era of the Hellenistic World, Greek culture had a massive influence on the Roman world (Italy) in terms of achievements in intellectual and cultural life, especially spreading from the Greek province (present-day Calabria) also where the Pythagorean school was to be found. Up until the first century BC, the Greek influenced and determined Roman intellectual life: Greek was used for (philosophical) writings, it was taught by Greek slaves (who were called *pedagogus*), and young Romans went to Greek universities. Greeks experienced their language from within (as native language) whereas the Romans reflected about language through the eyes of the Greeks (by reading Greek works) because they had the status of foreign language learners. The Roman grammatical tradition emerged as an amalgam of the logical analysis of propositions and more formal concerns of later writers.

The Romans predominantly adapted to the grammatical standard the Greeks had set. They innovated this standard only in so far as they had to allow for small changes by transferring the Greek system to their language. As a result, they very often kept grammatical rules for phenomena they did not even have in their own language. Most of the Roman grammars emerging in the first century BC exhibit a rigid structure including the three levels: phonology, morphology and rhetoric.

So, rhetoric was an integral part in most of the Roman grammars. At that time it was highly important that boys destined for a political career were schooled in rhetoric to become eloquent and to have a command of classical authors. One piece of work which shows how rhetoric was taught is the *Institutio oratoria* ('Educating the orator') by **Marcus Fabius Quintillian** (ca. 35 AD-100AD). He was a literary critic and educationalist; in his work he dedicates himself predominantly to describing the ideal education of an orator and the classical canon of Greek and Latin works. But since a good knowledge of grammar was part of a good education, grammar is dealt with in some chapters. More precisely, students had to learn letters, speech sounds, the parts of speech, and the prescriptive use of grammar.

One of the greatest of all Roman scholars at that time is **Marcus Terentius Varro** (116–27 BC). He was a polymath well versed in Greek and Latin literature, Roman history and antiquities, and Greek philosophy. His copious writings deal with practically all subjects known at that time. His principal work on language, *De lingua latina* (47–45 BC), is a treatise on fundamental linguistic issues. The book is divided into three parts according to the threefold nature of speech: 'The imposition of names upon things' including principles of etymology, 'Modifications in the form of original words' (which he called *declinatio*) including a discussion on **analogy** and **anomaly** in language, and 'Bringing words together to express a meaning' including a discussion of how to conjoin words in the Stoic tradition. The term *declinatio* that Varro uses here does not have the same meaning as it has for us today. For him, the term denotes the morphological variation of words in a very general way. He proposes a system of word formation processes which makes a distinction between derivation being subject to processes of anomaly, and inflection being subject to processes of analogy. This system reflects a long-standing debate between scholars at that time whether the structure of language follows a rigid system (analogy) or whether it does not (anomaly). In the latter case, systematic aspects of language are explained by convention.

This distinction had already been the topic in the naturalist-conventionalist debate during the Golden Age of Greece. According to the naturalists/analogists, language is ordered, it strictly follows rules and is completely regular. According to the conventionalists/anomalists, language is chaotic; it is full of irregularities and exceptions that cannot be explained by rules. Varro sees himself as a moderate proponent of the analogists and a mediator between the two camps. His aim is to discover the absolutely true aspects of language, which means that surface phenomena have to be linked to analogical processes in the world to redeem language from **arbitrariness**. Based on these assumptions, classes of words are strictly categorised along formal aspects disregarding semantic and functional issues. As a consequence, we do not find an elaboration of the eight classes of the parts of speech we have come across before but a system of linguistic entities which is entirely subject to morphological aspects. Words are classified according to the presence/absence of case and tense marking: words showing both types of marking are participles, words showing only case are nouns (including adjectives), words showing only tense are verbs, and words lacking both types of marking are adverbs.

For some time the classifications and theories proposed in the works of Varro and others were simply adopted by their successors dealing with language. What became more and more important was the teaching of a language, which was concomitant with the process of standardisation. This new interest in pedagogical issues finally led to the rise of a new genre of grammar which the German classicist Karl Barwick named **Schulgrammatik** ('school grammar'). But it was also the orientation of the language learners which shaped the grammars occurring at that time. You know from your own learning experience that pedagogical works for native speakers look different from those for speakers learning a second language. So the *Schulgrammatik* genre with a focus on semantic aspects was geared for native speakers of Latin whereas the so-called **regulae** genre was geared for foreign students of Latin. In the next chapter, we will come back to this classification.

Although Varro had paved the way for establishing a Roman grammar, Roman grammarians preferred to adapt the Greek style grammar. The reason for this may lie in the fact that both students of Latin and Greek (being native speakers) predominantly studied literary texts which required the knowledge of semantic, formal and functional categories, and not just formal aspects of language. So following Greek grammars the new *Schulgrammatik* type comprises the following features: it displays a rigorously hierarchical structure and a systematic structure within chapters. It follows a logical organisation which reflects the presumed logical structure of language. It further has a tendency to foreground semantic categories with the result that formal categories are relegated to second place or are omitted altogether. To make things more tangible, let's take a brief look at the two most famous grammars of the Roman world, the *Ars maior* ('Longer Grammar') and the *Ars minor* ('Shorter Grammar') by **Aelius Donatus** (fourth century AD). Both works were so popular that they were studied and consulted continuously up to the sixteenth century, and they served as a model for many works of grammar up until the early modern period.

The *Ars maior* is divided into three books and organised according to the norms of dialectic. The first book deals with sounds and syllables, the second book with the parts of speech (still eight classes!), and the third book with the so-called 'vices and virtues' of speech. Due to the fact that rhetoricians and literary critics were preoccupied with stylistics, they were very much interested in 'correct speech'. So for the reader it was important to be able to identify deviations from the norm: on the one hand the usages that should not be imitated (barbarisms and solecisms), and on the other hand stylistic devices that adorned discourse (metaplasms, schemes, tropes). The hierarchical structure of the work seeks to mirror the nature/structure of language (**isomorphism**), summed up in the saying 'Every sentence can be divided into words, and words can be divided into syllables, and syllables into litterae, but there is nothing into which litterae can be divided' (cited in Law, 2003, 67). This structure is motivated by the conviction that language is a natural phenomenon, that the world is logically organised and hence language is also logically organised.

The *Ars minor* is small in scale (only eleven pages long), geared for beginners and deals with parts of speech in a question-and-answer pattern. The treatment of the noun looks like this:

> What is a noun?
> It is a part of speech and signifies either an object or a notion,
> and is either proper or common.
> How many properties does the noun have?
> Six.
> What are they?
> Quality, comparison, gender, number, composition, case.
> [...]
> (from Law 2003:71f)

Although Donatus's grammars provide an inventory of basic notions like gender, derivation, composition, number, case, tense, person, mood, voice, conjugation, and an extensive semantic classification of noun, adverb, and conjunction, they are not a comprehensive description of inflectional morphology of Latin. This means that no non-native speaker could have learnt Latin by means of these grammars. But that was not Donatus's aim, he taught children (and their teachers) what to think about their language. So his works are clearly targeted at native speakers who want to learn more about their mother tongue.

Above, we mentioned another genre emerging at that time: the *regulae* grammars. This type of grammar was designed for foreign learners of Latin. The term *regulae* which is the plural form of *regula* has the meaning 'rule, model, pattern, paradigm' and covers a wide array of nouns, often in alphabetical form. The aim of a *regulae* is to point to patterns in a paradigmatic fashion so that learners of Latin can make generalisations. Under emperor Traian, the year 117 AD saw the Roman empire reach its greatest extent, with the result that Romans increasingly came into contact with other peoples and languages. So the need to teach Latin became more and more important.

Some grammarians tried to unite a work of the *Schulgrammatik* type with one of the *regulae* type. They did not succeed however, to fuse the two different ways of dealing with different aspects of language, and the result was a grammar with chunks of *Schulgrammatik* alongside chunks of *regulae*. One of these grammarians was **Priscian** (500 AD). Although he was not really successful in integrating form and meaning in a unified way, he became nevertheless one of the most influential Latin grammarians of the ancient world. Priscian did not have the same aim as Donatus; he was more oriented towards theory and wanted to teach his pupils how to think. In his three main works, the *Partitiones*, the *Institutio de nomine*, and the *Institutiones grammaticae*, he provides theoretical argumentations and a vast amount of data to test the theories. The first book mentioned here, is a linguistic analysis of a literary text (the *Aeneid*) in the same question-and-answer style we came across above in the *Ars minor*. The second work, the *Institutio de nomine* is a small piece of work of only fourteen pages and contains a systematic framework for a comprehensive description of Latin forms. Although it belongs to the *regulae* genre it is much more systematic than any other *regulae* work. The *Institutiones grammaticae* is the biggest and most famous of Priscian's works. It contains eighteen books and is somewhat a fusion of *Schulgrammatik* and *regulae*. Every aspect of inflectional and derivational morphology of Latin is recorded and illustrated with literary examples. But what makes the work so unique is that two books are solely devoted to syntax. Priscian discusses syntactic notions like **government**, ellipsis and **transitivity**, and the model he chose was a **dependency model** rather than a **constituency model** (we will come back to these terms below and in parts II and III of the book), because his main aim was to understand how one word affects another. When Priscian's work was rediscovered in medieval times (around 800 AD), many scholars were stimulated to devote themselves to syntactic problems.

Tax: 'So, Syn, what have we learnt in this chapter?'
Syn: 'In the first part we have learnt that Plato, Aristotle, and the Stoics claimed that language is a tool to find the knowledge of thought and reality, so language was not seen as a phenomenon worthy of investigation in its own right. But since language is a tool to get to the truth, it is important to understand it. So the first assumptions about grammar emerge in the context of philosophical questions. The analysis of a sentence as a unit (proposition) consisting of a noun and a verb provided the basis for the development of a sentence model where the subject and the predicate are in an interchangeable bidirectional relation.'
Tax: 'And what about Greek grammars and the Romans?'
Syn: 'In the second part we have seen that Roman Grammars are based on Greek Grammars. Whereas Greek Grammars included innovative aspects, Roman Grammars took up these aspects and sought to adapt them to didactic needs. Donatus and Priscian are the two most famous authorities of traditional grammar, but only Priscian really dealt with syntactic phenomena like government or transitivity.'

Literature: Since the topic is so intriguing much has been written on the history of grammatical theory and linguistics. This is why it is quite hard to find a way through the sheer mass of literature and to identify (text)books which provide a good overview, and at the same time invite the reader to get engaged in the topic in an appealing way. In my opinion, the book which fulfils all of these criteria is Vivian Law's *The History of Linguistics in Europe from Plato to 1600* from 2003. The book also includes a wealth of material, additional topics of discussion in extra text boxes, and many bibliographical references to all epochs, schools of thought and scholars discussed. The German equivalent can be seen in Jungen & Lohnstein's *Geschichte der Grammatiktheorie. Von Dionysios Thrax bis Noam Chomsky* (2007). It is even more comprehensive because it discusses a larger time span. Moreover, there is a smaller and more compact version of the book which serves really well to get into the topic (for those who can read German): *Einführung in die Grammatiktheorie* (2006). I should not forget to mention Robins's *A Short History of Linguistics* (1994) and Parret's (1976) collection of essays with the title *History of Linguistic Thought and Contemporary Linguistics*. Concerning works on Greek and Roman grammars I refer you to Robins (1985), Robins (1993) and Swiggers (2002), the collection of articles in Taylor (1987) and a work by Egli (1986) on the Stoics. On archive.org editions of the dialogues of Plato and Aristotle's *Physics* can be read online as well as Priscian's *Institutiones grammaticae* and Donatus's *Ars minor* (1446).

3 The Middle Ages

3.1 Language and the Christian Church

Many of the grammatical categories which are used today were developed during Antiquity. The modern concept of grammar, however, developed during the Middle Ages, and Christianity and the Christian Church played an important role. We can say that from late Antiquity to the central Middle Ages (ca. 400–1200), or from Priscian to the Northern Renaissance (ca. 500–1500) linguistics was converted to Christianity, meaning that traditional Greek-Roman ideas were permeated with Christian attitudes.

We can subdivide the Middle Ages into four main periods (Law, 2003): first, the early Middle Ages (500–800), which were very much influenced by the traditions of Late Antiquity. Recall from the previous chapter that two main types of grammar originate from that time: the *Schulgrammatik* and the *regulae* of Donatus as well as Priscian's short text *Institutio de nomine et pronomine et verbo*. A third type is constituted by Late Latin commentaries on these works. These works were used as a source by western European scholars with the aim to write descriptive grammars of Latin for non-native speakers. The second subperiod is the central Middle Ages (800–1100), spanning from the Carolingian Renaissance to the twelfth-century Renaissance. This period is characterised by the rediscovery of Aristotle's works (especially the *Categories* and the *De Interpretatione*) as well as Priscian's *Institutiones grammaticae*. These grammars were used as models to rethink the nature and role of grammar, and a new grammar type developed to fulfil didactic needs. Ælfric's *Latin Grammar* and *Colloquium* (Latin conversation book) along with a Latin-Old English glossary are good examples of this type. It was written around 1000 for English children speaking Old English. The third subperiod is known as the **Scholastic** era (1100–1350) in which further works of Aristotle were discovered. In the newly founded universities, scholastic philosophers dealt with linguistic studies from both a theoretical and a practical perspective. In schools preparing pupils for university another type of grammar, called **verse grammar**, developed. These grammars consisted of a long verse of Latin grammar dealing with parts of speech, syntax, quantity, metre, and figures of speech. The fourth period can be defined as the end of the Middle Ages (1350–1500) during which a vernacular consciousness developed which led to the fact that Latin began to be taught through the medium of vernacular(s). As we will see, this development is also highly relevant in the Renaissance (1450–1600) which we will address in the next chapter. In the following we will briefly discuss the main aspects of the study of language throughout the Middle Ages, and we will start out by asking the question of why Christianity and the Christian Church played such an important role.

The deposition of the last Roman emperor, Romulus Augustulus in 476 marks the end of the Roman empire. The collapse of the institutional structures was absorbed by the Church, and it took over the responsibility for the maintenance of literacy and learning. It simultaneously functioned as the teacher, librarian and transmitter of Graeco-Roman civilisation. As a result, intellectual life was taken care of by the Church, and even universities started out as religious institutions.

According to the position of the Western Church, Christians shouldn't make up their own minds on intellectual issues and questions such as whether Christ was wholly divine, wholly human, or somehow divine and human at the same time. To deal with such issues without having the authority was seen as being dangerous because it might lead to heresy. Thus, only through the Church could Christians learn the truth about intellectual and spiritual matters, and this meant that the Church proscribed what was correct (orthodoxy) and incorrect belief (heresy). We should, however, keep in mind that the Christian world at that time was not uniform at all. Whereas the Western Church was based on a Roman background and emphasised order and authority, the Eastern Church was much more influenced by the heritage of Greek philosophy and language, and emphasised that an individual himself is able to attain knowledge of higher matters directly. This clear difference between the Eastern and the Western Church led to tensions and resulted in the Great Schism (1054): the Catholic Church separated from the Orthodox Church.

When we think about the Catholic Church and which text might say something about language, it is of course the Bible that springs to mind. But from what we said above it is clear that no lay person at that time dared to read and interpret the Bible without the aid of a revered exegete. Saint Augustine (354–430) was such an authority, he is the first known Christian who wrote on linguistic issues from a Christian point of view. He was convinced that the best path to knowledge of divine and incorporeal matters was via what we perceive. He composed a number of textbooks on the **Seven Liberal Arts** which consisted of seven disciplines which were divided into two groups: the *trivium* comprising grammar, rhetoric, and dialectic (the language arts), and the *quadrivium* comprising arithmetic, music, geometry, and astronomy (mathematical arts). In his *De quantitatae animae* he makes an influential difference between the form and the meaning of words:

> The word consists of sound and meaning. The sound belongs to the ears and the meaning to the mind. Don't you think, then, that in the word, as in any living creature, the sound is the body and the meaning is, as it were, the soul of the sound?
> (in Law 2003:107)

For him and many other medieval scholars, the sound (*vox*, Greek *phono*), i.e. the word form, is much less important than the meaning (*verbum*, Greek *lógos*) because it is temporal, transient and thus not of interest. In more general terms, scholars at that time believed that everything which is constantly changing is ephemeral and unreliable and cannot point to enduring spiritual reality.

Let's take a quick look at one of the few passages in the Bible which directly addresses language: the origin of linguistic diversity in the story about the Tower of Babel:

> And the LORD came down to see the city and the tower, which the children of men builded. And the LORD said, Behold, the people *is* one, and they have all one language; and this they begin to do: and now nothing will be restrained from them, which they have imagined to do. Go to, let us go down, and there confound their language, that they may not understand one another's speech. So the LORD scattered them abroad from thence upon the face of all the earth: and they left off to build the city. Therefore is the name of it called Babel; because the LORD did there confound the language of all the earth: and from thence did the LORD scatter them abroad upon the face of all the earth.
> (Genesis 11:5–9, from the *King James Bible* online)

For Saint Augustine, the rise of linguistic diversity was a catastrophic event, the divine punishment for human arrogance. The true and original Adamic language was lost forever. Since linguistic forms were seen as being temporal and constantly changing, we will neither find a historical approach to language nor an interest in phonetics, phonology, morphology, nor in varieties and comparisons with other languages. Clearly, the need to escape from the arbitrariness of the word was still felt at that time (recall the debate of the Greeks from the previous chapter). The only aspect of language which was worth investigating was meaning: lexical and sentence meaning, illocutionary force, and sentence structure. Studying these aspects of language implies dealing with logic, perception, and real-world problems, and medieval scholars would have preferred to concentrate on these aspects which for them pointed beyond material life on earth to spiritual matters. But, as we will shortly see, the language policy of the Western Church compelled them to focus on grammatical aspects of language.

The aim of medieval scholars to concentrate on the transcendental nature of language can be seen in the way they dealt with form. Let's take a look at the following example from a grammar written at that time:

> How many vowels are there? Five.
> What are they? A e i o u.
> Why five?
> Because the body has five senses and the mind has five, too.
> What are the senses of the mind? Love, fear, joy, sadness, and hatred.
> Why do the vowels not occur together in the alphabet?
> Because the consonants are supported by the vowels in the same way that a house is supported by pillars.
> (in Law 2003:119)

This is a description of vowels and consonants that you have probably not come across so far. But what is so peculiar about it? What the grammarian does here is seek answers to questions in a **correlative** way, which is to say that he establishes a mutual relationship between a linguistic phenomenon and a non-linguistic phenomenon such as the senses. In this way, a form without meaning is attributed a 'spiritual truth'.

As mentioned above, the language policy of the Western Church focussed on the formal aspects of language and not on meaning. Whereas Eastern Christians used their native languages to translate the Scriptures and to write theological treatises (the problem of learning a foreign language hardly arose), Western Christians did not have an established literary tradition in their native languages, since Latin, being a foreign language to these people, had been the language of administration, education and culture for some time. The Western Church adopted this policy and assigned Latin the status of the language of cultural and ecclesiastical life. As a result, great efforts had to be made to teach Latin to native speakers of German, Celtic, and Slavic origins, and literate persons were obliged to deal with (foreign) linguistic form on a basic level by means of grammars. But the problem was that the works of the Latin grammarians were written for native speakers and therefore could not be used by people with no command of Latin. So a solution was needed for those who learned Latin, which were mainly oblates in monasteries and convents. The problem was solved by complementing passive exposure to a spoken form of Latin during church services with systematic instruction using **descriptive grammars**, and this implied using textbooks of Latin for foreign learners.

The starting point for teaching Latin was to supplement Donatus's *Ars minor* with the *Declinationes nominum*. These were little treatises with additional material that consisted of paradigms for nouns and verbs. Since learners of Latin lacked a good knowledge of the morphology of this language, teachers often reorganised noun groups according to grammatical aspects like gender or language origin. The conjugation of verbs was felt to be easier because verbs could be categorised into a group of regular and a group of irregular verbs. The importance of these little collections of paradigms must not be underestimated: for the first time, people started to think about the inner logic in the formal structure of language.

Generally, a medieval grammar was structured according to the following main aspects: letters (*litterae*), syllables (*syllabae*), parts of speech (*partes orationis*) and syntax (*constructio*). Metrics and figures of speech were also part of it. Forming a syntagma (i.e. a structured syntactic sequence of linguistic elements) by combining parts of speech required **agreement** (*congruitas*) between these units as well as conditions that define the proper formation of complete expressions (*perfectio*). The way phrases stand in relation to each other was characterised as dependency, and the relation was expressed by saying that one word governs (*regere*) another. Below, we will take a closer look at these terms and definitions.

As we have seen, the perspectives of ancient and early Christian thinkers differed from medieval thinkers: whereas ancient thinkers looked at their native language from an internal perspective and focussed on orality, the early Christian thinkers viewed Latin from the outside, as foreigners, and had to rely on the written language. But we must not forget that in medieval times the mode of reading (and teaching) was an oral/aural one, and this is also reflected in the way paradigms were represented. Teachers at that time relied on the so-called word-and-paradigm model which showed an example of an inflecting word with its different forms in linear order, one after the other in running text. Since the different forms were read out aloud, differences were easily identified. It was not common at all to present different grammatical forms of a word in columns as we do today. Only gradually did teachers and scribes become aware of the word as having a shape of its own which then led to an interest in morphological analysis.

3.2 Scholasticism

For the science of linguistics, the third subperiod of the Middle Ages, as we have defined it above, was more significant. It is the era of Scholasticism (1100–1350) during which theology and philosophy was taught in universities based on Aristotelian logic, Priscian's *Institutione grammaticae* and writings of Christian scholars. It is also a time where linguistic studies had an important place and where a notable amount of linguistic work was carried on.

Until the eleventh century most scholarly work had taken place in monasteries like Fleury in France, St Gall in Switzerland, Ramsey in Great Britain, and on the island of Reichenau in Germany. But between the ninth and the eleventh centuries schools started to be set up in towns close to cathedrals, and became more and more popular because they were more open than the monastic schools. In the thirteenth century some of these cathedral schools developed into universities, among them the universities of Paris and Oxford. There were clear differences between a university and a cathedral or monastic school: in universities a structured course with well-defined stages was offered which spread over several years. Students had to read certain texts on which they also had to attend lectures a set number of times. Moreover, universities granted degrees, and they were publicly recognised, generally in the form of a charter from the Pope or King. Universities had a Faculty of Arts, or even a Faculty of Grammar as in Oxford and Cambridge, where students attended courses on Aristotle's logical works and Priscian's grammar. After their graduation they could go on studying at one of the higher faculties like law, theology and medicine. In Oxford and Cambridge students were also trained to become teachers in grammar schools, where Latin, the language of the most influential scientific works, was taught.

Until that point, the aim of linguistic work had been pedagogical, applied to the teaching of Latin. So we can call these works **practical grammars**. In the scholastic period, however, a new type of grammar arose: the ***speculative*** grammar with a focus on theoretical aspects of language. The term *speculative* derives from Latin *speculum* 'mirror' which indicates the belief that language reflects the reality underlying the physical world. Thus, speculative grammarians assumed a one-to-one relation between linguistic categories, mental categories, and **universals,** i.e. properties common to all languages (a universal grammar in this sense would thus be a grammar valid for all languages). The driving force was the urge to rescue language from its arbitrariness (recall that this was already an issue in Antiquity) by showing the link between language and external reality. Scholars writing this type of grammar integrated grammatical description of Latin as formulated by Priscian and Donatus into scholastic philosophy.

Although two of Aristotle's treatises on logic (the *Categories* and *De interpretatione*) were known and available in the Latin West, it was only with the rediscovery of the translations of Boethius, a Roman scholar and Christian philosopher, of the remaining logical, physical, and metaphysical writings in the twelfth century that scholars became influenced by Aristotle's way of thinking about language and about extra-linguistic reality. Moreover, they started to become more critical about authoritative works like Priscian's *Institutiones grammaticae*. The result was that medieval grammarians started to see aspects of language in a new light. In his work *Physics* Aristotle defines motion as any kind of change, and related to language, '... of that which affirms or denies a predicate' (Law, 2003, 166), as well as the subject and the goal of motion (Ibid.). These ideas were transferred to syntax by medieval grammarians although Priscian had already described the relation between the elements of a sentence in terms of motion: 'the transition of the action from one word to another'.

In the twelfth century, in treatises on syntax, two concepts start to occur:
1. **regimen** 'government': the term describes relations where one word 'governs' another with the result that the governed word occurs in a particular case.
2. **congruitas** 'agreement': the term describes relations which involve agreement, i.e. two words enter into a relationship such that their properties have to be the same.

Regimen had been part of grammars since Hugo of Saint Victor's (1096–1141) work. Grammarians and teachers based their works on these definitions and listed all the (Latin) cases and the way they were used. One example is:

(1) lego   librum
     read-1-SG book-ACC-SG
     'I am reading a book.'

One grammarian comments on the relationship between the words in the following way:

> *Librum* is in the accusative case and is governed by the verb *lego* as the second element by virtue of transitivity in accordance with this rule: every transitive verb used transitively governs one or more accusatives to which the action of the verb passes [...]
> (in Law, 2003, 167)

Concerning *congruitas* or agreement, the following comment is found (note that *suppositum* stands for *subiectum* and *appositum* stands for *predicatum*):

> The first agreement is of the *suppositum* with the *appositum*, e.g. *homo currit* 'a person is running'. *Homo* 'person' is the *suppositum*, *currit* 'runs' is the *appositum*. The same number and person

are required in them both, and the nominative case of the noun signifying substantivally should correspond to a finite mood in the verb.
(in Law, 2003, 167)

The new aspect of motion was included in the description of syntactic relations between words, and the notion of **dependency** was introduced: motion passed from the dependent element (*dependens*) to the element which terminated the dependency (*terminans*). So in a sentence with a **transitive** verb like:

(2) *Socrates   legit   librum*
     Socrates-NOM-SG read-3-SG book-ACC-SG
     'Socrates is reading the/a book.'
     (in Law, 2003, 167)

two dependency relations hold: one between the subject and the verb, and one between the verb and the object. More precisely, the verb *legit* depends on the subject *Socrates* and on the object *librum*. Note that this notion of dependency deviates from the modern notion defined by Lucien Tésniere (see also chapter 9): in the modern model the verb is seen as the central element and thus the absolute governor. Thus, the verb *legit* in the example above governs both *Socrates* and *librum*.

In the quotation above it was mentioned that the terms *suppositum* and *appositum* stand for the logical terms **subiectum** and **predicatum** respectively. Here we see an important difference between the way the grammarians at that time analysed a sentence and the way the logicians did (recall Plato's and Aristotle's model briefly discussed in chapter 2). For logicians, the unit under scrutiny was a complete, meaningful utterance, the proposition, which was divided into two constituents: that about which something is said, which was called *subiectum* in Latin, and that which is said about it, which was called *predicatum* in Latin. So their constituent approach stood in contrast with the grammarian's dependency approach. It took centuries until the constituent approach was taken up and further developed, also then integrating the terms *subject* and *predicate* into today's grammatical model.

Concerning the formal side of language, at first sight, speculative grammars seemed to follow the grammatical tradition. They accurately preserved Priscian's Latin morphology, and they took for granted the classification of the eight parts of speech and the description of their grammatical properties. On closer inspection, however, speculative grammarians took these as a starting point and provided the basis for an ontological framework. Their aim was to establish how each grammatical category is related to reality. Some grammarians, like Petrus Helias writing in the 1140s, critically commented on Priscian's word classes and sought philosophical explanations for these categories. In his *Summa super Priscianum* ('Compendium on Priscian') he noted that Priscian's statements were partly unordered and that he gave definitions without explanations. For example, Priscian defined the verb on the basis of what is proper to it:

> It is proper to the verb to signify action or passivity or both with moods and forms and tenses and without case.
> (in Law, 2003, 172)

Helias realised that the criteria of form, syntax, distribution, semantics, and function were lumped together and made a significant change in defining the word classes based on one single *semantic* criterion: the **modus significandi** 'manner of signifying'. The different *modi significandi* are those aspects of meaning and denotation that were thus significant for the classification of the parts of speech. For example, to establish the identity of the word class of the verb he suggested the following definition:

> There is another *modus significandi* to signify action or passivity, and on account of this *modus significandi* the verb was created.
> (in Law, 2003, 173)

By introducing the *modi significandi*, Helias provided a grammar which was more coherent and which postulated a universally valid principle. This principle was based on the central hypothesis of the speculative grammarians which said that grammatical rules are extra-linguistically determined: by thought or the nature of real-world things. Helias paved the way for further work by speculative grammarians and for the rise of the modistic grammar.

In the thirteenth century the *modi significandi* were more and more linked with the properties of concepts. Some writers discussing a number of linguistic topics had made the important semantic distinction between the *significatio* and the *suppositio*. *Significatio* denotes the meaning of a word and can be defined as the relation between the sign or word and what it signifies. *Suppositio* denotes a substitute and defines the acceptance of a substantive verb for some thing. So for example, *homo* means 'man', and *homo* or *man* can stand for a referent in the real world, i.e. Socrates, Saussure or Chomsky. When *significationes* of more than one word are brought together in phrases or constructions, their *suppositio* may be restricted by this. Thus *homo adolescens* means 'young man' and can only be said for men who are young but not for men who are old or for young beings who are not men. This distinction is principally a current one, and be found in binary oppositions as meaning and reference, connotation and denotation, and intension and extension. During the times when modistic grammar developed, the focus of the relation defined by *significatio* shifted from the word itself (signifier) to what it signifies (signified). In the 1260s and 1270s the linking of the properties of words with the properties of real-world phenomena via the properties of concepts was undertaken by a number of scholars who are known today as **Modists**.

In the modistic system, we find real-world things or phenomena (*res*) and their various properties or modes of being (*modi essendi*). We further have concepts in the mind (*res intellecta*), and the mind apprehends the *modi essendi* by the modes of understanding (*modi intellegendi*). In language, we have the signified in the word (*res significata*) and its properties, the *modi significandi*. The Danish grammarian **Martin of Dacia** (1220–1304) explains the process of whereby linguistic categories are derived from real-world things in the following way: real-world things have many properties like action, rest, plurality, etc. When we start to think about such a real-world thing we, i.e. our mind, grasps its nature by apprehending its properties. We then form a concept of the real-world thing and of its properties. When we want to talk about this real-world thing, i.e. to signify its concept to someone else, we have to express it linguistically by uttering a spoken word (*vox*) to express it. Under these assumptions, the spoken word is the signifier of the concept. What is most important is that the properties of the sign are derived from the properties of the concept of the real-world thing. This is to say that the *modi significandi* (grammatical properties of the parts of speech) are ultimately derived by the real-world properties of the real-world thing which the spoken word via its concept ultimately denotes.

Having read the description of modistic grammar it must have become clear to you that it was an enterprise which aimed at systematically linking the properties of word classes with the properties of concepts, and finally with the properties of universals. All of the *modi* discussed above—the *modi essendi*, the *modi intellegendi*, and the *modi significandi*—were seen as being universal. This is why it has been said that it was the first **Universal Grammar** in the history of grammatical/linguistic theory. As you can well imagine, modern scholars interested in linguistic universals like Chomsky and others have paid a lot of attention to the Modists and their grammar.

Some scholars were highly critical of modistic grammar because they claimed that defining language on the basis of grammaticality would not suffice. Therefore, they proposed a grammar which accounted for the grammaticality and ungrammaticality of utterances, and the performative nature of utterances. Proponents of the intentionalist grammar like Roger Bacon and Robert Kilwardby included both speaker and hearer, and incorporated the notion of the speaker's intention into their theory. For them, two levels of sense had to be distinguished: the initial understanding (*intellectus primus*) which operates on the level of the *modi significandi*, and the secondary understanding (*intellectus secundus*) which operates on the level of the signified (compare Saussure's notion of the *signifié* in chapter 5). In a sentence like:

(3)   *The crowd are rushing.*

there is a mismatch: the finite verb does not agree with the singular form of the subject. Using the plural form of the verb can be explained by the intrinsic property of a crowd consisting of many individuals. For Bacon, Kilwardby and others the speaker's intention (*intentio proferentis*) causes the violation of a grammatical rule. This understanding of grammar (or grammatical theory) can clearly be seen as the precursor of pragmatics. As today, such an account challenges any syntactic or semantic theory which claims total explanatory validity on its own.

The so-called **Nominalists** were another group of scholars who attacked the Modistic grammar; for them the notion of universals was not tenable. **William of Ockham** (ca. 1285–1347), a proponent of this group, assumed that there is no one-to-one relation between linguistic and mental categories and hence there would also not be universals. For him, words existed on three levels: the mental word (*oratio mentalis*), the spoken word (*oratio vocalis*), and the written word (*oratio scripta*). Whereas the mental word signifies naturally, the spoken and written word only signify by convention. A linguistic phenomenon speaking in favour of these assumptions was taken to be synonyms which may be different on the spoken and written level but still denote the same concept. Thus, if there is a mismatch between the spoken/written word and the mental word, how can we be sure that there isn't such a mismatch between grammatical categories and properties? Although the ideas of the Nominalists spread across Europe and found quite a number of supporters, the quest for universals of language remained very attractive until modern times.

Syn: 'Now it's your turn, Tax. What have we learnt in this chapter?'
Tax: 'Well, first, we said that the modern concept of grammar developed during the Middle Ages, and that the Christian Church played an important part. Just like the Greeks, medieval scholars felt the need to escape from the arbitrariness of the word, and the only way to do so was to investigate the meaning of language because it pointed beyond material life on Earth to spiritual matters. Linguistic form, however, was seen as being temporal and consistently changing and thus not worth investigating. Although many scholars would have liked to concentrate on these aspects, the aim of the Church was to teach Latin to speakers with no command of the language. The result was that many practical grammars were written for this purpose. Due to the rise of scholastic philosophy the interest in writing speculative grammars grew. So for example concepts from logic like subject and predicate were transferred to language, and as a result the function of subject and predicate in sentences were discussed in more and more detail.'
Syn: 'And what about the dependency relations of government and agreement?'
Tax: 'We have seen that the terms 'government' and 'agreement' came up at that time and were thoroughly studied in Latin examples. But one of the most important aspects for modern grammatical theory was the aim of speculative grammarians to identify universals, i.e. different types of *modi*, which underlie grammatical rules. The belief in these universals led to the emergence of a number of modistic grammars. Although the notion of universals was debated the quest for them never ceased.'

Literature: Law (1993) deals with grammatical theory in the Early Middle Ages, and in Law (1997) grammars and grammarians in the same period of time are discussed. Bursill-Hall (1971) and Joly and Stefanini (1977) discuss speculative grammars, whereas the collection of articles in Hunt (1980) also include text material from that time which is hard to gain access to.

4 Grammar in the Renaissance and the first grammars of English

4.1 Grammar in the Renaissance

In chapter 2 we have seen that in the Golden Age of ancient Greece the way people looked at the world changed dramatically. People started to realise that they do not depend on the will of Gods, and that they rather have the freedom to use and develop their intellect. For them, language was a tool for finding reality. This way of thinking and of perceiving the world was fundamental throughout the eras of Classical Antiquity and the Middle Ages, although, as we have seen in the previous chapter, it was adapted to the needs of a Christian world which focussed on Latin as the language of knowledge and truth. Here, the importance of spiritual, transcendental, and universal matters were stressed, and only permanent aspects of language were worth studying. In the period which is called the Renaissance (ca. 1450–1600) things changed again fundamentally. Traditionally this period is regarded as the birth of the modern world, but by taking a closer look we find that it was also a period of rebirth: as the term Renaissance implies, it was a time where the interest in Classical Antiquity was revived.

Two movements especially define this period: on the one hand the rebirth of classical learning and value, and on the other hand, the reformation which resulted from a series of cultural, political, and intellectual transformations and led to the establishment of the Protestant faith. Apart from these movements which had far-reaching consequences, the Renaissance also witnessed the discovery of new continents, the rise in importance of city-states and national monarchies, the development of national languages, the break-up of the old feudal structures, and the invention of paper and printing. We can easily agree with Robins (1994, 94) who states that the Renaissance has a Janus-like character '... looking forward to an exciting future and backward to a glorious past.' And we can well imagine that all of these events shifted the people's perception of the world.

Now there were so many new experiences and observations to be made that the people changed their inner attitude to the material world. Had they before focussed on the universal and transcendental matters, they now came to focus on particular, visible, material phenomena. In medieval times the only valid route to knowledge could be observed via the *oculi mentis* 'the mind's eyes', now it could be observed through the *oculi carnis* 'the eyes of the body.' Evidence for this change in perspective is manifold. In the sixteenth century many books were printed with the title 'Observationes in ...', and botanical gardens were founded in Padua, Bologna, Florence, Montpellier and Leiden to survey and collect specimens. Voyages of explorations were undertaken, and travellers brought back descriptions not only of exotic flora and fauna, but also of exotic languages. Missionaries compiled phrasebooks and vocabulary lists, and even wrote grammars although they solely fulfilled practical needs. The scholars at home heard about reports from these new and exotic languages and started to collect 'specimens' of them. Since the Lord's Prayer was one of the most fundamental texts for Christians it was one of the first texts to be translated into other languages. It became a fashion to publish anthologies of this text in many languages, an example of which is Conrad Gesner's *Mithridates* from 1555 which includes 22 languages among them Armenian, Ethiopic, Polish, Hungarian, Welsh, Icelandic and two dialects of Sardinian. Another anthology written by the two German scholars Adelung and Vater from the beginning of the nineteenth century is *Mithridates oder allgemeine Sprachkunde mit dem Vater Unser als Sprachprobe in bey nahe fünfhundert Sprachen und Mundarten* (see Law, 2003).

The interest in observing the material world in all fields of life led to **empiricism**. Medicine was the discipline at university in which men could train the faculty of observation in the best way, and quite a number of them applied their newly acquired methodology to language. They aimed at answering questions like 'What is the definition of language?', 'How many languages are there?', and 'Is speaking a language a property of human beings?' Obviously, these questions have remained relevant for linguists until today.

Coming back to the revival of Classical Antiquity, scholars rediscovered and re-examined classical texts, and pedagogues sought to reform the education system along the lines of classical sources. This included teaching Classical Greek and Latin as well as the classical philosophy behind it. These scholars, who were also called **Humanists**, inherited the doctrine of the ***tres linguae sacrae*** (Hebrew, Greek, Latin) from the Middle Ages and followed **Durante degli Alighieri's** (or simply Dante) ideas laid out in the *De vulgari eloquentia* (1304, printed in 1529) about the status of these languages and the vernaculars. He states:

> We call that form of speech which toddlers pick up from those around them when they first start to make out words in the vernacular; or, to put it more concisely, the vernacular is that form of speech which we absorb by imitating our carers, without any rules. We also have a secondary form of speech called *grammar* by the Romans. The Greeks have this secondary form of speech too, and some other nations as well, but not all. Few people succeed in mastering it, or we learn its rules and doctrine only by devoting much time and effort to it. The vernacular is the nobler of the two because it was the first to be used by the human race; because everyone in the world uses it, even if it is divided into different words and accents; and because it is natural to us, whereas the other is created by art.
> (*De vulgari eloquentia* I i, in Law 2003:230)

Dante's comment is quite remarkable in that he actually refers to different types of **language acquisition,** i.e. the difference between acquiring our mother tongue and a second language. Recall that he did so at the beginning of the fourteenth century when there was still a long way to subdisciplines of linguistics like psycholinguistics with all its methodological machinery to define different forms of acquisition.

A further aspect which is implied in his comment is the difference between a written and a spoken **variety**. And since he attributes the labels 'nobler' to the latter and (implicitly) 'less noble' to the former we might also think of a **diglossic situation** in which there exists a strict functional differentiation between a (socially) high and a low variety. For Dante, Latin (and also Greek) was the form 'shaped by art' which is regulated by rules and learnt through formal study whereas the **vernacular** which was given by nature and acquired as a mother tongue was devoid of rules. Even more important was the opinion that a language like Latin was a stable form of language because it was not in constant flux as the vernacular(s). Because of this, Latin was often seen as the superior language, and the vernacular as the inferior language. However, this opinion could no longer be upheld when the Renaissance teachers realised that their world was completely different: Latin differed from their vernaculars in many ways, and so many of their questions remained unanswered. This gradually led to a growing disappointment concerning the role Latin played, the sacred language of the Middle Ages, and in more general terms, the achievements of Classical Antiquity. Very many aspects could simply not be applied to their language (and their world) and they were in need of a new perspective. Then they recalled what **Cicero** had said about Latin, namely that when he started to write, Greek was perceived as the cultured language and Latin as the rude, uncultivated language which was inadequate to talk about technical subjects. This is why Cicero himself took on the task to create Latin vocabulary which fulfilled the needs of philosophical discourse. Thus, they concluded that first of all, Latin must be subject to change because it changed from a rude language to a refined, well suited language, and second, that human activity can affect the nature of a language in a positive way since Cicero was able to refine Latin. So if Latin can be changed, other languages can be changed too, and this is when the process of the 'ennobling' of languages took its course. Grammars of the vernaculars arose, for example, the *Grammatica della lingua toscana* by Leon Battista Alberti (1437–1441), the *Gramatica de la lengua castellana* (1492) by Antonio de Nebrija or the work *Teutsch Grammatick oder Sprachkunst* by Laurentius Albertus (1573).

4.2 The first grammars of English

The situation in England differed from the situation in countries like Italy and Spain because the reputation of English was far from good. This can be seen by the name it was given: *spuma linguarum* meaning 'scum of languages'. Therefore, the writing of grammars was taken up quite slowly. What helped, however, was the long tradition of vernacular medium instruction, one nice example of which is **John Palsgrave's** *L'esclaircissement de la langue françoyse*. Although it is a grammar of French, it was written in England for English speakers in the English vernacular at the court of Henry

VIII. Henry's sister Mary Tudor was taught French by means of this grammar. It describes the grammatical properties of French in a detailed fashion pointing to relevant differences between the English and the French language. Moreover, it contains an appendix with different instances of discourse where the grammatical properties discussed in the book can be applied to authentic situations, e.g. how to speak with a messenger coming from the king.

It took some time until the first grammar of English was written. Before **William Bullokar** took on this task as we will shortly see, grammars were written in the English vernacular to teach Latin, often in a contrastive way. The first such grammar is **John Colet** and **William Lily's** *Shorte Introduction of Grammar* from 1547. At that time many new grammar schools were founded with the effect that their teachers wrote many new grammar books tailored to their way of teaching. If a child changed school, or if another teacher took over, the child had to start from the beginning. Evidently, this led to a quite confusing situation which was remedied by Edward VI who granted Colet and Lily's grammar a royal monopoly in 1547. As mentioned above, however, English in this type of grammar was only the language of instruction, and not the language of investigation.

The first grammar written with the aim to teach English is Bullokar's *Pamphlet for grammar* from 1586. Although he follows Lily and Colet's grammar to some extent he deliberately sets his work apart in measuring the vernacular English against Latin. For example he comments on the phonological and morphosyntactic differences between the two languages which are due to the synthetic character of Latin and the analytic character of English (see also chapter 5.1). Moreover, he seeks to create a grammatical analysis of English by recognising its peculiarities and by showing that English is rule-based as well, i.e. that it has a grammar which it is based on. The widely held opinion that vernaculars can be ennobled only if it can be shown that they have a grammar like Latin led to a conflict: on the one hand, grammarians wanted to demonstrate that English is rule-governed thus having the same status as Latin, but on the other hand they could only do so by referring to Latin. It was only in the following generations that this conflict was resolved.

With the rise of a new consciousness of other countries (languages) and one's own nationality in the seventeenth century the fashion for patriotic antiquarian research arose. This can for example be seen in the great interest in Old English which led to the publication of Ælfric's grammar and new grammars of Old English. Now scholars realised that languages must have changed and started to rethink the emergence of languages as described in the bible (the Tower of Babel); wasn't it the case that all present-day languages were created when the Tower of Babel was destroyed? If so, how can they change then, and how can new languages arise? With these insights came an interest in describing languages and in how far they differ. The Swedish antiquary, **Georg Stiernhielm,** for example published the Gospels in Gothic and compared it with other languages like Icelandic, Swedish, Latin, and dialects he was familiar with. During his studies he came to the conclusion that there must be a language family (Scythian) covering vast areas of Europe and Asia (today's Indo-European) and that Hungarian and Finnish do not belong to this family. Obviously, Stiernhielm was the precursor of **comparative linguistics** which, however, was established only in the nineteenth century as a discipline in its own right (see chapter 5).

In the previous chapter we have seen that in the Middle Ages, scholars were interested in finding universals in language, and in the previous paragraph we have seen that in the sixteenth century the focus lay on the observation of (different) languages. These trends are manifestations of two different orientations: empiricism and **rationalism**. Whereas empiricists focus on observation and concomitantly the minute description of the material world, and peculiarities of languages, universalists focus on reality, knowledge and inherent rules or universals that apply to each language. Although at first sight one might be tempted to infer a clear-cut distinction between these two orientations, in fact we cannot really talk about an alternation of the two: rationalists need empirical data, and empiricists need the tools of logical reasoning to analyse their data. Rather one orientation predominates over the other at times due to factors like prestige and the choice of methods of researchers which are in lead at particular points of time.

The biblical story of the Tower of Babel and the newly acquired knowledge of the world were now in conflict: people were aware of the fact that many continents existed in which the sacred languages Latin, Greek and Hebrew were not known, so these languages no longer played the dominant role they used to play before. As a result, a new awareness of **language diversity** arose, and the investigation of vernaculars became important for national pride. Latin lost its status as the language for intellectual communication and some scholars felt the need to compensate this loss. So the uniqueness of each language is stressed by those who base their work on observation (empiricism), and the quest for language universals by those whose orientation was towards rationalism. A proponent of the latter sort was the Spanish Humanist Francesco Sánchez de las Brozas (1523–1600), known as **Sanctius**, who sought '… to set out the underlying principles first and then to give examples (if possible) in order to make the matter clear' (cited in Law, 2003, 263). It is not surprising that he comments on empiricists in the following way:

> A perverse opinion, or rather a piece of unbelievable stupidity has taken over the minds of many people, namely, that there are no underlying principles in the Greek and Latin languages, and no reason for looking into the matter in depth. I have never seen anything more idiotic than this figment of the imagination, and it would be hard to dream up anything fouler. Does a human being, who is after all a rational being, really act, speak and plan without understanding and reason?
> (From Sanctius's *Minerva, sive de causis linguae latinae*, cited in Law, 2003, 263)

In a similar vein, a number of other scholars were in search of language universals, for example Francis Lodwick and Cave Beck who suggested to construct a 'universal character', a system of signs that could be read off in any language. Much more influential was the **school of Port-Royal**. At this school, which was a monastic community outside Paris, the empiricist grammarian Claude Lancelot and the philosopher Antoine Arnauld wrote the work *Grammaire générale et raisonnée* (1660) with the aim to define the rational order underlying language. According to these scholars language reflects three fundamental mental operations: first, forming a concept, second, forming a judgement, and third, reasoning. They further claimed that these three operations were found in all linguistic categories in all languages. So here mental processes are directly related to grammar for the first time. Their work became highly popular and influential in the following decades, and many scholars reading it identified two different approaches to dealing with language: **General grammar** and **particular grammar**. General grammar is the rationally ordered science of the unchanging principles of language in written or spoken form. Particular grammar applies the arbitrary conventions found in common use of a particular language to these unchanging general principles. These two different types of grammars, which might be seen as dichotomies, resemble concepts of modern linguistics: Saussure's distinction between *langue* and *parole*, and Chomsky's theory of **Generative Grammar** including **Universal Grammar** and the distinction between **competence** and **performance**. And indeed modern linguists like Noam Chomsky read the work of the Port-Royal grammarians and were influenced by it as we will see in more detail in chapter 6.

Before we will take a closer look at the study of language in the eighteenth and nineteenth centuries, we will focus our attention on particular grammars, or more precisely on grammar writing in England in the seventeenth and eighteenth centuries which was part of the process of standardising the language. After Bullokar's successful first grammar of English, Gil's *Lognomia Anglica* (1619, 1621) became so popular that it was the first grammar ever to be reprinted. In the years to come, the following grammars were widely read: John Wallis's *Grammatica Linguae Anglicanae* (1653), which was reprinted five times before the end of the seventeenth century, Ben Jonson's *English Grammar* (1640), which was reprinted four times, and Joshua Poole's *The English Accidence* (1646), which was reprinted three times. Generally, it can be shown that in the course of the seventeenth century the publication of grammars constantly increased (see Tieken-Boon van Ostade, 2008, 1).

So, many scholars at that time obviously felt the need for a reference work that told the learner how to use language. This implies the need for a (written) standard. But what is a standard? According to the *Routledge Dictionary of Language and Linguistics* it is 'the historically legitimated panregional, oral and written language form of the social middle or upper class' (Bussmann, 1996, 451). Since it serves as a public means of communication, it is subject to extensive processes of normalisation on the levels of grammar, pronunciation, and spelling. The following stages are differentiated in the process of standardisation which may overlap in time (Kloss, 1952, 15–31, Chambers and Trudgill, 1980, 10–14): First, there's the process of **selection**, i.e. a particular variety of a language must be selected from a pool of competing varieties. In the next step the selected variety must gain **acceptance** by a group of speakers/users who are capable of influencing other speakers. Next, the variety is subject to **diffusion**, it must spread socially and geographically via public media, institutions and the educational system. Concomitant with diffusion is the process of **maintenance**. In the **elaboration of function** stage, the standard-to-be variety has gained the status of the official language and is used in the fields of administration, science, philosophy, and literature. The next step, **codification**, is quite an important step because it lays down the rules of language in lexicons, dictionaries, and grammars. The final stage of this process is **prescription** when the normative rules are imposed on the language user and learner. By looking at these several stages it becomes clear that the writing of grammars is part of the codification stage. In the following, we will take a brief look at how this process took place in England in the eighteenth century which is the time where most grammars were written.

The increase in the production of grammars in the seventeenth century mentioned above steadily continued into the eighteenth century. More precisely, the rise in grammar production set off in the 1760s and continued up to 1860s (for details see Tieken-Boon van Ostade, 2008). Strikingly, between 1700 and 1750 the rate of grammar production increased from one to four which is probably due to the fact that at that time it became clear that Britain should never have an academy. Authoritative figures like Jonathan Swift advocated setting up an institution like the French *Académie française* to codify the English language by publishing an authoritative grammar and dictionary. In *A Proposal for Correcting, Improving and Ascertaining the English Tongue* addressed to the Lord High Treasurer Swift wrote:

> My LORD; I do here, in the Name of all the Learned and Polite Persons of the Nation, complain to Your LORDSHIP, as *First Minister*, that our Language is extremely imperfect; that its daily Improvements are by no means in proportion to its daily Corruptions; that the Pretenders to polish and refine it, have chiefly multiplied Abuses and Absurdities; and; that in many Instances, it offends against every Part of Grammar.
> (1712:8, in Beal, 2004, 91)

However, calls for an **academy** dwindled as more and more grammarians took on the task themselves to write and publish such a piece of work. In 1761 the philosopher, theologian and educator Joseph Priestley declared himself against setting up an academy:

> As to a publick *Academy* invested with authority to ascertain the use of words, which is a project that some persons are very sanguine in their expectations from, I think it not only unsuitable to the genius of a *free nation*, but in itself ill calculated to reform and fix a language. We need make no doubt but that the best forms of speech will, in time, establish themselves by their own superior excellence.
> (1761:vii, in Tieken-Boon van Ostade, 2008, 5)

His opinion was the opinion of most scholars by then, and the plea for an English academy fell silent.

A further peak of grammars published can be found in the 1790s (Tieken-Boon van Ostade, 2008, 4). At that time London was no longer the centre of grammar production, grammars were increasingly published in the provinces (e.g. in Bath, Bristol) because teaching material was needed there as well. Another interesting aspect is that 15 per cent of the entire output of grammars were written by women, mainly anonymously. We will discuss the role of the female grammarians below in some more detail.

The question is why there was such a need for this plethora of grammars. The answer can be sought in changes in society at that time. The eighteenth century was a time of social change and social mobility. The shift from a land-based to a money-based economy as well as the ongoing Industrial Revolution made it now possible for people of lower rank to rise to a higher position in society. From a linguistic perspective this meant that those aspiring to higher ranks often had to deny that they did not have a command of linguistic variants associated with a higher status. This led to the need for grammars to provide linguistic guidelines, i.e. for codification and prescription. Whereas modern linguistics aims at describing language, the normative grammarians in the eighteenth century were expected to take the route of 'prescribing and proscribing' (Baugh and Cable, 2005, 262). In the process of deciding which of the variants found in language should be used as the norm by learners, grammarians considered the following three principles: 'reason, etymology, and the example of Latin and Greek' (Baugh and Cable, 2005, 264, see also Tieken-Boon van Ostade, 2008, 247f and Beal, 2004, 11). **Robert Lowth** was one of the most important grammarians at that time, and in his grammar with the title *A Short Introduction to English Grammar* (1762), which became an extremely successful work, we find comments based on these principles. Concerning the principle of reason he comments on double negation by taking an argument from logic: 'Two Negatives in English destroy one another, or are an equivalent to an Affirmative' (Lowth, 1763, 139, second edition of his grammar). The stricture against preposition stranding is made on the basis of the principle of etymology: 'PREPOSITIONS, so called because they are commonly *put before* the words to which they are applied, serve to connect words with one another, and to shew the relation between them' (Lowth, 1799, 64f). Since the term 'preposition' is based on the description of Latin grammar this example could also be taken as an illustration of the third principle.

According to Tieken-Boon van Ostade (2008, 7) it is impossible to define the point of transition from codification to prescription but the amount of attention paid to **syntax** in grammars may be seen as a clue for this development. Stating this implies that the term grammar at that time had a meaning different from the term grammar we use today. Back then grammarians mainly discussed spelling, pronunciation, syllables and word categories of English and before the 1740s only sixty per cent of the grammarians had paid attention to syntax. This tendency, however, increased in the course of time (eighty-five per cent for grammars published between 1770 and 1800). Whereas **Samuel Johnson** only attributed very little space to the syntax of English, Lowth devoted about a third of his work to it. The attention paid to English syntax in more and more grammars is a sign for the growing interest in actual usage which leads to the birth of a new type of grammar at that time: **practical grammar**.

Ann Fisher, who was the first female grammarian, also included syntax into her work *New Grammar* (1745) which became one of the most popular grammars in the eighteenth century and which therefore was also copied many times by other (male!) grammarians. Fisher opened a school for young ladies who were learners with a background completely different from their male counterparts in that they neither emerged from the clergy nor were they taught Latin. Female grammarians like Fisher aimed at teaching 'unskilful ladies' for which purpose they developed a native terminology for grammar, and added exercises of bad English to their grammars. From 1775 onwards, a new category of grammarians, the **female teacher grammarians**, arose who were, as their students, not educated along traditional lines. Due to the needs of these learners and a general growing interest in pedagogical aspects, the target audience shifted to young learners.

By the end of the eighteenth century much has changed in grammar writing. And although it has been claimed by many modern linguists that grammarians at that time saw their task in prescribing language, we have also seen a descriptive aspect in their work, i.e. their awareness of and interest in current usage. We will see in the next chapter that the development towards descriptiveness will become more and more profound.

Tax: 'We have travelled quite a bit, don't you think, Syn?'
Syn: 'Yes, and many things have changed in the course of time. For example, in the period of the Renaissance people were looking back at the past and forward to the future: this is reflected in an interest in Classical Antiquity, on the one hand, and in the discovery of new continents, new languages and new experiences, on the other hand. The inner attitude of people changed to the material world, and observations became important. As a result, new languages were 'collected' and described and an awareness of varieties of languages arose.'
Tax: 'And in this context we also discussed the two different orientations of empiricism and rationalism which we linked to observing language and seeking for universals in language.'
Syn: 'Exactly. And we saw that the School of Port-Royal aimed at defining the rational order underlying language whereas many other scholars at that time saw their task in observing languages and describing differences between them. Moroever, the existence of different varieties or vernaculars stood in contrast with the classical languages Latin and Greek which were still seen as the sacred languages. Gradually people started to realise that even a language like Latin was subject to change and that therefore all languages could change. This led to the process of ennobling the vernaculars and to a new national awareness. And this process also led to writing grammars which, at first meant that Latin still was the language to be taught in the vernacular. In England this process also gradually set in and in the course of time grammars of English were published. More and more grammars were written in the course of the seventeenth and eighteenth centuries, and the focus shifted from grammars only suitable for educated male learners to grammars including aspects of syntax for uneducated female learners.'

> **Literature:** Padley (1976) investigates the Latin Tradition, and Padley (1988) takes a closer look at vernacular grammars in Western Europe between 1500 and 1700. In Bornstein (1976) readings from the seventeenth to twentieth centuries are provided. The monograph by Beal (2004) covers the time from 1700 to 1945 and discusses, amongst others, grammars and grammarians at that time in an engaging way. The collection of articles in Tieken-Boon van Ostade (2008) provides an interesting insight into grammar writing from all kinds of perspectives. Of course, it is worthwile reading the grammars written at that time as well, for example, Lowth (1799) or (an edition) of Ben Jonson's grammar available online at archive.org.

5 Modern linguistics and structuralism

5.1 The nineteenth century

The nineteenth century marks the rise of linguistics as a scientific discipline in its own right. In this century the focus of linguistic investigations lies on the development of single languages (atomism) and the comparison of languages from a grammatical point of view out of which grew the disciplines of historical and comparative linguistics (grammar). This is, however, not to say that before the nineteenth century no historical or comparative research was undertaken. In fact we have seen in the previous chapter that with the discovery of new continents and countries the interest in hitherto unknown languages started to grow and that scholars undertook comparative studies, for example Stiernhielm. What is new in this century is that new theoretical and methodological conceptions for studying historical and comparative aspects of language were developed.

Historical linguistics is the subdiscipline which is concerned with developing a theory of language change by investigating the history of a language (all languages). The aims of this discipline are to describe and account for observed changes in individual languages, to research the origin of individual languages and language groups (method of reconstruction), to develop a typology of language change and to study the origin and spread of language change. By looking at these aims we see that comparative studies are partly implied and this is also why some regard **comparative linguistics** as a subfield of historical linguistics. One of the most influential comparative studies was actually undertaken just over a decade before the turn of the century by the English philologist **Sir William Jones** (1746–1794). In 1786 he presented his famous paper to the Royal Asiatic Society in Calcutta wherein he postulated that Sanskrit had the same origin as Latin, Greek and the Germanic languages. This statement had far-reaching consequences one of which was a sudden and strong interest in studying the origin of languages and to reconstruct a proto language, called Indo-Germanic or **Indo-European**. Especially German scholars took on this task during the Romantic period, the most well-known proponents are **Franz Bopp** and his work *Über das Conjugationssystem der Sanskritsprache in Vergleichung mit jenem der griechischen, lateinischen, persischen und germanischen Sprache* (1816), **Jakob Grimm** and his *Deutsche Grammatik* (1819–37), **August Wilhelm Schlegel** with his famous work *Über die Sprache und Weisheit der Indier* (1808), and **August Schleicher** with his *Compendium der vergleichenden Grammatik der indoeuropäischen Sprachen* (1861). Schleicher also invented a system which made use of biological terminology, the *Stammbaumtheorie* (**family tree theory**). For the first time the origin of the individual Indo-European languages was reconstructed from the hypothetical Proto-Indo-European (PIE) in the form of a genetic tree. The branches of the tree are meant to represent the differentiation of these languages but since the model is based on abrupt branching gradual linguistic differentiation cannot be represented. To compensate for this shortcoming Johannes Schmidt introduced his **wave model** in 1872.

Indo-European is the most widespread language family in the world and is said to have its origin around 3000 BC in the area north of the Black Sea (note that this is hotly debated though). Proto-Indo-European is hypothesised to have been a highly inflectional language exhibiting eight or nine cases (nominative, genitive, dative, accusative, instrumental, ablative, vocative, locative, and probably directive or allative) probably three genders (masculine, feminine, neuter), and three numbers (singular, plural, dual). Apart from investigating and determining the nature of PIE it became necessary to systematically classify the languages under scrutiny, and as a result **language typology** came into existence. Schlegel and Schleicher, partly influenced by **Wilhelm von Humboldt**, proposed a classification based on formal grammatical characteristics (ignoring geographical, genetic connections), i.e. morphological criteria. Crucially, value judgements were attributed to each of the types, so for example richness of inflection was seen as a better system than one which shows isolating properties. The isolating type was seen as being inferior, and less developed. The first type proposed in this classification is the **isolating** or **analytic** type where grammatical relations are not expressed within a word. So different words are needed for lexical and grammatical meanings/functions as illustrated in the following examples of NHG and PDE:

(1) a. NHG *Ich werde gehen*
    b. PDE *I will go*

As you can see in both examples the words express either lexical information, as in the case of *gehen* and *go*, or grammatical information, as in the case of the personal pronouns and the auxiliaries.

The second type are the **inflectional** or **synthetic** languages where grammatical relations are expressed within a word. So inflectional endings express grammatical relations, and lexical and grammatical meanings/functions are thus expressed in one word as illustrated with the Latin (LAT) and Icelandic (ICE) example:

(2) a. LAT: *dominum* 'house', SG+ACC
    b. ICE: *himinn* 'sky', SG+NOM

The third type distinguished are the **agglutinating** languages where grammatical and lexical forms are stuck together, the result of which is the concatenation of elements. What is important is that the stem of a word does not change, that the affixes agglutinate to elements which are independent words, and that the single elements can easily be analysed since the forms do not change and retain their own meaning (note that at that time scholars didn't give much thought to things like vowel harmony). This is illustrated with the following example from Turkish:

(3) a. *ev* = house
     b. *evim* = house-my
     c. *evler* = houses-the
     d. *evlerim* = houses-the-my

The fourth type are the so-called **polysynthetic** (or **incorporating**) languages where syntactic relations in a sentence are expressed by compounding lexical and grammatical elements into long and complex words, and syntactic functions like object or adverbial may be incorporated into the predicate. An example of this type of language comes from the Canadian First Nation language Mohawk:

(4) *Sahonwanhotónkwahse*
     sa-honwa-nhoton-kw-a-hse
     again-PAST-she/him-open door-reversive-un-for-PERF
     'she opened the door for him again'
     (Rowicka, 2006, 194)

These language types were seen as being subject to a development on an evolutionary scale: isolating or analytic type → agglutinating type → inflecting type (Latin, Greek, Sanskrit). This notion implied two typological poles with Chinese as the purest isolating language on one end, and Sanskrit as the purest inflectional language on the other end. Nineteenth century linguists like Bopp and Schleicher saw language as an organism which was born and underwent a progressive development from a primitive state to some notional prime which then decayed and finally died. Without doubt, this sentimentalist view which is based on prescriptivism gives way to descriptivism in the twentieth century which states that languages should be described and regarded as being on an equal footing. Sapir put this quite to the point: 'a linguist that insists on talking about the Latin type of morphology as though it were necessarily the high-water mark of linguistic development is like the zoologist that sees in the organic world a huge conspiracy to evolve the race-horse or the Jersey cow' (Sapir, 1970, 131).

Since languages are subject to change such a classification is problematic because ideal types do not really exist. English, for example, can be seen as a mixture of the first three types:

(5) a. E: *beautiful - more beautiful - most beautiful* (analytic)
        nice - nicer - nicest (synthetic)
     b. *workable* = *work* + *able* (agglutinating)

Thus, the different typological types distinguished should be seen as tendencies rather than discrete types.

In the previous chapter we have taken a closer look at empiricism and rationalism. We have seen that although these two orientations might be perceived as standing in contrast (and many scholars have perceived them as such, recall the comment of Sanctius) we cannot really talk about an alternation. Wilhelm von Humboldt (1767–1835), brother of geographer and ethnographer Alexander von Humboldt, and a renowned German philosopher and linguist, held the opinion that only the synthesis of the rationalist-universalist and empiricist-individual model adequately accounts for the nature of language. For him a sentence is much more important than an isolated word, so isolated entities are always subordinated to synthesis (the whole). This, in more general (and philosophical) terms, leads to assuming that the universal lies in the individual. Further, he sees language as an **inner organ** of humans which precedes thinking and perceiving. These ideas are expressed in the title of one of his most influential works *Über die Verschiedenheit des menschlichen Sprachbaues und ihren Einfluß auf die geistige Entwicklung des Menschengeschlechts* (1836).

So according to Humboldt language conditions thought: only through the word does the concept exist and hence also, indirectly, reality (which is grasped in concepts). This is expressed by Humboldt in the following way:

> Die Sprache ist gleichsam die äußerliche Erscheinung des Geistes der Völker; ihre Sprache ist ihr Geist, und ihr Geist ihre Sprache, man kann sich beide nie genug identisch denken.
> (Humboldt, Gesammelte Werke 1960, Band 6, § 7, p. 38)
> 'Language is, as it were, the outer appearance of the spirit of a people; the language is their spirit and the spirit their language; we can never think of them sufficiently as identical.'
> (from the English edition by Michael Losonsky, 1999, Cambridge University Press, p. 50)

From what we have learnt so far about language and thought, his idea is new in so far as the relation between the two is reversed now. Some have seen this as 'cognitive turn', others have drawn connections to the **Sapir-Whorf hypothesis**, also called the '(Whorfian) **principle of linguistic relativity**', which holds that language affects or even determines cognitive processes such as thought and experience (see below). But if the world view of a speaker of a language was reflected in his or her language then the morphological shape of this language could also be seen as superior or inferior to other languages. Recall what we said about the four different types of languages above: inflectional languages were seen as superior to isolating languages. This now implied the dominance of speakers of perfect languages over the speakers of less perfect languages. This idea was widespread even until the early twentieth century but lost ground with the rise of universalist models of grammar (see next chapter).

For Humboldt the creative aspect of language was very important, as mentioned above he assumed a creative linguistic ability inherent in every speaker's brain or mind. More precisely he stated that speakers can make use of the finite resources available to them at any time, a thought which was later taken up by Chomsky saying that an infinite set of sentences can be created using a finite set of rules. According to Humboldt language can be identified as action or effective energy which he calls *enérgeia*. It is not to be surveyed in its entirety, but has to be seen as a continuously self-generating process. This stands in contrast with the concept of language as the product of a completed action (*ergon*). For him, language seen as a merely static entity, and a fixed and dead description of a language of a grammarian is not interesting.

By saying that the capacity of language is an essential part of the human mind implies that it is universal. More explicitly, Humboldt postulates an ***innere Sprachform*** which is the semantic and grammatical structure of language embodying the elements, patterns and rules imposed on the sounds of speech. Partly it is defined by its universality, but partly it is also defined by the **Sprachform** that defines each language individually. The universal nucleus of the grammar of speech are the verb ('Nerv der ganzen Sprache') and the pronoun due to its anaphoric character (for an explanation see Jungen and Lohnstein, 2006, 63).

Another German linguist whose ideas became quite influential in the second part of the nineteenth century is Jakob Grimm. His work *Deutsche Grammatik* is actually not a grammar of German but a comparative 'Volkssprachen Grammatik'. In contrast to Humboldt he was not interested in the abstract level of language but in the historical level, and in the etymology of words. He aimed at meticulously describing different languages in their development and identifying the inherent rules of language. In doing so he discovered fundamental grammatical factors defining German, like the difference between the *umlaut* (i-mutation) and *ablaut*. But he is most well-known for discovering the **First Germanic Consonant Shift**, also called **Grimm's Law**. These are systematic changes in the Indo-European obstruents which led to the development of Germanic and made it possible to distinguish German from the other Indo-European language families. Whereas Grimm still followed other nineteenth century linguists in claiming that climate, diet or race could explain language change, or that linguistic change can be equated with decay, in the late nineteenth century a group of linguists appeared who rejected this view on language and helped to shape linguistics as a modern science.

The **Neogrammarians** (other names are *Junggrammatiker* or Young Grammarians) were a group of predominantly German linguists working at the University of Leipzig in the last quarter of the nineteenth century. Leading linguists of this group were **Hermann Paul, Karl Brugmann, Karl Verner** and **Otto Behagel**. They argued against the Romantic idea that language is the key to the world. For them language was an objective phenomenon which requires detailed, minute description. Further, they believed that only historical linguistics could be truly scientific, that language is orderly and rule-governed, and that all instances of language change—which for them were mainly sound changes—can be explained by rules. To be more precise, they postulated that **sound changes** occur without exceptions and that sound laws are inviolable. As mentioned above one famous example of such a sound change is Grimm's Law. This law describes the development of voiced and voiceless plosives from PIE to G:

(6) **Grimm's Law:**
voiceless plosives > fricatives
PIE: *p,t,k > G: f,θ,h
voiced plosives > voiceless plosives
PIE: *b,d,g > G: p,t,k
voiced aspirated plosives > voiced plosives
PIE: *b^h,d^h,g^h > G: b,d,g

During their investigations the Neogrammarians found that their rule did not always hold. But, as mentioned above, they believed in the total regularity of sound change. Verner stated: 'There ... must exist a rule for the irregularities; the task is to find this rule' (1978,36 cited in McMahon, 1994, 17). This is spelled out by the **Regularity Hypothesis**:

(7) *Regularity Hypothesis*: sound change is regular and inviolable (no exceptions), it excludes sporadic changes and is restricted to a particular speech community at a particular time.

Thus, Neogrammarians described the irregularities of Grimm's Law in another law called Verner's Law:

(8) **Verner's Law** (explaining irregularities in Grimm's Law):
PIE voiceless stops between vowels, when the preceding vowel is unaccented, undergo voicing and develop into Germanic fricatives.
Grimm's Law: PIE *$patér$ 'father' > G *fadar* (> PDE *father*; NHG *Vater* because of the Second Germanic Consonant Shift)
PIE *$bhráter$ 'brother' > G *bróþar* (> PDE *brother*; but NHG *Bruder* because of the Second Germanic Consonant Shift)
Verner's Law: In the derivation of *father* PIE [t] developed into a voiced fricative because the stress lay behind the dental, while in *brother* PIE [t] developed into a voiceless fricative because the stress lay before the dental.

A reflex of these two laws is the contrast between word-internal plosives and fricatives in German words that have the same root (also called *Grammatischer Wechsel*): *Hefe* 'yeast' - *heben* 'lift', *schneiden* 'cut' - *schnitt* 'cut' (past tense), and *ziehen* 'pull' - *zog* 'pull' (past tense).

Their view of the primacy of diachrony arose from their interest in comparative studies and their claim that irregularities in synchrony could be explained by showing that they did not exist back in time. These assumptions motivated the methodology of reconstruction. The Neogrammarians saw their task in finding **cognate** words (i.e.

words which are historically derived from the same source) of related languages, for example:

(9) a. NHG: *zu, zehn* [ts]
    b. PDE: *to, ten* [t]

Further, they identified corresponding sounds like German [ts] and English [t], analysed these sounds and regarded them as being subject to sound change.

As mentioned above, they also showed that synchronic irregularities used to be regular before sound change, for example they took the plural forms of PDE which are irregular due to **i-mutation** (a regressive assimilation where the stem vowel of a word assimilated to a following /i/ or /j/ in pre Old English times):

(10) a. PDE: *foot* sg. *feet*, *foots
     b. (pre-)OE: *fōt* sg. *fōti*

They explained that in former times these plural forms were actually built in a regular way exhibiting the plural suffix -*i*. Due to the process of i-mutation these forms changed and became irregular.

The Neogrammarians believed that changes operate with 'blind necessity', i.e. without concerns for grammatical consequences of their actions. Further, they claimed that if irregularities arise they are cleared up by analogical processes, albeit in a sporadic fashion. So there is an interaction between sound change and analogy which was later defined by Sturtevant (1947) in the following way:

(11) **Sturtevant's Paradox:** Phonetic laws are regular but produce irregularities.
     Analogic creation is irregular but produces regularity (Sturtevant, 1947, 109).

This interaction can be observed with the irregular plural forms briefly discussed above: there used to be other irregular forms like OE *bōc* 'book' (sg), *bēc* 'books' (pl) but they were levelled out in accordance with regular plural formation with the -*s* suffix (*stone* (sg), *stones* (pl)).

5.2 Structuralism

The beginning of the twentieth century marks the birth of modern linguistics. At this point you might rightly ask 'but what is modern linguistics?' So far we have seen that people have been dealing with language for hundreds of years from different perspectives with different motivations. The general trend we can make out was that scholars mainly investigated individual languages and individual aspects or phenomena of language(s) in an atomistic fashion. The idea that language is a **system** can then indeed be seen as something new and modern. It was Ferdinand de Saussure's concept of language as a system in the early twentieth century that paved the way for structuralist grammar and structuralist thinking. We will see later on that his ideas not only extended into Europe, with centres in Geneva, Prague and Copenhagen, but also into North America. Moreover, the methods and ideas of structuralism also influenced other fields like philosophy, literary criticism, anthropology, and sociology.

As mentioned above, the tenets of **structuralism** were first laid down by the Swiss linguist Ferdinand de Saussure (1857–1913). He was trained in Leipzig and had connections to the Neogrammarians, but he gave lectures in Paris and Geneva. His famous *Cours de linguistique générale*, which was published posthumously in 1916 by his students, outlines Structuralist linguistic thought. In the following, we will take a closer look at Saussure's general theory of language which can be presented as a number of dichotomies.

First, Saussure defines language in a new way: for him ***langage*** is an umbrella term for ***langue*** and ***parole*** which must be distinguished. The *faculté de langage* signifies general human linguistic and language ability, that is to say, the ability to communicate using a system of sounds and symbols. *Langue* is the abstract (idealised) system of signs and rules, a static system of symbols with broad (social) value, due to the invariant and functional nature of its elements. *Parole* is the concrete realisation of language as it is used. Instances of *parole* are based on the system of *langue* and vary according to register, age, dialect, among other factors. His thoughts are captured nicely in the following quotation:

> ... le langage est multiforme et hétéroclite; à cheval sur plusieurs domaines, à la fois physique, physiologique et psychique, il appartient encore au domaine individuel et au domaine social; il ne se laisse classer dans aucune catégorie des faits humains, parce qu'on ne sait comment dégager son unité. (Saussure, 1969, 25)
> 'Taken as a whole, speech is many-sided and heterogeneous; straddling several areas simultaneously - physical, physiological, and psychological - it belongs both to the individual and to society'.
> (translated by Wade Baskin, edition published by The Philosophical Society, New York City, 1959, p. 9)

So, for Saussure the goal of structuralist linguistics is to research the systematic regularities of *langue* using data from *parole*, while *parole* itself can be researched in various disciplines, like phonetics, psychology, and physiology (see also Humboldt's distinction between *ergon* and *enérgeia*).

Second, Saussure suggests a distinction between the **syntagmatic** and the associative (paradigmatic) level. Relations on the syntagmatic level, i.e. on the linear/horizontal axis, exist between units co-occurring in a context. He calls this type 'associative relations *in praesentia*'. This type of relation holds between sequentially ordered units, for example in the sentence *Eric is a linguist*. Relations on the **paradigmatic** level, i.e. on the vertical axis, are restricted by synonyms. He calls this type 'associative relations *in absentia*', which means that associations exist but cannot co-occur. In the sentence *Eric is a linguist* we could substitute *linguist* with another noun like *teacher, doctor*, etc. So this relation involves a choice of items within a set of items at one structural point. Saussure also talked about the value of a sign (***valeur***) in the linguistic system. He stated that language is a synchronic system of single units (signs) which have a value in this system. The value of a sign is defined through the system, in paradigmatic and syntagmatic relations. Further, the sign is in opposition to the other signs in the system, i.e. they are defined by their differences.

Third, Saussure assumes the dichotomy of **synchrony** versus **diachrony**. For him, in the synchronic treatment of study, language is seen as a self-contained system of communication at a particular time (a state fixed in time). It is only on the axis of simultaneity that language can be analysed as a system of values in which the value of an individual element results from the relational context of all values in the system. Diachrony relates to changes, which a language is subject to in the course of time. Here language is treated historically by investigating changing states between different time periods. Saussure thought that the synchronic study of language is primary because it investigates the relationship of individual elements in a balanced linguistic system that can be described structurally. Historically oriented diachronic investigations are seen as being secondary because they can only address the replacement of single elements by other elements, or the change of individual elements. This devaluation of historical investigation has to be seen as a reaction against the strictly historical method of the Neogrammarians.

Probably the principal idea of Saussure's theory is the notion of the **linguistic sign** (dyadic model). According to Saussure, the linguistic sign has the following characteristics:

1. **Bilaterality** = every sign has two aspects, the material sign, the ***signifier*** (*signifiant*), which is realised phonetically (*image acoustique*) or graphemically, and a conceptual sign, the ***signified*** (*signifié*). For example, the *signifier* of 'tree' are the graphemic and phonetic representation <tree> and [tri:], and the signified is the concept of 'tree' that a speaker has in his mind of this object. Importantly, the *signifier* and the *signified* are inseparable, they are so to speak two sides of a coin (in the literal sense).

2. **Arbitrariness** = the relation between *signifier* and *signified* is not motivated although the co-ordination between the *signifier* and the *signified* is predetermined by convention. Proof for this assumption can be seen in the fact that the same object in reality has different names in different languages. For example, the connection between PDE <tree>/[tri:] and the concept of 'tree' is arbitrary, in NHG the signifier of the concept of 'tree' is <Baum>/[baum], in LAT it is <arbor>/[arbor] etc. (recall the discussion on this aspect in chapter 2.1).

3. **Linearity** = as a sensually perceptible signal the linguistic sign exists exclusively within the framework of time (synchrony). For example, the auditory *signifier* of 'tree' ([triː]) is linear because the sounds it consists of succeed each other or form a chain as well as other such *signifiers* preceding or following [triː] in the flow of speech.

To illustrate his thoughts, Saussure compared the linguistic system with a game of chess. Concerning the dichotomy between synchrony and diachrony he said that in chess the positions of the pieces constantly change during a game but at each point of time the actual state of the game can be described by looking at the position of the pieces without taking into account preceding moves. Transferred to language this means that subsequent states of a language can be described independently of each other, whereby the historical development of these states are irrelevant for an understanding of the system as such. Native speakers of a language are able to know and apply the rules of their language without historical knowledge. But he also notes that preceding moves are often not irrelevant for explaining later moves and states since they are often part of a long-term strategy. For investigating language this means that diachrony does play a role, because certain linguistic phenomena can only be explained by looking at their history.

Further, Saussure states that both chess and language are rule-based systems. Concerning the substance of units which are part of these systems, he claims that it is not important which material the pieces are made of and what they look like (arbitrary). What is important is how they differ from each other. In both systems the value is defined by the system, by the role it plays in the system and in relation to and opposition with the other pieces/signs. In the course of time, values of units can change, one example of which is the temporal system in English. In OE two tenses, present tense and past tense, were generally distinguished but in the course of time periphrastic constructions like the present perfect etc. developed which resulted in today's system. As a result, present and past tense in OE had a value different from that in PDE.

The **Prague School**, whose main proponents were **Josef Vachek, Villém Mathesius, Nikolaj Trubetzkoy,** and **Roman Jakobson,** was founded in the 1920s. It followed the methods and principles defined in the *Cours de linguistique générale* and applied Saussurean theory to the elaboration of the concept of the phoneme which was already known. So for these scholars the core discipline was phonology, which they also called *functional phonetics* and which dealt with distinctive units of sound. They claimed that speech sounds (phones) belong to *parole* whereas phonemes belong to *langue*, and they saw their task in developing ways to identify **phones, allophones** and **phonemes**. Thus, they claimed that minimal pairs would be an adequate tool for establishing the phoneme inventory of a language. And by investigating the distribution of phones they were for example able to define whether allophones occur in free variation or in complementary distribution.

Apart from dealing with phonetics and phonology, some scholars worked on the level of syntax. Mathesius introduced the model of *Satzperspektive* (sentence perspective) which analysed sentences according to their communicative function. He stated that a sentence is ordered based on its information structure: known/old information is expressed by the *theme* (topic, given), and what is said about the known information is expressed by the *rheme* (new, comment). Let's consider an example:

(12) a. I have a friend.
      Theme   Rheme
   b. He is a doctor.
      Theme Rheme

In (12) a. the personal pronoun *I* is old information whereas *a friend* is introduced as new information. Thus, *I* is the theme, and *a friend* is the rheme. In b. *a friend* is taken up again by the personal pronoun *he* functioning as an anaphor. This is possible because the referent of *he* has already been introduced in (12) a. and therefore *he* has the status of a theme now. The new information, i.e. rheme, is now *a doctor*. This information-structural classification is reflected in word order, the use of pronouns, articles and intonation. It was further developed in the model of the **functional sentence perspective** (FSP) by **Jan Firbas** and others.

Another school that should be mentioned here is the Copenhagen School of Linguistics. Based on Saussure's structuralist tenets, the Danish linguist **Louis Hjelmslev** developed a formal approach to language which he called **glossematics**. His aim was to provide a model for analysing the formal side of language (phonetics, grammar) and the meaning of language in a coherent way. More generally, he was interested in a general theory of the signs of communication, i.e. semiotics. A further development of Saussure's ideas can be seen in Bernard Pottier's model of *la sémantique générale*.

It is without doubt that the influence Saussure's ideas had on twentieth century linguistics is unsurpassed, and this not only applies to groups or schools of linguists in Europe but also in North America. In the 1940s and 1950s a specific form of structuralism developed in America which was pioneered by the outstanding scholars **Franz Boas, Edward Sapir**, and **Leonard Bloomfield**. Generally, a distinction is made between the Bloomfield Era and **taxonomic structuralism** or **distributionalism** whose main representative is **Zellig Harris**. American structuralism as such is characterised by at least two scientific developments that are peculiar to (the history) of this country: first, there was a strong interest in the dying Native American languages which led to the primacy of speech (*parole*) from a descriptive, synchronic, ahistorical perspective, and methodologically to focussing on field work. Especially the works by Boas and Sapir are important here. Based on Sapir's ideas his student Benjamin Lee Whorf developed the hypothesis that language determines the thought and perception of its speakers. As mentioned above, this idea is known today as the Sapir-Whorf hypothesis or the principle of linguistic relativity. Recall that in the previous chapter we have learnt that some decades before, Humboldt had similar ideas. Whorf, who investigated the native American language Hopi, found that it considerably differs from European languages in that it does not have the concept of time, for example. He concluded that 'people who use languages with very different grammars are led by these grammars to very different values for outwardly similar observations' (Carroll, 1956, 20). Second, linguistic theory and methodology became influenced by behaviorist psychology. This direction of psychological research is based on methods of self-observation (**introspection**) and the description of the consciousness. Leonard Bloomfield and **Burrhus Frederic Skinner** applied these ideas to language. They claimed that language is a special form of behaviour and they saw the learning process as a conditioning process: language is learned behaviour, the sum of individual language habits developed and acquired through conditioning, reinforcement and generalisation. More precisely, just as human behaviour is analysed as a reaction to environmental stimuli, so is language. Imagine a situation where you meet a friend under an apple tree with lovely, red apples. The friend looks at the apples, as you do, and says: 'Please, pick one of these lovely apples for me.' And you say: 'Yes, of course!'. And off you go and pick an apple for your friend. According to the behaviorists you have reacted to an extra-linguistic **stimulus** with an extra-linguistic **response** but the dialogue itself also consisted of a stimulus-response pair.

Since the behaviorists were only interested in verifiable, objective description of language, they excluded semantic aspects and investigated the relations of items on the level of phonetics and phonology, morphology, and syntax. So the items that could be observed directly were classified and defined according to their distribution. This way of dealing with language has been called distributionalism, as mentioned above. It superseded the Bloomfield era, and Zellig Harris's *Methods in Structural linguistics* (1951) is viewed as the standard work of this phase.

Harris proposed so-called **discovery procedures** which include two analytical steps: first, the **segmentation** of the material through substitution, i.e. through paradigmatic interchangeability of elements having the same function (recall Saussure's dichotomy between the syntagmatic and paradigmatic level), and second, the **classification** of elements as phonemes, morphemes, etc. on the basis of their distribution and environment in the sentence. Proponents of distributionalism thought that with this method the structure of each individual language could be described. On the level of phonetics and phonology the smallest distinctive units (phonemes) and their distribution (contrastive, complementary, free variation) could be identified. Furthermore, Bloomfield transferred the distinction between phone (concrete) and phoneme (abstract) to the level of morphology and applied the discovery procedures to elements on the morphological level. He claimed that we can talk about the morpheme as the smallest meaningful unit, that morphemes can be classified as being free or bound, and that all concrete realisations of a morpheme can be called allomorphs. This procedure was also applied to the level of the sentence and came to be known as the **immediate constituent analysis** (IC-Analysis). This method decomposes the sentence (in a top-down fashion) into immediate constituents which build the next segment on the next level. A sentence is divided into two maximal constituents, these constituents are divided into two constituents, etc., until the smallest constituents occur:

(13)

You are probably quite familiar with this kind of sentence analysis where the constituent is the core unit (see also part II, chapter 8.1). Constituents can be joined together, so the biggest constituent in (13) is the sentence consisting of the constituents *the man* (subject) and *hit* with the IC *the ball* (predicate). In turn, the constituent *the man* can be analysed into further ICs *the* and *man*. The same analysis is applicable to *hit the ball*. The irreducible elements which result from such an analysis are the ultimate constituents of the construction. Obviously, the relations which are expressed in a structure based on constituency implies hierarchical ordering: the constituent *the ball* is dominated by *hit* etc. This is central to all grammatical models of constituency one of which is Chomsky's model of generative grammar.

But, of course, there are other ways to model syntactic relations between elements in a sentence. There are grammars which are not based on constituents. One such grammar is **dependency grammar** which was developed in the 1950s, in particular by the French linguist **Lucien Tesnière** (1893–1954). This type of grammar explains grammatical relations between elements in a sentence by means of different types of dependencies. As a result syntactic structure is represented using dependency trees one of which is given below:

(14)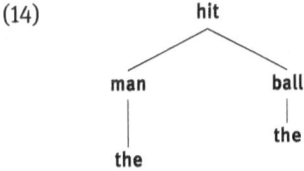

A dependency tree consists of sets of nodes (*the, man, hit, the, ball*) whose interconnections specify structural relations in terms of a **governor** and one or more **dependents**. In our example, the lexical verb *hit* is the governor of the dependents *man* and *ball* (which are the arguments of the verb, i.e. the subject and the object). In the same vein, the nouns *man* and *ball* are the governors of the definite determiner *the* (also called 'article' in the previous chapters). If you compare this tree with trees from constituency grammars you will see that they differ in two important respects: first, dependency relations hold between words, and second, words do not build constituents. We will briefly come back to dependency trees in parts II (chapter 9.2) and III (chapter 15) of the book. Since our focus lies on constituency grammars and generative grammar, we will take a closer look at this model in the next chapter.

Syn: 'So much has happened in the nineteenth and twentieth centuries, which paved the way for modern linguistics!'
Tax: 'Yes, and it's really hard to summarise it all, but I'll have a try: first of all, in the nineteenth century the disciplines of historical and comparative linguistics emerged which focussed on reconstructing the proto language Indo-European and which dealt with comparing Indo-European languages like Sanskrit, Latin, Greek, German etc. Further, these languages were classified according to their formal properties into inflectional, agglutinating, isolating and polysynthetic languages. Languages were seen as being superior over others depending on these properties, and language change was seen as decay. Second, we have taken a brief look at Humboldt's distinction between *enérgeia* and *ergon* and his belief that language conditions thought, which was later taken up in a stronger form as the principle of linguistic relativity.' *Syn:* 'And what about the Neogrammarians?'
Tax: 'They thought that language is totally regular, and any irregularity that may arise can be explained by diachronic regularity. But we have also learnt that in the twentieth century structuralism arose, and that the influence Saussure's general theory of language had is beyond compare (the linguistic sign, language as a system, dichotomies like langue and parole, synchrony and diachrony, etc.). His ideas were further developed by different schools in different places of the world (especially Geneva, Prague, Copenhagen, and also North America) which led to new theories, methods and insights into the nature of language on all levels (functional phonetics, functional sentence perspective, glossematics). The fact that especially the American structuralists saw speech and directly observable phenomena as the primary goal of of all research work done in linguistics led to taxonomic structuralism and distributionalism.'

Literature: The works by Jones, Bopp, Humboldt and others are, of course, an insightful read. Some, like the collected works of Bopp and Jones are also available via archive.org. Jankowsky (1972) re-evaluates the place of the neogrammarians in linguistics science, and Land (1986) deals with the major theories of language philosophy in Britain. One of the most influential works of a neogrammarian is, of course, Paul's *Prinzipien der Sprachgeschichte* (1888, see the reprint of 1990) which discusses basically all of the relevant phenomena you can think of in a surprisingly modern way. Sturtevant (1947) discusses the observation known as Sturtevant's paradox. Main works of the structuralists are first of all Saussure's *Cours de linguistique générale* (1916, see the edition of 1969), Sapir's *Language* (1921, see the edition of 1970), Tesnière's *Éléments de syntaxe structurale* (1965, also available now in English: Tesnière (2015)) Bloomfield's *Language* (1935), Harris's *Methods in Structural Linguistics* (1951), a selection of Whorf's writings (1956), and Hockett's *A course in modern linguistics* (1958). General discussions on American structuralism can be found in Newmeyer (1986) and Matthews (1993).

6 Chomsky and constituency grammars

In the previous chapters we have taken a look at language from quite different perspectives: from the perspective of (Greek) philosophers, language was seen as a tool for finding the truth, and from the perspective of medieval scholars like the Modists, the quest for universals in language was primary. During the Renaissance the focus of attention lay on vernaculars and on the way they should be examined. Some decades later it was the Port-Royal grammar that became quite influential with its aim to define the rational order underlying language. In the nineteenth century the focus shifted again: now the historical and comparative view became primary. Then in the twentieth century language, investigated from the synchronic perspective, was seen as a system having structure. Pondering the many ways language was perceived and researched throughout the centuries, we might think that after the structuralists everything had been said that could have possibly been said about the nature of language, and about how language should be studied methodologically. Yet, it is Noam Chomsky (*1928) who has been called 'the father of modern linguistics' and who is seen by many as the most influential linguist of all times. His thoughts on language and his grammatical theory, which were influenced by the Bloomfieldians, revolutionised the field of linguistics from the 1950s until today. Chomsky addressed the cognitive aspect of language for the first time: he sees language as a human, biologically based capacity. In this chapter we will deal with the development of Chomsky's generative grammar and pursue the question of why it has become so influential.

6.1 The early Chomsky

In the 1950s Chomsky was studying linguistics at the University of Pennsylvania, and influenced by the Bloomfieldians (behaviorism, distributionalism) and especially his teacher Zellig Harris. For these linguists language was a set of possible utterances/sentences, and in line with Harris and others, at the beginning Chomsky assumed that '... grammar generates all grammatically 'possible' utterances'" (1957, see the reprint of 2002, 48) and that a grammar 'is simply a description of a certain set of utterances, namely, those which it generates' (1957, see the reprint of 2002, 59). Furthermore, the discovery procedure(s) mentioned in the previous chapter meant that a corpus was obtained and research methods (segmentation, classification) were applied which determined the regularities that existed in the data. A problematic point was that these methods rearranged the data, and the resultant analysis was based on a set of defined utterances. Chomsky saw this procedure as 'a practical and mechanical method for actually constructing the grammar, given a corpus of utterances' (1957, see the reprint of 2002, 59). What was lacking, however, was the insight that possible patterns can be predicted. In his *Methods of structural linguistics* (1951) Harris states that when comparing utterances, it is important that linguists work with 'controlled material', which is illustrated with the following examples:

(1) a. *What books came?*
 b. *What book came?*
 c. *What maps came?*
 d. *What books are you reading?*
 (Matthews, 1993, 132)

The utterance *What books came?* is not compared with arbitrary other utterances. Instead, the linguist's task is to find partly similar patterns to test variations in predefined utterances. What is implicit in this method is a definition of a **corpus** as deliberately sampled material and not, as we would understand it today, with huge corpora at hand like the *British National Corpus* or the *Corpus of Contemporary American English* as a random collection of material.

Although Chomsky was definitely influenced by scholars like Harris, there are also crucial aspects where he clearly parted company with proponents of distributionalism (and even more so, behaviorism) and where his theory of grammar became revolutionary. First, Chomsky set out to define language as '… a set (finite or infinite) of sentences, each finite in length and constructed out of a finite set of elements' (1957, see the reprint of 2002, 13). Recall what Humboldt said about language (see chapter 5.1) and you will find that Chomsky was influenced by his ideas. Second, the aim of the linguist is to study the structure of all grammatical sentences of a language, i.e. sentences acceptable to native speakers. The motivation behind this claim is that the grammar of a language generates only grammatical sentences, therefore the task is to separate the grammatical from the ungrammatical sentences. The method Chomsky proposes to determine (un)grammatical sentences is not the method of the distributionalists, i.e. to use a corpus of deliberately collected material. Instead, Chomsky claims that **grammaticality** is a property of a grammar: 'Any grammar of a language will *project* the finite and somewhat accidental corpus of observed utterances to a set (presumably infinite) of grammatical utterances' (1957, see the reprint of 2002, 15). By seeing language from this rather abstract perspective and thus arguing against the behaviorists' idea of language as learned behaviour, Chomsky redefined linguistics: it developed from a science which had the aim to classify linguistic units to a science which is explanatory empirical.

In claiming that the study of grammar is independent of semantics Chomsky followed the tradition of the distributionalists. He further stressed the formal nature of grammar and stated that the term 'grammatical' could not be identified with 'meaningful' (1957, see the reprint of 2002, 15). To prove this claim Chomsky provides the following examples:

(2) a. *Colorless green ideas sleep furiously.*
     b. **Furiously sleep ideas green colorless.*
        (Chomsky, 2002, 15)

Both examples are clearly nonsensical but only the example in (2) a. is grammatical. Even though these assumptions are in line with those of Harris and others, Chomsky's claims go further in that he seeks to provide a general theory of language and explanations for semantic facts. To illustrate the second point let's take a look at the following examples:

(3) *the shooting of the hunters*
     a: the hunters shoot
     b: they shoot the hunters

The example in (3) exhibits what Chomsky called **constructional homonymity**: a form (sentence) which has been assigned more than one structure. So due to the assumption that *the shooting of the hunters* has two **transformational derivations**, *the hunters* can either be analysed as being the subject or the object which has also an effect on the semantic description. The distributionalists could not have explained this phenomenon because they would have only classified the items in the sentence according to their discovery procedure. Chomsky goes further in saying that there are two levels, and that the syntactic description of a sentence determines its semantic interpretation. This led Chomsky to stipulating the concept of **deep structure** in the mid 1960s to which we will come back shortly. The term 'transformational derivations' used here actually also alludes to this idea and will become relevant in the discussion of phrase structure grammar to which we will turn in the following.

In the previous chapter we have briefly dealt with the so-called IC-analysis. We have said that it aims at analysing a linguistic expression into a hierarchically defined series of constituents. If the constituents are assigned syntactic categories we can say that we have applied **phrase structure rules** to the structure. For example, in the IC-analysis of the sentence (S) *The man hit the ball* (see the example in (13) in the previous chapter) the complex constituent *the man* can be assigned the status of a noun phrase as well as the constituent *the ball*, and the constituent *hit the ball* can be assigned the status of a verb phrase. In more general terms, we can formulate *phrase structure rules* which state that a sentence consists of the immediate constituents N(oun)P(hrase) and V(erb)P(hrase), and that these constituents in turn consist of further immediate constituents: the NP consists of a determiner (D) and a noun (N), and the VP of a verb (V) and an NP. The phrase structure rules of our example would look like this:

(4) (i) S → NP + VP
    (ii) NP → D + N
    (iii) VP → Verb + NP
    (iv) D → *the*
    (v) N → *man, ball*
    (iv) Verb → *hit, took*

A **phrase marker** can then represent a structure which is built by these phrase structure rules:

(5)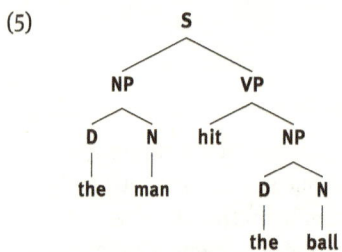

Proponents of distributionalism analysed sentences along these lines and worked on a phrase structure grammar of (all sentences of) English. Note that rules for a phrase structure grammar can be derived by a bottom-up or top-down analysis: in the first case we start from the bottom and ask ourselves: which words in a sentence are constituents and belong together? From these smaller entities bigger ones are built until the maximal level, i.e. the sentence, is reached. In the second case the sentence is the starting point, and it is replaced by structural categories of the next level (smaller category) until the minimal level (words) is reached. These quite static and descriptive rules were originally formulated as a recognition procedure but Chomsky proposed to reinterpret them as **rewrite rules** (1957, see the reprint of 2002, 26): for example, S → NP + VP corresponds to 'a sentence [which] consists of a noun phrase and a verb phrase.' In this way he stressed the creative aspect of language, the ability of the native speaker to build and understand an infinite number of sentences. But since phrase structure grammars cannot reconstruct the speaker's creativity, a new type of rule was needed which implied a further level of representation. Above, we briefly discussed constructional homonymity, another problematic case for this type of grammar--or better, the assumptions behind it--was the passive construction:

(6) a. *John loves Mary.*
    b. *Mary is loved by John.*

There is a systematic connection between a sentence in the active voice as in (6) a. and a sentence in the passive voice as in b.: both sentences have the same meaning. This connection cannot be reconstructed if the two 'surface' structures are derived independently by means of phrase structure rules. The grammar can only account for this connection in an adequate way if the passive construction is reconstructed as a change of the active construction, which means to say that one structure is derived from another and that transformation must come into play. According to Chomsky we need phrase structure rules which determine the formation of sentence structure, and transformational rules which reconstruct the systematic connection between sentence structures. Let's take a look at another example:

(7)   a.   *John is easy to please.*
        b.   *John is eager to please.*
           (Chomsky 1964:66)

Just by looking at the ordering of the elements on the surface and the form of the elements, the two sentences look the same. However, if we examine them in more detail we see that *John is easy to please* can be paraphrased as 'It is easy to please John' where *John* is the object. In the sentence *John is eager to please* John pleases someone else, so *John* functions as the subject. On the syntactic surface the two structures are the same then, but at another level the two structures are obviously different. Chomsky claims that a native speaker knows these relations, which implies that our knowledge of language refers to a more abstract level, the deep structure, and not to the surface level (**surface structure**). The transformations he assumes mediate between the deep structure and surface structure of sentences. A further claim Chomsky makes is that a grammar which cannot assign different structural descriptions to the sentences in a. and b. is not descriptively adequate. These are the core assumptions of **generative transformational grammar**.

Summarising what we have discussed so far we can say that Chomsky assumes three levels in his model of grammar introduced in *Syntactic Structures* (1957):
1. phrase structure: by means of phrase structure rules sentence structures are built up from the smallest elements of words (morphemes).
2. transformational structure: transformations resulting in deletion, substitution and permutation are applied to the structures created on the first level, and a string of words is the result.
3. morphophonemics: the morphophonemic rules convert this string of words into a string of phonemes.

As mentioned above, this model of grammar is a reconstruction of the complex ability of a native speaker to produce and understand an infinite number of sentences which are seen as structured linguistic units, the function of which is to systematically connect sound and meaning. The deep structure determines the semantic interpretation of a sentence, the surface structure determines the actual pronunciation of the sentence.

By reading the previous paragraphs you probably realised how innovative and ingenious Chomsky's ideas in the mid-1950s were opposed to the ideas of behaviorism and distributionalism. Especially his aim to study sentences acceptable to native speakers was completely new and developed into the mentalist or nativist concept of language learning: grammars are seen as mental states of speakers. So the goal of linguistic theory is to explain the process of language acquisition, and especially its creative aspect, i.e., the ability of a speaker to produce an infinite set of sentences.

A number of observations of child language acquisition clearly spoke against the behaviorist assumption that language can be learnt through conditioning or association and generalisation (recall what we said about the stimulus-response model in the previous chapter). First, language acquisition proceeds fast and successfully. Second, the grammar that is acquired is highly complex, and third, the relation between impoverished input and the grammar (output) acquired calls for an explanation. The third point relates to what Chomsky called the **poverty of the stimulus**: the quality and quantity of the input is often not very good/high, and many sentences the child hears are ungrammatical. Moreover, it is impossible that a child has come across all possible sentences and constructions in the **primary linguistic data** (PLD) before he or she starts to produce them. But how is it still possible then that a child acquires a complex grammar without having full exposure to it? And how can it be explained that speakers of a language have the same knowledge about that language? Chomsky refers to this observation as **Plato's problem**, and his answer was to stipulate a **language acquisition device** (LAD) which constructs a theory of a language of which the data the child is exposed to is a sample. The LAD is part of what has come to be known as **Universal Grammar**, a theory of knowledge which is concerned with the internal structure of the human mind. Such a grammar relates to what a speaker knows about his/her language and also where this knowledge comes from. It is universal because grammatical properties which are common to all human languages are assumed. Since the theory is concerned with the intrinsic knowledge a speaker has, Chomsky called it **I(nternalised)-language** which stands in contrast to **E(xternalised)-language**, a system of utterances or forms, which is understood independently of the properties of the mind. Clearly, American structuralists were concerned with E-language because they saw their task in collecting samples of language and in describing their properties. In *Aspects of the Theory of Syntax* Chomsky (1965, 10) states that '... investigation of performance will proceed only in so far as understanding of underlying competence permits.' Here he draws the influential distinction between **competence**, the knowledge of the speaker about his/her language, and **performance**, the actual use of language, which partly corresponds to the distinction between I-language and E-language.

In the same book, Chomsky gave thought to the question of how to justify and evaluate theories of grammar. He developed a way to evaluate grammatical descriptions which consists of three levels: observational, descriptive, and explanatory adequacy. The level of **observational adequacy** is reached if a theory of grammar can predict grammaticality of samples of a language, i.e. the PLD of adult speech. The level of **descriptive adequacy** is met if a theory of grammar can account for the competence of a native speaker regarding the rules of the language. The highest level of adequacy, **explanatory adequacy**, is met if a theory of grammar offers an explanation of why linguistic competence takes the form that it does, i.e. the process of language acquisition. Chomsky (1965, 26) critically states:

> Clearly it would be utopian to expect to achieve explanatory adequacy on a large scale in the present state of linguistics. Nevertheless, considerations of explanatory adequacy are often critical for advancing linguistic theory.

6.2 The Theory of Principles and Parameters

In the following decades Chomsky constantly revised his theory of grammar to get closer to a theory of grammar which could be called explanatorily adequate. In his famous Pisa lectures (1979) he first introduced his **Theory of Principles & Parameters** (P&P) which refined the theory of Universal Grammar. The theory assumes a language faculty which is seen as a separate module in the mind of human beings. Thus, UG is a theory only of the language module which has its own principles and is independent of other cognitive modules. Chomsky further stated that

> The theory of UG must meet two obvious conditions. On the one hand, it must be compatible with the diversity of existing (indeed, possible) grammars. At the same time, UG must be sufficiently constrained and restrictive in the options it permits so as to account for the fact that each of these grammars develop in the mind on the basis of quite limited evidence.
> (Chomsky, 1981, 3f)

The result of these claims was to say that UG contains principles and parameters. **Principles** are the properties that all languages have in common, they define the invariant core of universal grammar, whereas **parameters** are the choices that have to be set for each language based on the input the child is exposed to during language acquisition. Parameters are described as switches with the options 'on' and 'off' (since they are binary there are always two possibilities). In the following we will take a look at the properties of such principles and parameters (see also part II, chapter 9 where we will come back to this model).

Now, let's investigate the nature of a grammatical principle. Above, we saw that Chomsky made a distinction between two structures, a deep and a surface structure (later they were called **D-structure** and **S-structure**). He further said that these two structures are mediated by transformations. The notion of transformations was further developed in this theory as the notion of **movement**. At first sight movement seems to be defined in very general terms, so we could assume that all linguistic entities can move around to whatever place they like. This, of course, is not the case, we can observe that there are limitations to the operation of movement. More precisely, movements have to be short or local, and this limitation has been called the **Locality Principle**. It states that movement must be within a local part of the sentence from which the moved element originates. Take a look at the following examples:

(8) a. *The linguist will ponder the problem in her armchair.*
    b. *Will the linguist ponder the problem in her armchair?*

Yes-no questions in English require an auxiliary like *will* to occur in the first position of the sentence. Put in terms of movement, we can say that the auxiliary *will* has moved from its position behind the subject to a position directly preceding the subject. This type of movement is known as **subject-auxiliary inversion**. What happens if we have more than one auxiliary in a sentence? Take a look:

(9) a. *The linguist will have pondered the problem in her armchair.*
    b. *Will the linguist have pondered the problem in her armchair?*
    c. **Have the linguist will pondered the problem in her armchair?*

Here, only the first auxiliary can move to the first position (example (9) b.)), the second one, *have,* cannot (example (9) c.)). If we now compare the distances that the two auxiliaries must move, we can say that movement of *will* is shorter than movement of *have*. In other words, the shorter movement renders the sentence grammatical, whereas the longer movement renders the sentence ungrammatical. This is the **Locality Principle**.

Since grammatical principles are taken to be universal we expect to find them in all human languages (for details see for example Cook and Newson, 2007). Indeed, the Locality Principle can limit movement in other languages as well:

(10) a. NHG *Hat Eric das Buch gelesen?*
     b. **Gelesen Eric hat das Buch?*
     c. PDE *Has Eric read the book?*
     d. **Read Eric has the book?*
     e. FRE *A-t-il lu le livre?*
     f. **Lu-t-il a le livre?*
     g. ITA *Ha Gianni letto il libro?*
     h. **Letto Gianni ha il libro?*

In all of these cases from German (NHG), English (PDE), French (FRE) and Italian (ITA), the first verb, i.e. the auxiliary, must move to the front of the sentence. If the lexical verb moves—as for example *gelesen* in NHG in (10) b.—the sentences become ungrammatical because the movement is not as short as with the auxiliary (compare (10) a.). The explanation is that in these cases the Locality Principle is not adhered to.

We have said above that whereas principles are invariant, parameters account for the variation we find between languages. One parameter which specifies the order of certain elements in a language is the **head parameter**. In the 1970s Chomsky claimed that all phrases have a central element, the **head**, which can minimally stand for the whole phrase. Around the head we find elements that directly relate to the head. So for example, the VP *ponder the problem* has *ponder* as a verbal head, the NP *the linguist* has *linguist* as a nominal head, and the PP *in the library* has *in* as a prepositional head. The motivation behind this claim is, on the one hand, to say that all phrases have the same structure, and on the other hand, to express generalisations about the phrase structure of all human languages.

The example of the VP also serves well to illustrate another aspect of the theory. We know that the verb stands in a special relation to its (direct) object, for example *the problem* in (9) or *the book* in (10). In more general terms, we can observe that the relation between the head and its **complement** is subject to variation. In English, the head of a VP occurs to the left of the complement, whereas in German the verbal head occurs to the right of its complement:

(11) a. 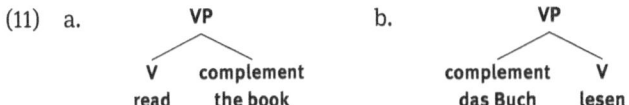   b.

Cross-linguistically we can observe that there are two possible structures of phrases in human languages: either head-left (head-first) or head-right (head-last). So according to this analysis the relative position of the head and the complement can be specified in an elegant way, i.e. by the head parameter which can be set either to 'heads are first in a phrase' or 'heads are last in a phrase'. For many languages this seems to hold, for example the heads of NPs, VPs, and PPs in English are all head-first. German is more tricky because the VP is head-last and the NP and the PP are head-first (with some exceptions, consider *den Fluss entlang* vs. *entlang des Flusses* 'along the river'). Some have suggested that if the phrases in a language are not 'harmonically aligned' in this respect the language might undergo a change (see Hawkins, 1979, Hawkins, 2014).

The idea that we can generalise over the structure of phrases (all kinds of phrases in all languages) led to **X-bar Theory**, which replaced phrase structure grammar. During the time when the **Theory of Government & Binding** was developed (of which the P&P theory is a part) grammar was broken down into modules with the aim to achieve simplicity and generality within a module. One such module is X-bar Theory which is responsible for the shape of actual structures. It constrains the structure of phrases to the following format:

(12)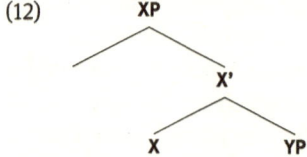

Two projection levels are assumed: first we have the head X, also called the zero level (X°). Above this, we have X', the first projection of the head. The 'bar' marks the level of projection. Above this we have a further level which is the maximal projection, in former times labelled X". During the process of derivation lexical items are selected from the lexicon and inserted into a structure adhering to X-bar Theory. The **Projection Principle** makes sure that the lexical information projected into such a structure remains constant at all levels of syntactic representation.

Other modules within the Theory of Government & Binding are **Case Theory** or **Theta Theory**. Theta Theory accounts for rules determining the integration of lexical units into a syntactic structure which are based on the meaning of these units. More precisely, Theta Theory deals with the relationship between predicates and their arguments and assigns semantic roles (or theta roles) such as AGENT, PATIENT, THEME to arguments in a sentence (see also part II, chapter 8). Take a look at the following examples:

(13)   a.   *Eric drinks a cup of tea.*
       b.   **Eric drinks a cup of tea a beer.*

In (13) a. the predicate *drinks* expresses relationships with its arguments *Eric* and *a cup of tea*. The argument *Eric* deliberately carries out the action of drinking and is the AGENT. The argument *a cup of tea* is the object of drinking or the argument that is acted upon by the AGENT, and therefore called the THEME. The example in b. shows that theta-roles and arguments are in a one-to-one correspondence with each other: the predicate has exactly two arguments and they must be assigned (exactly) one theta-role each. Since we have one argument too many (*a beer*) it cannot be assigned a theta-role which results in an ungrammatical sentence. This one-to-one correspondence is captured by the **Theta Criterion**.

A further consequence of Theta Theory is the postulation of empty categories:

(14)   *Parla molto*
       talks much
       'He/she talks a lot.'

We assume that Theta Theory applies to all languages. Now we know that in languages like Italian verbs like *parlare* assign a theta role to their subject, but actually it is not 'there', at least on the surface. But since theta roles always have to be assigned, subjects are assumed to always be there, either in an overt or covert way. This leads to the stipulation of **null subjects** (see also part II, chapter 8 and part III, 14).

To illustrate how much has changed in the course of time, compare the two models presented below. Note that these models represent how speakers generate sentences, i.e. they reconstruct the competence of speakers. Figure 6.1 illustrates the model of grammar based on Chomsky's *Aspects of the Theory of Syntax* from 1965:

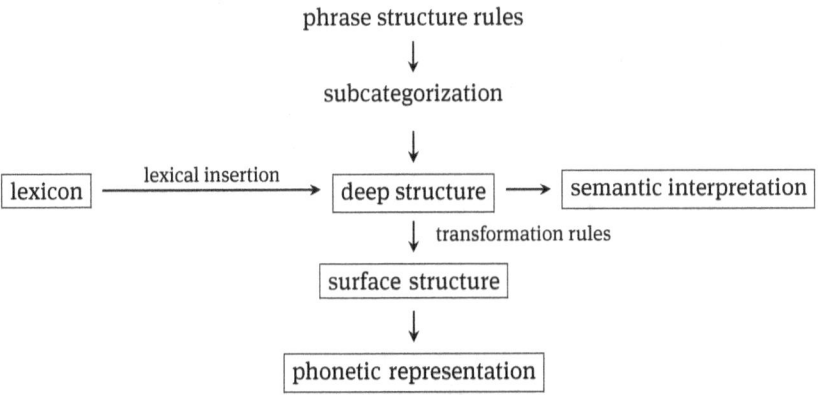

Fig. 6.1. Grammatical model of the *Aspects of the Theory of Syntax (1965)*

The *Aspects model* shows that grammar consists of a generative syntactic component, as well as of an interpretive, semantic and phonological component. As you can see deep structure is built by two rules: lexical insertion and phrase structure rules. Lexical elements are taken from the lexicon and are inserted in a tree structure in slots for elements of the type noun, verb, adjective etc. The syntactic structure is built by applying the phrase structure rules, and the result is a syntactic tree (phrase marker). The result is the deep structure of a sentence which determines the meaning of a sentence. It contains the lexical elements and their meanings, as well as the most relevant syntactic relations of these elements. Let's say we built a sentence in active voice (*the man hit the ball*) according to the processes described above. If we now built a sentence in passive voice (*the ball was hit by the man*) we would need transformations that transfer the active into the passive sentence. The passive sentence has a surface structure which is the result of transformations that were applied to deep structure. Whereas deep structure determines the meaning of a sentence, surface structure determines the phonetic form of the sentence. This demonstrates that grammar is seen as a mechanism which relates sounds with meanings. As you can also see in the model, deep structure is the input for the semantic component where a sentence is assigned a semantic interpretation. Surface structure is the input for the phonological component where a sentence is assigned a phonetic representation.

Figure 6.2 shows the **T-model** of Chomsky's theory of grammar (1981) taking into account all modifications (some of which we have discussed in this chapter) since the 1965 model.

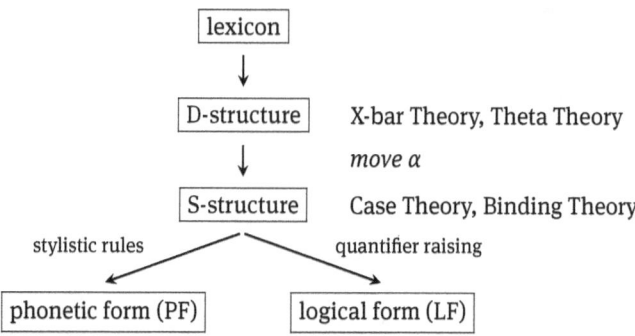

Fig. 6.2. Grammatical model of the P&P Theory (1981)

One crucial difference between the two models is that in the T-model D-structure (formerly deep structure) no longer feeds semantic interpretation. Rather, D-structure is fed by the level of **Logical Form** (LF). The first step in the syntactic derivation is that elements are retrieved from the lexicon building a syntactic structure (sentence) according to the principles of X-bar Theory and Theta-Theory. The operation *move α* then transforms D-structure into S-structure (formerly surface structure). On the level of S-structure the principles of Case Theory and Binding Theory hold, and it is also on this level where pieces of information relevant to the components of **Phonetic Form** (PF) and Logical Form are sent to these interfaces respectively. PF and LF are called interfaces because they establish the contact between the grammar (computational system), i.e. language, and aspects which are not language: '... the outside world of sounds and the inside world of concepts' (Cook and Newson, 2007, 6).

This model was further modified resulting in the so-called Y-model of the **Minimalist Program** (Chomsky, 1981, 1993) which I will not discuss here. Below I will provide some references which deal with this model in detail.

Many linguists were in accordance with the fundamental notions of generative grammar as laid down by Chomsky in his *Syntactic Structures* and *Aspects of the Theory of Syntax*. However, there were also aspects that were criticised, for example the role deep structure played. As a result **Generative Semantics** was proposed by the linguists Lakoff, Ross, McCawley, Katz and Postal. Bresnan & Kaplan developed **Lexical Functional Grammar** which replaced deep structure by *functional structure*. Other

Fig. 6.3. The development of grammatical theory since 1800 (adopted from Stein (2010, 5) and slightly modified)

theories of grammar which developed based on Chomsky's early work are **Head-driven Phrase Structure Grammar** (HPSG) and **Tree Adjoining Grammar** (TAG). What these theories all have in common is that they are based on constituents and a phrase structure grammar. Lexical-Functional Grammar and Head-driven Phrase Structure Grammar are members of a group of theories called **Unification Grammars** because they reject the idea of an underlying syntactic representation and of transformational rules. Further, they assume that morphosyntactic information is represented by syntactic features, that the lexicon plays an important role, and that unification is a central mechanism in the grammar. Since a detailed discussion of this type of theory is far beyond this book, I refer you to van Valin (2001) who deals with these and other theories in an engaging way.

The figure in 6.3 (p. 61) summarises the development of grammatical theory since the nineteenth century and shows which theories were directly influenced by Chomsky's ideas.

Tax: 'From what I have learnt travelling through time, I have the feeling that I now have a better understanding of what modern linguists assumed some decades ago, and still assume (in the case of Chomsky), because I see these things embedded in the historical context.'

Syn: 'Yes, and even ideas as complex and abstract as Chomsky's have become comprehensible if not intriguing, although, I must say, it was a lot to digest.'

Tax: 'I totally agree, and this is why I try to summarise the main facts: first, we learnt that Chomsky was influenced by the distributionalists because he stated that the formal study of grammar is independent of semantics. But instead of only describing structures on the surface he realised that there must be two structures, one deep and one surface structure. Second, he assumed that transformations, which later came to be movement operations, mediate between the two structures.'

Syn: 'Don't forget that he was also influenced by scholars like Humboldt.'

Tax: 'Exactly. Chomsky was influenced by the famous German scholar in assuming that language is an infinite set of sentences built by a finite set of elements. And his idea of a universal grammar was also not really new, here he has been mainly influenced by the Port-Royal grammar. But we have also learnt that something he completely rejected was the behaviorist idea, namely that language is an instance of behaviour. Instead he said that grammars must be seen as mental states of speakers, thus stressing the mental or cognitive aspect of language. To corroborate this claim he took a look at language acquisition and stated that the process of acquiring a language can only be explained if a universal grammar is assumed which includes invariant principles and parameters which account for variation between languages. He also defined several stages to evaluate models of grammar and has tirelessly been working on reaching explanatory adequacy.'

Syn: 'It seems that we are at the end of our journey through the centuries.'

Tax: 'Yes, but now the task is to apply the knowledge we have acquired to phenomena of Present-Day English. So, come along to the next part of the book.'

Syn: 'Great idea! Let's go!'

Literature: There is a plethora of work on the theory of Universal Grammar, by Chomsky himself and by others. Therefore, I will only provide a selection of works. To understand what his aims were right from the start it is inevitable to read his *Syntactic Structures* (1957, see also the edition of 2002) and his *Aspects of the Theory of Syntax* (1965). In his *Cartesian Linguistics* (1966, see also the edition of

2009) Chomsky discusses important aspects in the study of language and mind since the end of the sixteenth century in order to explain in how far scholars like Humboldt or the Port-Royal grammarians influenced his work. In his Pisa lectures (published in 1981) Chomsky introduced the P&P theory, and in his *Knowledge of language: its nature, origin and use* (1986) and in his Managua lectures (1988) he discusses the nature, origins, and current concerns in the field of linguistics. In *The Minimalist Program* (1993) his minimalist approach to linguistic theory is formulated and developed. The book by Cook and Newson (2007) is a masterly introduction to Chomsky's Universal Grammar, really well and clearly written with many exercises. Further, I highly recommend Haegeman's work, her textbook on the Theory of Government and Binding (2001), a generative perspective on English grammar (Haegeman and Guéron, 1999), and especially *Thinking syntactically* (Haegeman, 2006). Both are really well written, with many trees and exercises: students (will) love it! Grewendorf (2002) is a good introduction to Chomsky's philosophy of language, and Grewendorf (2006) is an introduction to the Minimalist Program (both in German). For those who are also interested in Chomsky as a person I recommend Barsky's (1997) biography. Concerning a discussion of different grammatical models there are some (but few) textbooks like van Valin's (2001), and Müller's (2013, German version) and (2014, English version) which provide a comparison of different generative and non-generative models in an appealing way.

Part II: Synchronic analysis of English syntax

7 Introduction

In the second part of the book, we are going to deal with the synchronic analysis of English syntax. As mentioned in the preface, we will select some of the many syntactic phenomena of Present-Day English, describe their patterns and discuss analyses. The aspects chosen in this part of the book relate to aspects we have come across in the first part of the book. So we will start out with general aspects of sentence structure including the properties of subjects and predicates, differences between the structure of main sentences and subordinate clauses, and the special role the verb plays in a sentence (see again part I, chapter 2). In the following chapters we will address the notion of government, universals (see again part I, chapter 3) and instances of syntactic variation in PDE (see again part I, chapter 4). We will further compare prominent syntactic constructions in PDE and other Germanic and non-Germanic languages (see again part I, chapter 5) and take a closer look at the theoretical notion of movement and how it can be applied to PDE (see again part I, chapter 6).

As previously mentioned in the preface, one of the aims of this book is to provide a solid descriptive basis for an analysis of data from PDE and historical data. This is why in this part and part III of the book you will find a lot of data describing the phenomena discussed. Since another aim is to *explain* why PDE is as it is, and why it differs from other (Germanic) languages, also by looking back in history, sometimes the generative syntactic model is applied to the data. Having read part I of the book you should be in a position to see the merits of a theory generally, and the advantages (and disadvantages) of generative grammar. Thus, you should also be able to choose another grammatical model and apply it to the data presented in the book, if you wish.

Recently, it has become common practice to illustrate linguistic aspects in textbooks by using data from authentic speech, i.e. from corpora. Especially for novice students of syntax, it is very important to show that the constructions we are dealing with really exist and are not just something made up by linguists trying to prove their point. However, introspection also has its justification, especially if a constructed example is easier to understand because it is less complex than authentic data or if parallels between languages are pointed out. Therefore, I will provide both constructed examples where necessary and authentic data collected from the *British National Corpus* (BNC).

8 Sentence structure of Present-Day English

In this chapter we are going to deal with sentence structure of PDE. The main types of sentences are discussed as well as the properties of subject and verb, and the properties of negated sentences.

If you have read the first part of the book you will know by now that quite a number of terms and definitions of grammatical theory derive from Plato and Aristotle (see part I, chapter 2). Recall that in the Platonic dialogue *The Sophist* the *lógos* ('proposition' in logic, 'sentence' in grammar) is defined as consisting of *ónoma* ('subject' in logic, 'noun' in grammar) and *rhēma* ('predication' in logic, 'verb' in grammar). Thus, we have two parts of a sentence which are not interchangeable. Moreover, only a sentence containing both parts is meaningful. In this model, a thing is not only named by a noun but a noun is also predicated of the verb. This analysis of a sentence (or of sentences) can be seen as the first approach to grammatical theory in a systematic way. You will see in the following that this approach is still valid today and serves as the basis in many models of grammatical theory.

8.1 Constituents and constituency tests

In traditional grammar a sentence is defined in terms of a predication relation between a subject and the property related to the subject, the predicate. So the sentence *The syntactician ponders the problem in her armchair* tells us something about the subject, namely that the syntactician will undergo the activity of pondering the problem in her armchair. We can also say that pondering the problem is predicated of the syntactician. *The syntactician* is the subject of the predication.

In the following, we will take a look at the structure of a sentence and discuss the properties of the elements in a sentence. Before we do so, however, a note on the terms **sentence** and **clause** is in order: in traditional grammar a sentence is a language unit which comprises a minimum sense of completeness and unity (see Quirk et al., 2004, 12). Sentences can be divided into **simple**, **compound**, and **complex** sentences. A simple sentence contains one lexical, finite verb plus obligatory and optional constituents. The types and number of constituents occurring in a sentence are to some extent determined by the lexical verb. Let's take a look again at our example from the introduction:

(1)   *The syntactician ponders the problem in her armchair.*

This is a simple sentence. It contains the obligatory constituents *the syntactician* (NP with the function of subject), *the problem* (NP with the function of object), the lexical, finite verb *ponders*, and *in her armchair* (PP with the function of locative adverbial).

Clauses are units smaller than the sentence, generally a distinction is made between **main (independent)** and **subordinate (dependent)** clauses. In a compound sentence like

(2) *The syntactician ponders the problem in her armchair and the chemist does an experiment in his lab.*

two main clauses are joined through **coordination**. The first main clause is *the syntactician ponders the problem in her armchair* which is conjoined by the coordinating conjunction *and* with the second main clause *the chemist does an experiment in his lab*. The compound sentence thus consists of two lexical, finite verbs which are part of two independent clauses, and both clauses are conjoined by coordination, not by subordination because they are on an equal footing.

A complex sentence contains at least two lexical, finite verbs with all additional (dependent) clauses being joined to the main (independent) clause via **subordination**. One example would be:

(3) *The syntactician ponders the problem in her armchair because the chemist who said that linguistics is irrelevant has occupied the syntactician's office to carry out experiments.*

In this case, the dependent clause *because the chemist who said that linguistics is irrelevant has occupied the syntactician's office to carry out experiments* is joined to the main clause *the syntactician ponders the problem in her armchair* by the subordinating conjunction *because* forming a reason clause. Moreover, the dependent clause contains further dependent clauses like the relative clause *who said that linguistics is irrelevant*, and the nominal *that*-clause *that linguistics is irrelevant*. All of these clauses contain a subject and at least a lexical verb and are dependent on other parts of the subordinate and main clauses. You can prove this by trying to form a simple sentence with these clauses:

(4) a. **Because the chemist who said that linguistics is irrelevant has occupied the syntactician's office to carry out experiments.*
 b. **Who said that linguistics is irrelevant has occupied the syntactician's office to carry out experiments.*
 c. **That linguistics is irrelevant has occupied the syntactician's office to carry out experiments.*
 d. **To carry out experiments.*

Clearly, you fail to do so because they cannot stand alone.

In the following, we will use these terms and definitions in the analysis of synchronic and diachronic syntactic phenomena.

Syn: 'Hello, here we are again!'
Tax: 'Yes, and we will guide you through this part of the book which means that we will summarise the findings of each chapter and we will also provide some exercises for you.'
Syn: 'And your first task now is to apply the types of sentences and/or clauses defined above to the following example from the BNC:'

(5) She had plenty of time to ponder things last night after flying off to Perth where she and Jeremy Bates are the stand-bys for next week's Hopman Cup.
(BNC,AAN 16)

Coming back to the definition of a sentence as a unit consisting of a subject and a predicate, we will now examine the properties of the subject and the relation it has to the predicate. To illustrate the nature and properties of the subject, let's again use the constructed example from above:

(6) **The syntactician** *ponders the problem in her armchair.*

In this sentence, the subject *the syntactician* is expressed by an NP consisting of the definite determiner *the* and the noun *syntactician*. The noun carries meaning and denotes a referent in the world (for example, if we look up the meaning of the word in the OED we find that a *syntactician* is 'an expert in or student of syntax'). From the sentence above we further gather that the syntactician we are talking about is female because the referential possessive pronoun *her* refers back to it.

Subjects need not be expressed by NPs, we could also clearly state

(7) a. **She** *ponders the problem in her armchair.*
     b. **She** *had plenty of time to ponder things last night ...*

by using a referential pronoun to define the subject in these sentences. What we cannot do in PDE is to leave out the subject:

(8) a. **Ponders the problem in her armchair.*
     b. **Had plenty of time to ponder things last night ...*

Interestingly, there are languages like Italian where this is possible and perfectly grammatical:

(9) Considera il problema.
     ponder-3-SG the problem

Languages which permit a sentence to lack an explicit subject are called **null subject** languages or **subject-drop** languages (from pronoun-dropping). In part III, chapter 14 we will see that in Old English subjects could also be omitted.

There are constructions which reorganise the information of a sentence and shift the subject towards the end of the sentence. In these cases a 'placeholder' for the subject appears in first position. These constructions are called existential sentences, an example of which is given in (10) b:

(10) a. *Two syntacticians are investigating the data.*
     b. ***There** are two syntacticians investigating the data.*
     c. *Are two syntacticians investigating the data?*

In PDE, a sentence usually begins with reference to 'given' information and continues to provide 'new' information ((10) a.). Existential constructions are introduced by an unstressed *there* followed by a form of *be* and serve to bring the existence of a full proposition to the attention of the hearer/reader (also note that the finite verb form *are* agrees with *two syntacticians* and not with *there*). *There* is inserted as a dummy theme to indicate the 'new' status of the proposition, including its subject. The subject of the proposition (i.e. of the original sentence) has been called the **notational subject** or the **logical subject**, and *there* has been called the **thematic subject** or the **grammatical subject**. The term 'grammatical subject' refers to the role it plays in the sentence: if it is deleted, the sentence becomes ungrammatical. If we form a direct question on the model of (10) a. we see that *there* no longer occurs and that subject-verb inversion has taken place ((10) c.). This is not surprising since direct questions serve a completely different function (i.e. seeking information on a specific point), a dummy theme is not needed. Apart from the fact that the logical subject cannot be left out in 'normal' sentences, the grammatical subject can also not be left out in existential constructions.

The fact that the subject cannot be left out in sentences in PDE tells us something quite fundamental about language: it is structured by linguistic units (this may sound trivial but it is not!). There are primary units like sentences which consist of a minimum sense of completeness and unity. The subject and predicate are the main units of a sentence that fulfil the need for grammatical completeness, they are the main, obligatory **constituents** of a sentence. If someone says

(11) *ponders the problem in her armchair*

we would like to know '*Who* ponders the problem in her arm chair?'. And if we hear someone saying

(12) *the syntactician*

we would want to ask 'What about the syntactician?' because we know that something, i.e. the predicate, is missing here.

Very often, predicates consist of constituents themselves which can be seen by looking again at our example:

(13) *ponders the problem in her armchair*

Therefore, we need to examine the constituents of the predicate and the sentence.

The term 'constituent' is used in structural sentence analysis for every linguistic unit. Several constituents together form a linguistic unit. Moreover, constituents can be joined together with other constituents to form larger units (see Bussmann, 1996, 98).

For English, we apply the following tests to discover syntactic constituents: Substitution (for example Pronominalisation), Fronting/Movement, Question formation, Deletion/Ellipsis, Coordination, and Focalising. All the tests are **one-directional**, meaning that if an entity is analysed as a constituent with one test, it is a constituent but if this entity fails a test it could still be identified as a constituent in another test.

Let's start with the first test, **substitution (pronominalisation)**. It can be defined as follows: A unit that can be pronominalised is a constituent. Anaphoric elements like pronouns can replace constituents.

(14) a. [*The syntactician*]$_{NP}$ *ponders* [*the problem*]$_{NP}$ *in her armchair.*
 b. ***She*** *ponders **it**.*

The syntactician and *the problem* whose most important elements are *syntactician* and *problem* are noun phrases (NPs). They can be replaced by pronouns and are thus constituents in the sentence. In more general terms, substitution also includes cases where *the syntactician* can be substituted for a proper noun like *Mary*. *In her armchair* which is a prepositional phrase (PP) can also be replaced by a proform (*there*) and thus is a further constituent in the sentence. The unit *do so* functions as a proform for the predicate:

(15) a. *The syntactician ponders the problem in her armchair.*
 b. *The morphologist **does so**, too.*

By replacing the predicate in the sentence by this proform, it can be identified as a constituent. Note that *do so* occurs in both finite and non finite forms.

The next test to be discussed is **Fronting/Movement**: A unit that can be fronted/moved is a syntactic constituent. The examples below illustrate this test:

(16) a. *The syntactician ponders the problem in her armchair.*
 b. ***The problem*** *the syntactician ponders in her armchair.*
 c. ***In her armchair*** *the syntactician ponders the problem.*
 d. ***Ponder the problem in her armchair*** *the syntactician will.*

To see whether a constituent has been fronted/moved or not, we need to define the neutral or **unmarked** order of elements in a sentence. The concept of markedness used here is based on the distinction between what is neutral, natural or unmarked, and what departs from the neutral or unmarked along some well-defined properties or characteristics. Some of the characteristics for unmarked elements are that they are expressed by simpler means or that they occur more frequently in the languages of the world (see Bussmann, 1996, 294). For a different notion of markedness and its relation to parameters see Roberts (2007), chapter 3.4. Coming back to our data, in PDE, the subject typically precedes the finite verb and the object follows it. In (16) b. the order is O(bject)-S(ubject)-V(erb), so the NP *the problem* which functions as the object in the sentence must have been fronted/moved to the first position. This order can be defined as a **marked** order because it clearly deviates from the neutral order. The same applies to the PP *in her armchair*: PPs with the function of an adverbial typically follow the verb (and object). Since it occurs right at the beginning of the sentence, it must have been fronted/moved. The example in d. illustrates that even the whole VP can be fronted/moved to the first position in the sentence.

The third constituency test under discussion is **question formation**: A unit that can be replaced by an interrogative pronoun and moved to the front of the sentence is a constituent (combination of pronominalisation and movement). Let's take a look at some examples:

(17) a. *The syntactician ponders the problem in her armchair.*
 b. ***Who*** *ponders the problem in her armchair? The syntactician.*
 c. ***What*** *does the syntactician ponder in her armchair? The problem.*
 d. ***Where*** *does the syntactician ponder the problem? In her armchair.*
 e. ***What*** *will the syntactician do? Ponder the problem in her armchair.*

The NP *the syntactician* in (17) b., the NP *the problem* in c., and the PP *in her armchair* in d. can be replaced by the interrogative pronouns *who, what,* and *where*. Since all of these questions ask for the replacement of a constituent, they are called constituent questions (as opposed to yes/no-questions for example). The example in e. confirms that the predicate can also be the answer to a constituent question.

Deletion/Ellipsis can serve as a further test for constituency: Only constituents can be deleted/elided. The following examples illustrate this test:

(18) a. *The syntactician ponders the problem in her armchair.*
b. *The syntactician claims that her problem is **the hardest** to solve.*
c. *The syntactician prefers the papers of Chomsky, while I prefer **those of Jackendoff**.*
d. *The syntactician will present a talk at the conference when Chomsky **will**.*

A constituent can only be omitted if it is precisely recoverable. In (18) b. the head of the NP *(her) problem* is elided. This also applies to the example in c. (*the papers of Chomsky*) although in this case the proform *those* must be inserted to render the sentence grammatical. (18) d. is an example of predication ellipsis, the presence of the auxiliary *will* is obligatory.

Many cases of ellipsis involve some degree of parallelism between the original construction and the elliptical construction. This aspect also plays a role in **coordination** which is a further test of constituency: Only constituents can be coordinated.

(19) a. *The syntactician ponders the problem in her armchair.*
b. *The syntactician **ponders and tackles** the problem in her armchair.*
c. *The syntactician ponders **the problem and the solution** in her armchair.*
d. *The syntactician ponders the problem **in her armchair and in the hot tub**.*
e. *The syntactician **ponders the problem in her armchair and investigates the data at her desk**.*

The examples show that the constituents which are parallel in meaning can be linked by the coordinating conjunction *and*. In (19) b. the finite verb *ponders* is coordinated with *tackles* (both verbs are transitive), in c. the NPs *the problem* and *the solution* are coordinated. (19) d. is an example of PP coordination, and e. an example of the coordination of predication (note that in the latter case the subject is shared).

The last test to be discussed here is the **foregrounding** of a constituent: units that can be foregrounded are constituents. Two constructions which have the effect of foregrounding a constituent while the rest of the sentence is backgrounded are cleft sentences and pseudo-cleft sentences. In both cases, the sentence is divided into two clauses, each with its own verb:

(20) a. *The syntacticians ponder the problem in her armchair.*
 b. *It is **the syntacticians** that ponder the problem in her armchair.*
 c. *It is **the problem** that the syntacticians ponder in her armchair.*
 d. *It is **in her armchair** that the syntacticians ponder the problem.*
 e. *What the syntacticians do is (to) **ponder the problem in her armchair**.*

Generally, clefting reorganises the information in a sentence. The truth value in the examples in (20) is unchanged but clearly the presentation is different. Cleft sentences follow the pattern *It is X who/that Y* where *X*, i.e. the focussed (foregrounded) element, can be the subject ((20) b.), the object (c.), and the locative adverbial (d.). Pseudo-cleft sentences are more limited and follow the pattern *What X Verb is/was Y (rest of sentence)*. Example e. shows that pseudo-clefts permit marked focus to fall on the predicate.

Tax: 'So far we have seen that the structure of a sentence consisting of a subject and a predicate can be further decomposed into smaller units which we call constituents. The tests we have discussed help us identify the constituents in a sentence.'

Syn: 'Now, to see whether you understood the notion of constituency we want you to apply the tests to the data from the BNC. More precisely, **1)** apply all tests to (21), and **2)** identify instances of pronominalisation, fronting, ellipsis, coordination and clefting in all of the examples in (22)':

(21) At a conference at Oxford in December 1989, Professor Randolph Quirk, the famous linguist, attacked me fiercely for including material like this, which could be easily misrepresented by the press.
(BNC,CCV 449)

(22) a. *It is the registration that must be obtained by fraud.*
(BNC, FD7 375)
 b. *He repeatedly found himself asking the question Who? – and What? – was he?*
(BNC, A0P 1148)
 c. *The provisional title referred to the life-span of Jaromil, who dies young, as lyric poets will,*
...
(BNC, A05 621)
 d. *Anomalocaris is the biggest predator among the Burgess animals, and one of the hardest to interpret.*
(BNC, ABG 2989)
 e. *Well, I'm sure I shouldn't have, but I was feeling so guilty about you that I would have agreed to do anything you asked.*
(BNC, HTG 1652)
 f. *And both these books pale before novels that contend for the mantle of Disraeli: those of Jeffrey Archer himself.* (BNC, ARX 202)

8.2 Subjects, verbs, and negation

Next, let's take a look at the predicate of PDE sentences from another perspective, i.e. at the position of the finite verb. The following examples serve to illustrate its position(s). The syntactic functions of subject, verb, and object are indicated by indices, constituents bigger than one word are enclosed in square brackets:

(23) a. $Eric_S$ $plays_V$ [the piano]$_O$ every day.
b. $Eric_S$ is_V [quite relaxed]$_{Su\text{-}compl}$ because he_S $plays_V$ [the piano]$_O$ every day.
c. Every day, $Eric_S$ $plays_V$ [the piano]$_O$.
d. [The piano]$_O$, $Eric_S$ $plays_V$ every day.
e. Unfortunately, $Eric_S$ $plays_V$ [the piano]$_O$ every day.
f. Although he_S $annoys_V$ [all members of the family]$_O$, $Eric_S$ $plays_V$ [the piano]$_O$ every day.

In the main declarative sentence in (23) a. the finite verb *plays* directly follows the subject *Eric*. This also applies to the main and subordinate clauses in the complex sentence in b. (where in the main clause the copula verb *be* creates the relation between the subject and the predicate in the form of the participle). In the main declarative sentence in c. the NP with the function of an adverbial of time is fronted to the first position, followed by the subject and finite verb. The examples in d. and e. also exhibit fronting: in d. the object *the piano*, and in e. the sentence adverb *unfortunately* occur in first position. In both cases the first constituents are followed by the subject and the finite verb. The complex sentence in f. is introduced by a subordinate clause and followed by the main clause. Again, in both clauses the subject *he/Eric* is followed by the finite verb. The result of the investigation is quite clear: in main declarative and in subordinate clauses the finite verb follows the subject.

Tax: 'Okay, here is another exercise for you: what do you think, do the examples below from the BNC confirm this finding? **1)** analyse the examples in (24) and **2)** compare them with the examples above.'

(24) a. *The Tories say they're philosophical but not angry.*
(BNC, KRM 441)
b. *If both sides agree, any deterioration or delay regarding the return of the part exchanged goods can be ignored.*
(BNC, J7D 375)
c. *Every day, I get a postcard from some tropical place called Brown Sugar Island or Crab Cove.*
(BNC, FPB 2201)
d. *Others I like for their sheer messiness.*
(BNC, FS5 865)
e. *Unfortunately, a fuss proved to be unavoidable.*
(BNC, A0D 870)

What about the order of the subject and its predicate in yes/no-questions and wh-questions? Let's use the constructed examples from above again:

(25) a. Does$_{Aux}$ Eric$_S$ play$_V$ [the piano]$_O$ every day? Yes/No.
b. Has$_{Aux}$ Eric$_S$ played$_V$ [the piano]$_O$ every day? Yes/No.
c. Will$_{Aux}$ Eric$_S$ play$_V$ [the piano]$_O$ every day? Yes/No.
d. *Plays$_V$ Eric$_S$ [the piano]$_O$ every day? Yes/No.
e. When does$_{Aux}$ Eric$_S$ play$_V$ [the piano]$_O$? Every day.
f. What does$_{Aux}$ Eric$_S$ play$_V$ every day? [The piano]$_O$.
g. What has$_{Aux}$ Eric$_S$ played$_V$ every day? [The piano]$_O$.
h. Who plays$_V$ [the piano]$_O$ every day? Eric$_S$.

To form questions in PDE we restructured some of the sentences in (23). In yes/no-questions like (25) a. the sentence is introduced by a verb form of the auxiliary *do* or any other auxiliary, for example *has* in b. or *will* in c. What is not possible is to place the inflected lexical verb in first position as you can see in (25) d. This results in an ungrammatical sentence. If an **argument** or **adjunct** of the lexical verb is questioned, the respective interrogative pronoun has to occur in the first position and it has to be followed by a finite form of *do* or another auxiliary. This is illustrated with the examples (25) e., f. and g. The exception are questions introduced by *who* which question the subject of the sentence (25 e.). Here, the finite form of the lexical verb has to occur (this observation has given many theoretical syntacticians quite a headache! For interesting solutions to the problem see, for example, Chomsky (1995) and Rizzi (1996) and the references given below).

Comparing the relative order of subject and finite verb in the examples above, we see that questions are marked by the word order: the finite verb precedes the subject. It has been said, that in interrogative contexts the subject inverts with the finite verb, and this is why the process is called **subject-verb inversion** or **subject-auxiliary inversion**. The latter term restricts the operation to auxiliaries and to PDE (and also ignores some data like questions introduced by *who*). We will see that there are other languages like New High German (NHG) and Old English which show subject-verb inversion with the subject and the finite lexical verb. In NHG inversion also occurs in questions as in:

(26) a. Spielt$_V$ Eric$_S$ jeden Tag Klavier$_O$? Ja/Nein.
Plays Eric every day piano? Yes/No.
b. Wann spielt$_V$ Eric$_S$ Klavier$_O$? Jeden Tag.
When plays Eric the piano? Every day.

Since we are also interested in comparing PDE to other languages, I prefer to use the broader definition of inversion and will refer to it as subject-verb inversion.

Table 8.1 summarises the orders found in main declaratives and questions (1st C stands for first constituent):

Table 8.1. Word order patterns in PDE

	main declarative	yes/no question	wh-question	subordinate
PDE	[1st C = S]–V–(O)… [1st C]–S–V–(O)…	Aux–S–V–(O)…	[wh=S]–V–(O)… wh–Aux–S–V–(O)…	S–V–O

So far, we have talked about sentences without negation, i.e. where the proposition of a sentence is positive. But what about negated sentences in PDE? First of all, there is a difference between sentence negation and constituent negation. Sentence negation negates the proposition of a sentence whereas constituent negation negates (only) a constituent in a sentence. This difference is illustrated with the following examples:

(27) a. *He did **not** have dinner.*
     b. *He had **no** dinner.*

In (27) a. the sentence negation *not* negates the proposition of the sentence which results in the reading 'It is not the case that he had dinner'. Here, the negation extends over the entire predicate. In (27) b. the constituent negation *no* negates the constituent to its right, i.e. *dinner* which results in the reading 'It is the case that he had no dinner'. You can clearly see that the scope of *no* is more narrow than that of *not*. Concerning the position of the sentence negation *not* we see that it occurs directly after the auxiliary *did*. As illustrated below it can also occur as a contracted form on *did* as *didn't* (see also part III, chapter 18.2). The constituent negation *no* precedes the constituent it negates.

In non-standard varieties of British English, sentence and constituent negation can be combined, so you can hear speakers saying things like:

(28) *He didn't have **no** dinner.*

A quite prominent example from the Rolling Stones is:

(29) *I can't get **no** satisfaction.*

Although two instances of negation occur in these sentences, they are negated only once: 'it is not the case that he had dinner', and 'it is not the case that he can get satisfaction'. Note that in Standard English the same sentence would have a positive interpretation (if it occurred) because two realisations of negation in a single sentence give rise to a positive statement. Languages where different negative expressions combine to express a single logical negation are called **negative concord languages**, languages like Standard English are **non-negative concord languages**.

In non-standard varieties of British English, negative concord occurs. It is generally held that negative concord is a typical social class marker rather than a dialectal feature. In her study on spoken non-standard British English (based on the spoken part of the BNC), Anderwald (2008) found that it occurs in all dialect areas and that regional variation can in fact be found. The different dialect areas were assigned to three main groups: North, Midlands, and South. Some comparable examples from these three dialect areas are given in (30):

(30) a. *Because ee er, some of the subjects I brought to him but he **didn't** know **nothing** about them!* (North)
(BNC, FL4 34)

b. *and er [pause] we scouted and scouted till daybreak and we **didn't** find **nothing**.* (Midlands)
(BNC, F8P 114)

c. *she only had the one daughter and two brothers, but she, the brothers she **don't** hear **nothing** of them they just, you know they were gonna put her in a home, ...* (South)
(BNC, J8F 75)

Interestingly, negative concord was considerably rarer in the Northern varieties than in the Southern varieties. Anderwald's findings thus support the hypothesis that negative concord never died out despite the influence of prescriptive grammars in EModE times. Moreover, language contact with Old Norse in OE times might be an explanation of why nowadays it is rarely found in the North and a more frequent feature in the South. In part II, chapter 10 and part III, chapter 14 we will gain further insights into the occurrence of negation in dialects and in the history of English.

Syn: 'So what have we learnt in this chapter?'
Tax: 'First of all, we revisited the traditional structuring of a sentence into a subject and a predicate introduced by Greek philosophers. Second, we have examined the properties of different types of subject in PDE and we have applied the standard tests of constituency to define constituents of the predicate. Further, we analysed the relation and position of the subject and the finite verb which resulted in a number of generalisations we will need in the following especially when we look at historical data. Finally, we have dealt with sentences containing a negator, and we have seen that negative con-

cord is a feature of non-standard varieties of British English. These findings are all taken up again in the diachronic part of the book.'

Literature: There is a plethora of work on the topics discussed in this chapter. The most comprehensive authoritative work for English clearly is Quirk et al. (2004), the smaller version of it is Greenbaum and Quirk (1990). Although Lamprecht (1986) is some decades old and written in German, it is a fantastic reference work because it comments on the grammatical phenomena in English from the perspective of a German L2 learner of English. Another well accessible book is König and Gast (2008) which addresses the major contrasts between English and German (also including two chapters on phonology). Haegeman's textbooks have always been my favourite because she provides fine-grained analyses in a highly accessible and engaging way. Haegeman (2006) is one of them, especially suited for novice students of syntax. Although it is generative in spirit, it does not focus on the nitty-gritties of this approach but rather enables students to think in a scientific way, to evaluate different approaches and to deal with authentic data.

9 Dependency relations and linguistic universals

In this chapter we'll first of all take a closer look at the two dependency relations discussed in part I, chapter 3, agreement and government, and determine their occurrence in PDE and NHG. Further, we will come back to the notion of universals in Chomsky's framework by discussing some PDE data that could be seen as being proof for their existence.

9.1 Agreement and government in Present-Day English and New High German

We have seen in part I, chapter 3 that in the eleventh and twelfth centuries syntax was based on the two key notions:
1. *regimen* 'government': the term describes relations where one word 'governed' another with the result that the governed word occurs in a particular case. So government is actually case government.
2. *congruitas* 'agreement': the term describes relations which involve agreement, i.e. two words enter into a relationship such that their properties have to be the same. Depending on the language, agreement can be expressed by morphology marking grammatical specifications like for example case, number, gender, and person.

Today we would say that the following example from Latin repeated here is an instance of government:

(1) lego   librum
     read-1-SG book-ACC-SG
     'I am reading the/a book.'

Since *lego* is a transitive verb, it governs one or more accusatives, hence *librum* is governed by *lego*.

Concerning agreement, which is sometimes also called **concord** or **congruency**, generally the distinction is made between **subject-verb agreement** and **nominal agreement**. Both types of agreement are based on dependency relations. Take a look again at the following example from Latin:

(2) homo   gaudet
     man-NOM-SG rejoice-3-SG
     'A/The man rejoices.'

In this example, subject-verb agreement is expressed by a relation between the verb *gaudet* and the noun *homo*. This relation is expressed by morphological marking, i.e. the inflectional endings on the noun and the verb (both noun and verb agree in third person singular). A case of nominal agreement is illustrated in the Latin example in (3):

(3) *homo*   *stultus*
     man-SG-MASC-NOM stupid-SG-MASC-NOM
     'A/The stupid man'

Here, the relation between the noun *homo* and the adjective *stultus* is again expressed by the inflectional endings; they agree (or are in concord) in case, number and gender. The adjective depends on the noun because it describes its quality.

Today, in grammar and theoretical linguistics the notion of government or **rection** is still valid and widely used. In (traditional) grammar, case government is discussed as an important relation between verbs, prepositions and their complements. In some models of generative syntax, especially in the **Theory of Government & Binding** developed by Noam Chomsky in his *Lectures on Government and Binding* (1981), it was one of the main structural relations and, as we will see, was defined in rather complex terms (for an introduction to X-bar Theory see part I, chapter 6.2). In this theory, verbs govern their complements, or more generally, lexical heads (**governors**) govern their dependents (**governee**) in structural, hierarchical terms (and not only in linear terms, i.e. from left to right or vice versa!). This relation is illustrated by the following tree representation in accordance with X-bar Theory:

(4)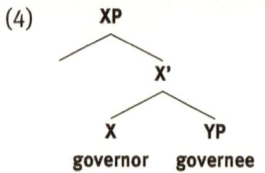

Let's take a look at some data from PDE and New High German (NHG):

(5) a. *Eric$_S$ sees$_V$ [the girl]$_O$.*
     b. *Eric$_S$ helps$_V$ [the girl]$_O$.*
     c. *Eric$_S$ sieht$_V$ [das Mädchen]$_O$.*
     d. *Eric$_S$ hilft$_V$ [dem Mädchen]$_O$.*
     e. *Eric$_S$ sees$_V$ her$_O$.*
     f. *Eric$_S$ sieht$_V$ sie$_O$.*
     g. *Eric$_S$ helps$_V$ her$_O$.*
     h. *Eric$_S$ hilft$_V$ ihr$_O$.*

By applying the definitions from above, we can identify two dependency relations: first, the relation between the subject *Eric* and the finite verb *sees/sieht*, and second,

9.1 Agreement and government in Present-Day English and New High German — 83

between the transitive verb *sees/sieht* and its object *the girl/das Mädchen* (the examples in (5) a. and c.). The relation between the subject and the finite verb is formally expressed by agreement, the second relation between the lexical verb and its object is government. This also applies to the examples in b. and d. with the verb *helps/hilft*.

Concerning agreement, the finite verb depends on the (proper) noun *Eric*. This relation is also expressed by the inflectional endings of the finite verb forms in both English *sees* and German *sieht* (as opposed to *ich sehe*, *du siehst*), both (proper) noun and verb agree in third person singular.

Concerning government, the transitive verb *see/sehen* governs the object *the girl/das Mädchen*. In NHG the object is morphologically marked as accusative (*das Mädchen*), however, in PDE morphological case marking is absent (but note that pronouns have distinctive case forms, see (5) e.). The difference between the verbs *see/sehen* and *help/helfen* is that they require different types of objects: the verbs *see/sehen* require direct objects, the verbs *help/helfen* require indirect objects. We may say that a direct object undergoes the action described by a verb, whereas an indirect object identifies for whom or what the action of the verb is performed (note that there are many different views on this!). As mentioned above, NHG has morphological case, so the object of *sehen* is marked for accusative case, and the object of *helfen* is marked for dative case. You will see that in early stages of English, like Old English, case government was morphologically marked, so the data generally resembles the NHG data in this respect.

The intuition that the verb has a close connection with its object is expressed, as we have said above, in structural, hierarchical terms in generative grammar. The verb, i.e. the head of the VP, is the governor, and the direct object, the governee, is its sister:

(6)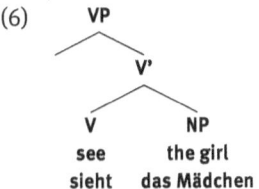

This geometrical relation has also been defined in terms of **c(onstituent)-command**: 'X c-commands Y iff every constituent that dominates X also dominates Y' (Reinhart, 1976). Put in simpler terms, any constituent c-commands its sister constituent, and everything that the sister constituent contains. Since the verb governs the direct object under these conditions, it is a case assigner and case marks the direct object.

In this framework, **abstract case** is postulated which is part of universal grammar. According to this theory abstract case exists without overt morphology which means that (even) languages which do not mark case morphologically have (abstract) case (we could say that it is always there even if we don't see it). In languages like PDE, abstract case marking is often not morphologically realised; in languages like NHG abstract case is morphologically realised which is well observable by looking at the data presented here.

Prepositions are also case assigners because they govern an NP:

(7)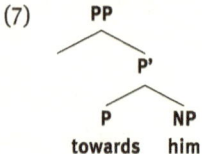

Before we move on, a digression on other grammatical models is in order to remind you that there are always different possibilities to model properties of language. Recall from part I of the book (chapter 5.2) that there are grammars which are not constituent-based and which therefore treat syntactic relations differently. For example, in dependency grammar instead of assuming constituents in a sentence, we talk about dependencies between words. And although we talk about a governor and dependents here, which is quite similar to talking about a governor and a governee in constituent grammar, the tree representations look different:

(8)

Make sure that you understood the differences between these two models (grammars) before you go on reading.

Coming back to our discussion from above, if we compare the verbs *see/sehen* and *help/helfen* in active and passive constructions we see a further difference between PDE and NHG, and in addition, the difference between two types of case:

(9) a. *Eric$_S$ sees$_V$ her$_O$.*
 b. ***She**$_S$ is seen$_V$ [by Eric]$_O$.*
 c. *Eric$_S$ sieht$_V$ sie$_O$.*
 d. ***Sie**$_S$ wird [von Eric]$_O$ gesehen$_V$.*
 e. *Eric$_S$ helps$_V$ her$_O$.*
 f. ***She**$_S$ is helped$_V$ [by Eric]$_O$.*
 g. *Eric$_S$ hilft$_V$ ihr$_O$.*
 h. ***Ihr**$_S$ wird [von Eric] geholfen$_V$.*

In (9) we see that in a passivised sentence like b. the direct object occurs as the subject in the nominative case. This also applies to the NHG data: the direct object bearing accusative case (c.) occurs as subject bearing nominative case (d.). Differences surface in the examples with *help/helfen*: the PDE examples e. and f. behave like the examples in a. and b: the indirect object occurs as subject in the nominative case. In NHG, however, things are different: the indirect object bearing dative case in g. (*her*) occurs as subject bearing dative case in h. Chomsky (1986) explains this observation by assuming two types of case assignment: structural case which is solely defined by government (nominative and accusative), and inherent case which is partly defined by government and partly by the property of being sensitive to thematic relations (dative and genitive, see also below). This means that it is a property of the lexical entry of verbs like *helfen* to assign inherent case (as well as certain adjectives and nouns). It has also been said that structural case shows **neutralisation** under **passivisation** whereas inherent case is not. We will come back to this issue in part III, chapter 15).

Coming back to the other dependency relation we have dealt with traditionally in linear terms only, in generative grammar subject-verb agreement is also a relationship of government since the inflection of the finite clause hierarchically governs the subject position:

(10)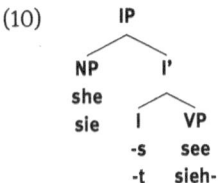

More precisely, since I is a head it is a governor and assigns nominative case to its specifier which is to its left. It is assumed that lexical heads, such as nouns, verbs, adjectives and prepositions are governors along with the inflection of the finite clause. The structural notion of government is a very local relation because the governor and the element it governs have to occur in the same maximal projection (this relationship has been defined in terms of m-command[1]). As you can see in the tree diagram, this condition is adhered to.

The second type of agreement is found between the head noun and its modifiers[2].

---

[1] 'α m-commands β if the first maximal projection dominating α also dominates β.' This is a version of c-command, 'm' stands for 'maximal (projection)'.

[2] Note that words like determiners and adjectives are modifiers of the noun in functional terms, but they occur in the specifier position in a tree in structural terms. In (11) the positions of specifier and head are indicated to make things clearer.

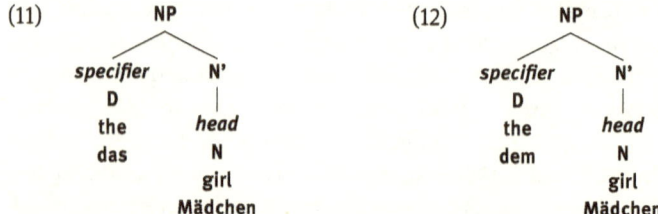

The relevant relation here is the **specifier-head relation** between the determiner (in the specifier position of NP) and the head N. In NHG specifier-head agreement between the determiner and the head noun in an NP is morphologically realised. In (11) and (12) agreement between the determiner and the noun is established in case, number and gender: in (11) *das* and *Mädchen* without context either agree in nominative, singular, neuter or accusative, singular, neuter. In (12) the determiner and noun agree in the specifications of dative, singular, and neuter. An update of this approach is to say that the phrases discussed above are not NPs but DPs, i.e. functional projections headed by the determiner D (known as the **DP-Hypothesis**, Abney 1987). As a result, NPs are complements of D:

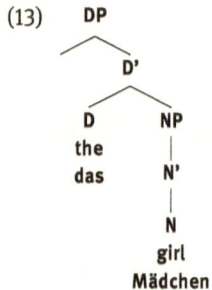

As a consequence, agreement between the determiner and the noun is not established via the specifier-head relation but via the head-complement relation. Since the purpose of this chapter (and this book) is neither to provide a comprehensive introduction to generative syntax nor a detailed analysis of the DP, I refer you to Haegeman and Guéron (1999), and Cook and Newson (2007) for further details on these rather complex theoretical issues. For the sake of simplicity in the following I will stick to the analysis of NPs as illustrated in (11) and (12) above.

Before we dedicate our attention to linguistic universals, I would like to come back to the thematic relations between the verb and its arguments, i.e. its subject and object(s). In the following we will concentrate on objects. In chapter 8 we have taken a closer look at the traditional partitioning of a sentence into subject and predicate by defining the constituents of the predicate. The number and types of constituents occurring in a sentence are determined to some degree by the choice of the lexical verb. So you intuitively know that a verb like *kill* requires an object, whereas a verb like *smile* does not. Then again, a verb like *give* requires two objects, a direct and an indirect one. This property of verbs to require objects (complements) or not is related to their meanings. Think of a situation where the action of killing takes place. It always involves somebody who does the killing (subject) and somebody who is affected by the killing (object). If you think of a situation in which you smile it is clear that you express your feelings by doing so, so the type of activity is completely different from killing (or giving).

The property of a verb requiring certain elements in a sentence has been called the **valence** (or **valency**) of a verb by Tesnière and others (see also part I, chapter 6). An **intransitive** verb requiring no object (or complement) is monovalent (note that the subject is part of the valence), a transitive verb requiring one object (or complement) is called a bivalent verb, and a **ditransitive** verb requiring two objects (or complements) is a trivalent verb in this framework (for the notion of transitivity see Greenbaum and Quirk (1990, 10.3)). What you see right away is that the concept of valence overlaps with the concept of transitivity we have discussed above. Moreover, Tesnière described the predicate of a sentence as expressing 'un petit drame' where the meaning of the predicate corresponded to the action in a drama, and the entities which are part of the drama corresponded to the characters in a drama. This is why he called them ***actants*** (and ***circumstants***). In his **Case Grammar** Fillmore (1968) introduced the concept of **semantic roles** which define the semantic side of the 'actants' (arguments) of a sentence (the semantic valency so to speak). In a sentence like

(14) *Eric gave the flowers to the girl*

the argument in the position of the subject has the semantic role of AGENT (the instigator of an event), the direct object has the semantic role of THEME (an entity to which the verb's meaning assigns a location or a change of location), and the indirect object has the semantic role of GOAL (the destination of a motion; for a full account see Fillmore, 2003). Each argument in a sentence is assigned a semantic role or a thematic relation. Which of the roles occur in a sentence depends on the meaning of the verb. So apart from the syntactic criterion of quantity ('How many arguments?') the semantic criterion of quality ('What types of argument?') is added. The predicate and its arguments build the **argument structure** which contains syntactic and semantic information.

In the generative Theory of Government & Binding (GB) semantic roles are called **thematic roles** (or theta-roles for short, see also part III, chapter 6). All the thematic roles belonging to a verb must be realised in a sentence, so a verb must always have a sufficient number of arguments to assign all thematic roles. The **Theta Criterion** says that one argument must correspond to each thematic role and vice versa implying a one-to-one relation between arguments and thematic roles. Take a look at the following examples:

(15) a. *Eric sees the girl the boy.
     b. *Eric sees.
     c. *Eric smiles the girl.

In (15) a. the verb *see* is transitive (or bivalent), so two thematic roles must be assigned, one to *Eric* and one to *the girl*. The NP *the boy* cannot be assigned a thematic role and thus cannot be related to the verb. This is why the sentence is ungrammatical. In b. there is one thematic role too many or put differently no argument which can be assigned to it. Since the one-to-one relation between number of arguments and thematic roles is violated, the sentence is ungrammatical. In c. the intransitive or monovalent verb *smile* has one argument too many. The NP *the girl* cannot be assigned a thematic role resulting in an ungrammatical sentence.

The **circumstants** mentioned above are adjuncts in GB terms (e.g. adverbials of time, manner, place). They modify the verb and are less central to the meaning of the verb than arguments. This is why they are not assigned a thematic role. In a sentence like

(16) a. *Eric sees the girl at university*

the adverbial of place (adjunct, circumstant) is not assigned a thematic role whereas the arguments *Eric* and *the girl* receive the thematic roles of AGENT and PATIENT, respectively. If you take another look at the tree structure of the VP of this sentence

(17)

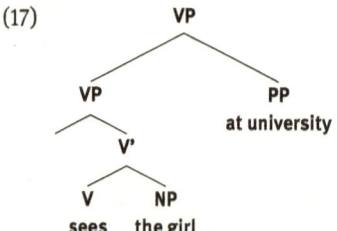

and apply what we have said so far about government and thematic roles you will see that the assignment of thematic roles to the argument(s) by the verb is an instance of government. You will also see that the adjunct *at university* stands in another relation to the verb: it is adjoined to the VP which illustrates that it is less central to the meaning of the verb and thus is not assigned a thematic role.

Syn: 'And now again it's your turn to check if you have understood the things discussed in this chapter. First, take a look at the examples from the BNC below with which you can check if you have understood the notion of government.'
Tax: 'More precisely, **1)** identify the different types of dependency relations.'
Syn: 'And **2)** identify the arguments and complements in all of the sentences.'

(18) a. *But not all women want change; at one performance, a woman stopped the show by shouting that her husband would claim half her savings if the law were altered.*
       (BNC, HCH 171)
   b. *Still others seek autonomy but do not seek creativity.*
       (BNC, EAA 533)
   c. *Cley said, 'If that weapon kills aggression, as you claim, then it will have no effect on me.'*
       (BNC, HA0 3637)

Tax: 'I reckon, everything is clear to you! In the second part of the chapter we will turn to universals in current linguistic theory.'

9.2 Universals revisited

Chapter 3 in part I introduced the notion of universals in the theory of language of the so-called Modists in the Middle Ages. In their grammar they were mainly interested in significance, i.e. in what a word signifies, and the properties of the signified. They established a classification into *modi essendi* (the ways things are), *modi intellegendi* (the ways we conceive them), and *modi significandi* (the ways we express them), and sought to reveal the links between reality, thought, and language. Put in different terms, the Modists were looking for a logical structure hidden beneath the surface of sentences. They thought that all languages communicate in the same way, and that they are therefore based on universals.

Modistic grammar had an impact on the Port Royal grammarians (a group of Renaissance philosophers, see part I, chapter 4) who assumed that there were universal features in the grammars of all languages and that linguistic creativity was subject to universal rules. Their goal was to determine the nature of a system in the mind that only human beings have. Founding his theory of generative grammar, Chomsky was undoubtedly influenced by the work of these grammarians, as he himself acknowledges them in *Cartesian Linguistics* (1966). For him, one of the main goals of linguistic theory is to develop a general theory of linguistic structure that identifies formal universals of human language (see again part I, chapter 6). As noted in part I, chapter 6.2 many linguists have been influenced by Chomsky's theory which led to the development of different generative theories like **Interpretive Semantics** (Jackendoff, 1972), **Case Grammar** (Fillmore, 1968), and **Lexical Functional Grammar** (Bresnan, 1978), as we have also seen in the summary in Figure 6.3. What they all have in common is the quest for universals. In the following, I will briefly repeat the main claims that the **Theory of Principles & Parameters** makes. Recall that it was developed by Chomsky and others in the 1980s and that it aims at accounting for language acquisition and cross-linguistic variation in quite an elegant way.

In this theory, Universal Grammar (UG) is the innate part of our linguistic knowledge; it contains the properties that all languages have in common. The notion of UG is tightly linked to language acquisition because its rules or universals can explain why language acquisition proceeds so fast and so successfully. But UG does not suffice to explain why speakers are constrained: the child's immediate environment determines the native language he or she finally speaks. We all know that there is a lot of variation between languages. For example, in PDE the (finite) lexical verb always precedes the object whereas in Japanese it always follows the object. Apart from the rules of UG, the primary linguistic data the child is exposed to must play a role in the acquisition process. On the basis of the input the child's language is selected (whether it has English, Japanese or any other language as its mother tongue), the exposure to that language can be seen as a 'triggering experience'. If the input didn't play a role, we would all speak the same language, in all countries and in all generations. In a way, we can think of UG as the hardware, and the input the child gets as the software.

From what was said above, UG as the innate cognitive capacity of human beings to acquire language must have the following properties: on the one hand, it has to capture the properties that are common to all languages, and on the other hand it has to capture the properties that vary cross-linguistically. In P&P, **principles** are the properties that define the invariant core of universal grammar, and **parameters** are the choices that have to be set for each language. Whereas the principles are given at birth and don't have to be acquired, parameters are set according to the language(s) a child is exposed to. Parameters are often described as switches with two options: on and off, or more abstractly, 0 and 1. A principle of UG could be the universal theory of syntactic categories (verbs, nouns, etc.) and grammatical functions (subject, object, etc.). So for example we could say that UG determines the nature of V and O, and how they combine to build a verb phrase. The respective parameter would define the relative order of the lexical verb and its object, either OV or VO. There are languages like NHG, Dutch (DUT) and Frisian (FRI) which require the object to precede the lexical verb:

(19) a. NHG *(Ich habe)* $[_{VP} [das\ Buch]_O\ gelesen_V]$.
 b. DUT *(Ik heb)* $[_{VP} [het\ boek]_O\ gelezen_V]$.
 c. FRI *(Ik ha)* $[_{VP} [it\ boekje]_O\ lezen_V]$.

But there are also languages like PDE, French (FRE), and Danish (DAN) where the object follows the lexical verb:

(20) a. PDE *(Ich have)* [$_{VP}$ read$_V$ [the book]$_O$].
b. FRE *(J' ai)* [$_{VP}$ lu$_V$ [le livre]$_O$].
c. DAN *(Jeg har)* [$_{VP}$ læst$_V$ bogen$_O$].

Examining this example it seems that there have to be as many parameters (P) as there are properties (p) in a language. However, it is much more interesting to say that a number of properties are determined by one parameter: If properties p1 and p2 are determined by parameter P1 the child need not acquire both properties to set the parameter P1, only one of these properties would suffice.

(21)

In this way, we would be in a position to explain why language acquisition proceeds so fast and so successfully. To put it differently, theoretically it is more attractive to derive as many properties or surface phenomena as possible from as few parameters as possible.

The OV/VO parameter seems to be connected with finite word order of the auxiliary in subordinate clauses. In NHG, Dutch and Frisian the finite verb is clause-final:

(22) NHG ... *weil ich* [$_{VP}$ [das Buch]$_O$ lesen$_V$ soll$_{Aux}$.
DUT ... *omdat ik* [$_{VP}$ [het boek]$_O$ lezen$_V$ zal$_{Aux}$.
FRI ... *omt ik it* [$_{VP}$ [boekje]$_O$ leze$_V$ mat$_{Aux}$.

In PDE, French, and Danish the auxiliary precedes the VP directly following the subject:

(23) PDE ... *because I must*$_{Aux}$ [$_{VP}$ read$_V$ [the book]$_O$].
FRE ... *parce que je dois*$_{Aux}$ [$_{VP}$ lire$_V$ [le livre]$_O$].
DAN ... ... *fordi jeg skal*$_{Aux}$ [$_{VP}$ læse$_V$ bogen$_O$].

So we may assume the following parameter where the two properties are related:

(24) Parameter 1 (either a or b)

    property 1   property 2
    a: O-V   a: VP-Aux
    b: V-O   b: Aux-VP

The parameter that has most extensively been investigated is the **null subject parameter**. It has been observed that languages differ as to whether they require the presence of subjects in finite, declarative sentences or not. Take a look at the following examples:

(25) a. *Mangio la pasta.*
 b. *Io mangio la pasta.*
 c. **Eat pasta.*
 d. *I eat pasta.*
 e. **Esse Pasta.*
 f. *Ich esse Pasta.*

In (25) we see that in a finite, declarative sentence in Italian we can leave out the definite, referential, pronominal subject (see also part III, chapter 14.1). As the examples in c. to f. show this is generally not possible in English and German (although in colloquial speech you might come across such sentences. But it is not the rule). Here we find a clear contrast between the grammatical sentences with the subject and the ungrammatical sentences without the subject. Thus, a language like Italian is a null-subject language whereas languages like PDE and NHG are non-null-subject languages. This difference could be expressed by a parameter defining the presence/absence of this type of subject. However, the state of affairs is much more complex because in NHG there are also contexts where an expletive must be dropped:

(26) a. *Es wurde gestern gelacht.*
  it was laughed yesterday
 b. *Gestern wurde (*es) gelacht.*
  yesterday was (*it) laughed
 c. *Gestern wurde *(es) verkauft.*
  yesterday was *(it) sold

The phenomenon illustrated in (26) a. and b. is a so-called impersonal passive construction. In a. *es* as the non-referential subject occurs in the first position of the finite, declarative sentence. In b. it occurs in a position after the finite verb *wurde* and must be dropped. But if *es* is referential as in c., for example referring to a car (*Gestern wurde das Auto verkauft*), it cannot be dropped. So it does not suffice to talk about the presence/absence of subjects in different languages. Based on these observations, it has been suggested that rather talking about one parameter we talk about two 'related but autonomous parameters' (Rizzi, 1982, 143): one parameter defines whether an empty pronoun is allowed at all, and the other parameter defines whether this empty pronoun, if it occurs, is referential. In NHG, the first parameter has a positive value and the second parameter a negative value. Hence NHG allows non-referential null subjects as shown in (26) b., but not referential ones (see (26) c.). In PDE, both parameters are negative whereas in Italian both parameters are positive.

Recent research has shown that there is much more variation concerning this property than previously assumed and that we should talk about clusters of properties that go along with the positive/negative value of the null subject parameter rather than one property associated with it. In the following chapter we will take a look at further instances of syntactic variation that may be interpreted as properties associated with parameters.

Syn: 'Woah, some aspects in this chapter, especially the more abstract ones, were quite taxing.'
Tax: 'Haha, great pun.'
Syn: 'Let's see if you, dear reader, understood the notion of parameters: **1)** analyse the examples from the BNC under the assumption that the two null subject parameters discussed above have negative values in PDE. Do the data confirm this assumption?'
Tax: 'If not, **2)** describe these cases and explain why they are problematic for this assumption.'

(27) a. *She can expect to obtain an E in history at A level, possibly a D in law.*
(BNC, JJT 420, spoken part)
b. *They emerge and merge, co-operate and co-ordinate for a while, but they have a relatively short active lifetime.*
(BNC, B3D 1368)
c. *Went to Blackpool one or or on one or two occasions but me mother suffered with er with her heart and the doctor said, Well don't go to Blackpool again, the air's too strong.*
(BNC, FYH 499, spoken part)
d. *Eating smoked salmon while talking to Johnny Prescott had seemed to last a lifetime.*
(BNC, BP7 1275)

Tax: 'In this chapter we have learnt about some quite abstract notions like government, principles and parameters, and universals in the generative framework. Some of these were quite hard to grasp, and this is why I'll summarise the main facts: In the first part of the chapter, we have seen that (case) government can be applied to the following dependency relations: the relation between the verb and its direct object, the relation between a preposition and its NP complement, the relation between the subject and the verb, the relation between the determiner and the noun, and the thematic relation between the verb and its direct object in valency grammar and GB.'
Syn: 'And we have also discussed the notion of universals in Chomsky's UG and taken a look at the model of P&P and why it can explain the nature of language acquisition. Some examples have served to illustrate the difference between principles and parameters.'

Literature: The traditional grammars cited at the end of the previous chapter all deal with agreement and government in detail from a descriptive perspective. Chomsky (1986) elaborates on the difference between structural and inherent case in the generative framework. Haegeman and Guéron (1999)

discuss the notions of specifier-head and complement-head relation. Cook and Newson (2007) is a brilliant introduction to Chomsky's UG because it also provides an overview of the development of the theory over the last six decades. Although Roberts (2007) focusses on the diachrony of syntax he nevertheless provides the theoretical synchronic background in a very accessible and engaging way. One main topic is the nature of parameters. Baker (2001) proposes networks of parameters and claims that they are ranked in a hierarchy in terms of intrinsic ordering. Rizzi (1982) includes a discussion of the null subject parameter in Italian and other languages. Fillmore (1968), Jackendoff (1972), and Bresnan (1978) are introductions to other generative models: Case Grammar, Interpretive Semantics, and Lexical Functional Grammar.

10 Syntactic variation

In this chapter we will deal with **syntactic variation** in non-standard varieties of English. We will also see how syntactic variation can sometimes be interpreted as **parametric variation**. These aspects relate to the increasing interest in non-standard varieties of languages, i.e. vernaculars, and to the 'ennobling' of languages during the Renaissance (see again part I, chapter 4.1).

10.1 Standard and non-standard varieties

As second language (L2) learners of English we are used to consulting grammar books if we are not entirely sure about the grammaticality of sentences we hear, utter and write because in our second language(s) we lack the intuitions we have for our native language(s). For example, if we want to know about sentence negation we find the following description in one of the authoritative works on English grammar:

> A simple positive sentence (or a positive finite clause within a complex sentence) is negated by inserting the clause negator *not* between the operator and the predication.
> (Quirk et al., 2004, 776)

Inserting the clause negator results in sentences like:

(1)   a. *I have **not** finished.*
       b. *They **do not (don't)** know you.*
       c. *Jane **isn't** responsible.*
          (Quirk et al., 2004, 776f)

Further, the clause negator is frequently followed by one or more nonassertive items like *any, anything, anyone* etc. '[These] items must normally be used after the negative element in place of *every* assertive item that would have occurred in the corresponding positive clause' (Quirk et al., 2004, 787f). The note below this description states that:

> [i]n nonstandard English, a negative item can be used wherever in standard English a nonassertive item follows a negative:
> STANDARD: No one *ever* said *anything* to *anybody*.
> NONSTANDARD: No one *never* said *nothing* to *nobody*.
> Such double or multiple negatives are condemned by prescriptive grammatical tradition.
> (Quirk et al., 2004, 787)

So when we go to countries where the target language is spoken we do find **negative concord**, i.e. we hear things like:

(2) a. *and er [pause] we scouted and scouted till daybreak and we **didn't** find **nothing**.* (Midlands)
    (BNC, F8P 114)
   b. *I was **never no** good after that.*
    (Beal, 2006, 70)
   c. *They **never** learnt you **nowt** (nowt=nothing).*
    (Beal, 2006, 70)

The same applies to another phenomenon called **double modals**. In the standard, modals are normally followed by the bare infinitive:

(3) a. *You **will be** asked questions.*
   b. *They **might have** stolen it.* (Quirk et al., 2004, 127)

If we read on we learn in a note at the bottom of the page that:

> [b] In dialectal use (*eg* Scots English, Tyneside English, and Southern AmE), there are varieties of popular speech in which one modal auxiliary can follow another: *He might could come* ['He might be able to come'] etc.
> (Quirk et al., 2004, 127)

So if going to these regions, we would expect to hear utterances like:

(4) a. *We **might could** do with some washing powder.*
    (Beal, 2006, 67)
   b. *until one day they couldn't think of any way that you **could may** improve it.*
    (BNC, F7K 32)
   c. *You **might should** eat before you go.*
    (Hasty, 2012, 1717, Southern AmE)

If we produced these sentences in an English test back home, they would probably all be marked 'wrong', but for speakers uttering these sentences they are correct. How can this be?

Generally, most languages have a (written) **standard** they use as a 'reference guide'. More precisely, a standard is a panregional form of oral and written language which functions as the public means of communication. It is subject to normalisation which is controlled and passed on via the media, institutions, and most importantly via school systems. The goal of formal language instruction is the command of the standard language. This definition somehow implies that there is something else, namely other forms or **varieties** of a language which are felt to stand in opposition to the standard and are thus often called non-standard varieties (see chapter 9.2). To gain a full understanding of a language we should therefore take a look at the full range of possibilities a language provides for communication because language is, after all, highly heterogeneous.

The differences we find between syntactic constructions in the standard and in the non-standard varieties are numerous. Some further examples of such syntactic variation are **non-agreement:**

(5) a. *If you're a staunch union member there **is advantages**.*
       (BNC, GYU 248)
    b. *It's very hard for us to live without parents, but with our sister at least we feel secured cos if she's our guardian and **she look** after us.*
       (BNC, KN2 311)
    c. *I **likes** a nice pair of shoes on if, if I go out.*
       (BNC, KBE 5712)

Another instance is **pronoun exchange:**

(6) a. ***Her** said to **I**.* (I said to her)
       (Beal, 2006, 79)
    b. *Well, if I didn't know **they**, they knowed **I**.* (they=them, I=me)
       (Wagner, 2005, 157)
    c. *We used to stook it off, didn't **us**?* (us=we)
       (Wagner, 2005, 158)

Since the foundation of **variationist sociolinguistics** by William Labov in the 1960s, the concept of the **sociolinguistic variable** has been investigated in numerous studies. In his seminal work on the Black English vernacular (BEV) Labov (1972a) investigated the appearance and disappearance of the copula in the vernacular (recall that *be* can function as a copula, creating the relation between the subject and the predicate). He found that there were some environments where the finite form of the copula *be* was absent, and some environments (for example in embedded questions) where the copula is present:

(7) a. *She the first one started us off.*
       (Labov, 1972a, 67)
    b. *That's what he **is**: a brother.*
       (Labov, 1972a, 72)

By applying a quantitative analysis to controlled data from the speech community in question, Labov's aim was to locate the source of this kind of variation by exploring at what level of the grammar the copula occurs first and what controls its disappearance. To gain these insights, he defined so-called **variable rules** that accounted for this phenomenon. For Labov, these rules are based on a general principle of accountability which states '… that any variable form (a member of a set of alternative ways of 'saying the same thing') should be reported with the proportion of cases in which the form did occur in the relevant environment, compared to the total number of cases in which it might have occurred' (Labov, 1972a, 94). Stating that variables say the same thing in alternative ways makes clear that in this approach variation is seen as two or more surface variants of one underlying variable (which is actually the traditional way of defining variation). It should be pointed out that Labov's method was designed especially for investigating phonological variables. In the following we will see that a number of linguists extended these methods to syntactic variation.

10.2 Variation and parameters

Fundamental differences between the nature of phonology and syntax have made it a difficult task to extend Labov's methods to syntax. For example, it is very difficult to determine strict **semantic equivalence** between two syntactic variables, which led some syntacticians to postulate different types of such variables. Hasty (2012) assumes that there are some morphosyntactic variables that vary with their absence, for example negative concord and non-agreement which we have briefly discussed above. In these cases, alternative variables can clearly be recognised, and semantic equivalence seems to hold between the form showing the feature and the form showing a null realization. However, there are other cases where this doesn't seem to be applicable. Let's take a closer look at the phenomenon of double modals again:

(8)   a. *He should can go tomorrow.*
           'He ought to be able to go tomorrow.'
      b. *He would could do it if he tried.*
           'He would be able to do it if he tried.'
           (Brown, 1991, 74)

In Hawick Scots, speakers regularly use the combinations *might/should* plus *can/could*, any of which can be preceded by *will* in the examples in (8). Brown (1991) assumes that the first modal in the expression has an **epistemic value** (probability, possibility) whereas the final modal has a so-called **root sense** (basic meaning). If you compare the Scots examples with their Standard English translation you see that the modals are replaced by semantically equivalent expressions like *ought to* for *should*, and *be able to* for *can/could*. According to this assumption, the double modals are an alternate variable to the Standard English expressions, so the traditional definition of variation holds. However, there are cases where such an assumption is problematic. It was stated above that Southern AmE exhibits **double modals** as well:

(9) a. *You might go to the store.*
     b. *You should go to the store.*
     c. *You **might should** eat before you go.*
         (Hasty, 2012, 1717, Southern AmE)

Hasty (2012) and others have claimed that there is no clear semantic equivalent with which (9) c. alternates. Rather, the construction is used by the speaker to express politeness and certainty without wanting to show definite certainty. So this variable of the non-standard does not have an equivalent in the standard. Since there seem to be two systems at work, i.e. two dialects or languages, this type of syntactic variation could be called **parametric variation** (recall what we said about parameters in part I, chapters 6.2 and 9).

Parametric variation is often found between a standard and a non-standard form. We also know that these two varieties are in consistent contact because standard varieties are often viewed by speakers as being inherently superior, which is why they try to adopt the standard. So obviously social constraints play a role in the use and acceptance of non-standard features.

In a study with informants from Northeast Tennessee, Hasty (2011) elicited acceptability judgements of double modal constructions by different social groups of native speakers who themselves produce double modals. Three independent social variables were investigated: **Age** (Young 19–29, Middle 30–59, Old 60+), **Gender** (Male, Female), and **Education** (College, No College). The strongest predictor of the acceptance of double modals was Age. Interestingly, the Young age group were most accepting of double modals, followed by the Old age group, and the Middle age group. Concerning the other two social variables, Hasty found that there is an overall Education effect, where informants with no college education were more accepting of the double modal construction than informants with college education. Further, he found a Gender effect within the Education groups, with male informants accepting the construction more in both Education groups. Concerning correlations between Age and the other two variables, Hasty found that the Old and Middle age informants were more likely to accept the double modal construction when they were part of the No College group. For the Young group, there was a high rate of acceptance, regardless of the Education group. The variable of Gender only showed differences in the Old and Middle age groups but not in the Young age group.

How can these results be interpreted? In line with earlier studies on other phenomena (e.g. Trudgill (1974) on the use of *-ing*) the gender and education pattern in Hasty's study is suggestive of a low **prestige** evaluation of the double modal construction. The Middle Age group shows a low acceptance of the phenomenon because they are in need of establishing cultural and linguistic capital. This is why these informants probably gain most from using prestigious varieties (and not double modals). For the Old age group these aims are less or no longer relevant and that is why they accept double modals to a higher degree. The Young age group stood out in the study because they were much more accepting of the double modals and were also a more homogeneous group with no significant differences between Gender and Education. One explanation of this pattern is that Young informants are using double modals to create a Southern identity. So for them, the linguistic phenomenon is not linked to low prestige, but on the contrary to a **positive attitude** towards producing double modals in general and their Southern **identity**.

Taking a look into the future, based on these results, we could expect that in this variety double modals become more and more accepted by more and more speakers of following generations; at least, this is one possible scenario. So one syntactic variable not only becomes accepted but also established in the grammar of these speakers. It may even gradually replace the function of single modals and occur in all contexts in which the single modals used to occur.

Claiming that language is heterogeneous implies a potential for language change. Three famous linguists, Weinreich, Labov, and Herzog stated the following:

> Not all variability and heterogeneity in language structure involves change, but all change involves variability and heterogeneity.
> (Weinreich et al., 1968, 188)

Coming back to our analysis of double modals as an instance of parametric variation, this statement also holds although variation seems to be restricted to only a small defined set of variables. Here, we would assume that the non-standard, i.e. Southern AmE, allows the feature of double modals to occur whereas the standard precludes that syntactic feature from ever occurring. So the two varieties exhibit different parameter settings. In part III, chapter 16 this analysis will be linked with language change and it will be shown that the development of some phenomena occurring in OE and Middle English (ME) times can be explained along these lines.

Tax: 'Before I will summarise what was discussed in this chapter I will provide some examples of phenomena in non-standard varieties of PDE which we have not discussed so far. Now it's your turn to analyse the data!'

Syn: 'Yes! So what you should do is 1) define the different phenomena in question and find the standard form; 2) you should answer the question of whether these instances of syntactic variation are based on a semantic equivalent or not.'

(10) a. *Does he not liking yoghurt?*
(BNC, KBW 15480)
b. *So what are you wanting from me?*
(BNC, F7E 393)
c. *I have been waiting for a lift for four hours.*
(BNC, ARB 1867)

(11)   a.   *But I did tell him about Jordi.*
            (BNC, AC6 620)
       b.   *William, my son, do live down there.*
            (Wagner, 2005, 171)

(12)   *He do go now. He 'ave been a good watch.*
        (Wagner, 2005, 161)

Syn: 'Well, Tax, what have we learnt in this chapter?'
Tax: 'Again quite a lot. First, we have dealt with syntactic variation in PDE and some other varieties of English. We have seen that although the standard somehow prescribes what syntactic structures should be like, more often than not differing non-standard forms or variables exist that cannot, and should not, be ignored. Moreover, we have taken a look at a number of examples and seen that it seems to be feasible to make a distinction between syntactic variables that are based on semantic equivalence, and syntactic variables that have no semantic equivalent. In the case of syntactic variables some authors have suggested to define them as parametric variation. We have further seen that variationist sociolinguistics provided an adequate methodology to study linguistic variation which has not been restricted to phonology but can also successfully be applied to syntax. Finally, we briefly discussed the historical dimension of variation and found that synchronic variation is a prerequisite for diachronic change.'

Literature: As noted above, Weinreich et al. (1968) is the seminal work on synchronic variation and language change because they addressed this correlation for the first time in theoretical terms. Labov has written many papers on variation, sociolinguistics, and language change (with a focus on phonology) in which he mainly dealt with variation in American English. Labov (1972a) is one of his first studies investigating the Black English vernacular, Labov (1972b) is a summary of his work (several studies) including a theory of sociolinguistics. Labov (2001) deals with the social factors leading to language change. Trudgill has extensively worked on the dialects of British English. Trudgill (1974) is a sociolinguistic study on the English of Norwich, Trudgill and Chambers (1991) is a textbook on dialectology covering an overview of the field of dialectology, aspects of social and spatial variation and mechanisms of variation. In the handbook of the varieties of English (Kortmann et al., 2005) which comes in two volumes, the varieties of English worldwide are discussed on the level of phonology, morphology and syntax. In Beal's textbook (2006) an introduction to regional Englishes is provided. Anderwald (2008) is a study on negation in non-standard British English, and Anderwald (2009) is a comprehensive work on verb-formation in non-standard English. Brown (1991) is a study on double modals in a variety of Scots, Adger and Smith (2010) is a more current study on the same variety and with a focus on a theoretical generative analysis of the empirical facts. Hasty (2011) and Hasty (2012) discuss the phenomenon of double modals in Southern AmE, the former paper with an empirical focus, the latter one with a theoretical focus.

11 Comparative syntax from a synchronic perspective

In this chapter we will apply the comparative method to the phenomenon of Verb Second. We will compare a number of Germanic languages in this respect and define similarities and differences.

11.1 Verb Second in the Germanic languages

In chapter 5 of part I we have seen that in the eighteenth and nineteenth centuries the subdisciplines of historical linguistics and comparative linguistics emerged. Since the focus at that time was on the history of language(s) the main aim was to reconstruct the origins and relationships of and between languages on the basis of comparative studies (reconstruction). Although recently a number of linguists applied this method to syntax mainly within the Theory of Principles & Parameters (see for example Roberts, 2007), another prominent approach is **word order typology.** In this approach the order of the syntactic constituents of a language are studied, as well as how different orders are employed in different languages. Generally, six theoretically possible basic word orders for the transitive sentence are distinguished: SVO, SOV, VSO, VOS, OSV, and OVS. The vast majority of the (known) languages in the world are either SVO or SOV. Apart from these word order patterns, other patterns can of course be compared cross-linguistically to get a better understanding of the similarities and differences between languages. Comparing a set of cognate languages (i.e. languages that are historically derived from the same source language) for example can reveal striking differences which then leads to the question of why one or some of these languages behave differently. Often, these differences can be accounted for by looking at the development of these languages, i.e. in special internal and/or external factors that resulted in a different system.

In chapter 8 we used the comparative method on a small scale concerning the relative order of subject and finite verb in main declaratives and questions in PDE and NHG. We have learnt that there are differences to be found although these languages also have many things in common. In the following, we will take a closer look at one phenomenon which is peculiar to the modern Germanic languages: The **Verb Second** phenomenon. This word order pattern of main declaratives has been labelled 'Verb Second' (den Besten, 1983) because the finite verb has to occur in the second position. This is a property of most of today's West Germanic and Scandinavian languages, the question we will pursue is whether PDE is part of this set of languages.

Let's start with a comparison of main declarative sentences with the full subject as the first constituent. I will provide data for the modern Scandinavian languages **Swedish** (SWE), **Danish** (DAN), **Icelandic** (ICE), for **Dutch** (DUT), NHG and PDE. I

will also add modern **French** (FRE) as a Romance language to make the contrast clear between Germanic and non-Germanic patterns.
Main declarative with full subject as first constituent:

(1) a. SWE $Eric_S$ **har_{Aux}** $läst_V$ $[denne\ bok]_O$.
 b. DAN $Eric_S$ **har_{Aux}** $læst_V$ $[denne\ bog]_O$.
 c. ICE $Eiríkur_S$ **$hefur_{Aux}$** $lesið_V$ $[þessa\ bók]_O$.
 d. NHG $Eric_S$ **hat_{Aux}** $[dieses\ Buch]_O$ $gelesen_V$.
 e. DUT $Eric_S$ **$heeft_{Aux}$** $[dit\ boek]_O$ $gelezen_V$.
 f. PDE $Eric_S$ **has_{Aux}** $read_V$ $[this\ book]_O$.
 g. FRE $Eric_S$ **a_{Aux}** lu_V $[ce\ livre]_O$.

In the first set of examples above, all languages under investigation show that the full subject *Eric* is followed by the finite form of the auxiliary 'have', the participle form of the lexical verb 'read' and the full object NP *the book*. Clearly this pattern is grammatical in all of these languages, therefore a difference between Germanic and non-Germanic (Romance) languages cannot be observed. Importantly, the finite verb occupies the second position and is preceded by the subject.

Let's take a look at the next set of examples:

(2) a. SWE $[Denne\ bok]_O$ **har_{Aux}** $Eric_S$ $läst_V$.
 b. DAN $[Denne\ bog]_O$ **har_{Aux}** $Eric_S$ $læst_V$.
 c. ICE $[Þessa\ bók]_O$ **$hefur_{Aux}$** $Eiríkur_S$ $lesið_V$.
 d. NHG $[Dieses\ Buch]_O$ **hat_{Aux}** $Eric_S$ $gelesen_V$.
 e. DUT $[Dit\ boek]_O$ **$heeft_{Aux}$** $Eric_S$ $gelezen_V$.
 f. PDE *$[This\ book]_O$ **has_{Aux}** $Eric_S$ $read_V$.
 g. FRE *$[Ce\ livre]_O$ **a_{Aux}** lu_V $Eric_S$.

These examples differ from the ones in (1) in that the first constituent is the object of the sentence. In Swedish, Danish, Icelandic, Dutch and German the object is followed by the finite form of the verb 'have', followed by the subject *Eric* and the participle form of 'read'. In these languages, this ordering of the constituents is grammatical. In contrast, in both English and French fronting the object to the first position is not possible if the finite verb inverts with the subject. Fronting of the object is only possible if the subject precedes the finite verb:

(3) a. PDE $[This\ book]_O$, $Eric_S$ **has_{Aux}** read.
 b. FRE $[Ce\ livre]_O$, $Eric_S$ $l'a_{Aux}$ lu.

In PDE, the boundary between the object in first position is prosodically marked by an intonation break indicated by a comma in the spelling. In FRE it is also prosodically marked by a rising contour on *livre*. Moreover, a so-called **resumptive pronoun** which repeats or recapitulates the meaning of a prior element has to precede the finite verb: *l'a*. Note that in both PDE and FRE this order is highly marked, speakers tend to use other constructions to highlight the object. In PDE and FRE we would expect to find cleft sentences like

(4) a. PDE *It is this book that Eric has read.*
　　b. FRE *C'est ce livre qu'Eric a lu.*

If we changed the order of the sentences of the other languages under investigation we would gain ungrammatical sentences because then the finite verb would occur in third position:

(5) a. SWE *[Denne bok]$_O$ Eric$_S$ **har**$_{Aux}$ läst$_V$.
　　b. DAN *[Denne bog]$_O$ Eric$_S$ **har**$_{Aux}$ læst$_V$.
　　c. ICE *[Þessa bók]$_O$ Eiríkur$_S$ **hefur**$_{Aux}$ lesið$_V$.
　　d. NHG *[Dieses Buch]$_O$ Eric$_S$ **hat**$_{Aux}$ gelesen$_V$.
　　e. DUT *[Dit boek]$_O$ Eric$_S$ **heeft**$_{Aux}$ gelezen$_V$.

It seems that the Verb Second rule is inviolable, i.e. violation strictly results in ungrammaticality. Let's see if this assumption is also borne out if we add further sentences:

(6) a. SWE Nu$_{Adv}$ **har**$_{Aux}$ Eric$_S$ läst$_V$ [denne bok]$_O$.
　　b. DAN Nu$_{Adv}$ **har**$_{Aux}$ Eric$_S$ læst$_V$ [denne bog]$_O$.
　　c. ICE Nú$_{Adv}$ **hefur**$_{Aux}$ Eiríkur$_S$ lesið$_V$ [þessa bók]$_O$.
　　d. NHG Nun$_{Adv}$ **hat**$_{Aux}$ Eric$_S$ [dieses Buch]$_O$ gelesen$_V$.
　　e. DUT Nu$_{Adv}$ **heeft**$_{Aux}$ Eric$_S$ [dit boek]$_O$ gelezen$_V$.
　　f. PDE *Now$_{Adv}$ **has**$_{Aux}$ Eric$_S$ read$_V$ [this book]$_O$.
　　g. FRE *Maintenant$_{Adv}$ **a**$_{Aux}$ lu$_V$ Eric$_S$ [ce livre]$_O$.

The examples in (6) have the temporal adverb 'now' as first constituent. As in the examples in (2), the finite verb form of 'have' directly follows the first constituent—here the adverb—thus preceding the subject. In the Scandinavian languages as well as in German and Dutch Verb Second resulting from the inversion of the finite verb and the subject is the only grammatical option. In English and French, however, sentences adhering to the same ordering of constituents are ungrammatical. The only way to render these sentences grammatical is **Verb Third** order:

(7) a. PDE Now$_{Adv}$ Eric$_S$ **has**$_{Aux}$ read this book.
     b. FRE Maintenant$_{Adv}$ Eric$_S$ **a**$_{Aux}$ lu ce livre.

The same pattern can be seen by looking at a further set of data, with a PP as local adverbial in first position:

(8) a. SWE [På biblioteket]$_{Adv}$ **har**$_{Aux}$ Eric$_S$ läst$_V$ [denne bok]$_O$.
     b. DAN [På biblioteket]$_{Adv}$ **har**$_{Aux}$ Eric$_S$ læst$_V$ [denne bog]$_O$.
     c. ICE [Á bókasafninu]$_{Adv}$ **hefur**$_{Aux}$ Eiríkur$_S$ lesið$_V$ [þessa bók]$_O$.
     d. NHG [In der Bibliothek]$_{Adv}$ **hat**$_{Aux}$ Eric$_S$ [dieses Buch]$_O$ gelesen$_V$.
     e. DUT [In de bibliotheek]$_{Adv}$ **heeft**$_{Aux}$ Eric$_S$ [dit boek]$_O$ gelezen$_V$.
     f. PDE *[In the library]$_{Adv}$ **has**$_{Aux}$ Eric$_S$ read$_V$ [this book]$_O$.
     g. FRE *[Dans la bibliothèque]$_{Adv}$ **a**$_{Aux}$ Eric$_S$ lu$_V$ [ce livre]$_O$.

Again, the only two languages which exhibit ungrammatical sentences when the finite verb directly follows the first constituent and precedes the subject are English and French. The sentences can be 'rescued' if the order of the finite verb and the subject are reversed:

(9) a. PDE [In the library]$_{Adv}$ Eric$_S$ **has**$_{Aux}$ read this book.
     b. FRE [Dans la bibliothèque]$_{Adv}$ Eric$_S$ **a**$_{Aux}$ lu ce livre.

So far it seems that the languages under scrutiny here build two well-defined sets: the Scandinavian languages, German and Dutch behave alike and consistently show Verb Second in all the patterns described. English and French behave alike as well in that they never show Verb Second in the same contexts. The only exception where all languages show the same pattern is the context with a sentence initial subject (examples in (1)). There are two possibilities to interpret this finding: either all languages share properties expressed in the subject-initial context or this context is not relevant for the distinction between Verb Second and non-Verb Second languages. We will return to this question below.

Finally, let's bring in the context of constituent questions:

(10) a. SWE [Vilken bok] **har**$_{Aux}$ Eric$_S$ läst$_V$?
     b. DAN [Hvilken bog] **har**$_{Aux}$ Eric$_S$ læst$_V$?
     c. ICE [Hvaða bók] **hefur**$_{Aux}$ Eiríkur$_S$ lesið$_V$?
     d. NHG [Welches Buch] **hat**$_{Aux}$ Eric$_S$ gelesen$_V$?
     e. DUT [Welk boek] **heeft**$_{Aux}$ Eric$_S$ gelezen$_V$?
     f. PDE [Which book] **has**$_{Aux}$ Eric$_S$ read$_V$?
     g. FRE [Quel livre] **a**$_{Aux}$ lu$_V$ Eric$_S$?

In these sentences the first position is occupied by the object NP which is questioned: 'which book'. Interestingly, all the languages given here behave the same, i.e. the finite verb inverts with the subject which results in Verb Second. Before we draw some conclusions based on our observations, the following table summarises our results:

Table 11.1. Comparison of languages in Verb Second contexts

1st constituent	SWE	DAN	ICE	NHG	DUT	PDE	FRE
Subject	yes	yes	yes	yes	yes	yes	yes
Object	yes	yes	yes	yes	yes	no	no
Temporal adv.	yes	yes	yes	yes	yes	no	no
Wh-question	yes	yes	yes	yes	yes	yes	yes

The contexts in which the first constituent is occupied by an object, an adverbial and a wh-constituent, i.e. not by the subject, clearly show that the finite verb always inverts with the subject. In the literature, it has been claimed that this is a prerequisite for Verb Second. This implies that in these languages **subject-verb inversion** occurs in all main declarative sentences regardless of the status of the first constituent. So the structure underlying the Verb Second rule is:

(11)   [Any constituent]-V_{fin}-Subject-...

In theoretical terms this also implies that sentences with the order S-V_{fin}-Object in PDE and FRE are different from sentences with the same order in Verb Second languages. In chapter 12 we will come back to this point and discuss an analysis which makes this difference explicit.

Among the Germanic languages PDE is the exception because it displays Verb Second only in a restricted set of contexts like constituent questions. Rizzi (1996) called this property **'residual Verb Second'** because in early stages of English, as will be shown in part III, chapter 17, Verb Second was found in all the contexts investigated above, so OE and ME behaved much more like NHG, SWE, and the other modern Germanic languages. We can then assume that the pattern we find today is a residue of a full-fledged version of Verb Second. Interestingly, this has also been claimed for French.

11.2 Verb Second in subordinate clauses

So far we have seen that there are Germanic languages which show 'proper' Verb Second, and PDE which shows residual Verb Second in main declarative sentences.

But what about subordinate clauses? Let's first take a look at some examples from NHG and PDE:

(12) a. ... *dass Eric dieses Buch gelesen **hat**$_{Aux}$.*
          that Eric this   book read   has
    b. ... *that Eric **has**$_{Aux}$ read this book.*
    c. * ... *dass dieses Buch **hat**$_{Aux}$ Eric gelesen.*
           that this   book has   Eric read
    d. * ... *that this book **has**$_{Aux}$ Eric read .*

In NHG the subordinate clause which is introduced by the conjunction *that* shows that the finite verb *hat* 'has' must occur in clause-final position. If it occurs in the second position after the object NP *dieses Buch* (in analogy to Verb Second in main sentences) the clause is ungrammatical. In PDE the subordinate clause introduced by *that* shows the ordering S-V-O ((12) b.). If the finite verb *has* occurs in second position the clause is ungrammatical ((12) d.).

From a comparative perspective, we find this pattern in the other Germanic Verb Second languages as well, for example in Danish:

(13) a. **Johan beklager [at   denne bog   **har**$_{Aux}$ Eric læst].*
        John   regrets   that this book has   Eric read
        (from Vikner 1995:72)

So at first sight Verb Second only occurs in main declarative sentences. However, there are some exceptions: in clauses which are complements of so-called *verba dicendi* and *verba sentiendi* or **bridge verbs**, i.e. verbs of saying or verbs of perception like *say* or *believe*, Verb Second is an option. This is not possible in PDE as example (14) e. shows:

(14) a. NHG *Sie behauptete, dass Eric dieses Buch gelesen **hat**$_{Aux}$.*
          She claimed   that Eric this   book read   has
    b. NHG *Sie behauptete, dieses Buch **habe**$_{Aux}$ Eric gelesen.*
          She claimed   this   book had   Eric read
    c. DAN *Hun påstod at   Eric **har**$_{Aux}$ læst denne bog.*
          She claimed that Eric has   read this book
    d. DAN *Hun påstod at   denne bog **har**$_{Aux}$ Eric læst.*
          She claimed that this book has   Eric read
    e. PDE **She claimed (that) this book **has**$_{Aux}$ Eric read.*

Note that in NHG the subjunctive form of the finite verb (here *habe*) is required in embedded Verb Second. In DAN and the other Scandinavian languages this type of Verb

Second even occurs if the subordinate clause is introduced by a conjunction (here *at* 'that').

So we can summarise our findings so far: almost all of the modern Germanic languages are Verb Second languages, consistently exhibiting the finite verb in the second position directly after a first element which can be any constituent. These languages also show Verb Second in subordinate clauses but only in a very limited way, i.e. only in the context where the lexical verb of the main sentence is a bridge verb. English is the exception: it shows Verb Second only in constituent questions and never in subordinate clauses (we will come back to this point below).

Before we draw some final conclusions we must consider two further Germanic languages to complete the picture. Modern Icelandic is the only Scandinavian language which consistently shows Verb Second in subordinate clauses. The following examples serve to prove this:

(15) a. Jón efast um [að á morgun **fari** María snemma á fætur].
 John doubts that tomorrow get Mary early up
 'John doubts that Mary will get up early tomorrow.'
 b. Jón harmar [að þessa bók **skuli** ég hafa lesið].
 John regrets that this book shall I have read
 'John regrets that I have read this book.'
 (Rögnvaldsson and Thráinsson, 1990, 23)

In both examples the finite verb (*fari* in (15) a. and *skuli* in b.) are in second position of the subordinate clauses.

Yiddish, a variety of German which arose during the Middle Ages as a trade language of Jews, is another Germanic language which displays Verb Second in both main sentences and subordinate clauses. Below, I give a number of examples:

(16) a. Dos bukh **hot** Max geleyent.
 this book has Max read (Diesing 44 1990)
 b. ... oyb dos yingl **vet** oyfn veg zen a kats.
 if the boy will on-the way see a cat
 c. ... oyb oyfn veg **vet** dos yingl zen a kats.
 if on-the way will the boy see a cat
 d. *... oyb oyfn veg dos yingl **vet** zen a kats.
 if on-the way the boy will see a cat
 (Santorini 1995:54)

In (16) a. the object NP *dos bukh* 'this book' is directly followed by the finite verb *hot* 'has' which in turn directly precedes the subject *Max*. Subject-verb inversion has taken place resulting in Verb Second. In the subordinate clauses in b. and c. the finite verb *vet* 'will' must occur in the second position directly following the object *dos yingl* 'the boy' (b.) or the PP *oyfn veg* 'on the way' with the function of a locative adverbial. If the finite verb occurs in another position as is illustrated with d. the clause is rendered ungrammatical.

Now we can summarise our findings for the phenomenon of Verb Second and propose the following classification: languages like Swedish, Danish, German and Dutch consistently show Verb Second in main sentences but only to a limited degree in subordinate clauses. This is why they can be called 'asymmetric Verb Second languages'. Although we haven't discussed Afrikaans, Faroese, Norwegian and Flemish, we can add these languages to this type of Verb Second because they have the same properties. Germanic languages like Icelandic and Yiddish consistently show Verb Second in both main sentences and subordinate clauses. They have been labelled 'symmetric Verb Second languages'. English, or more precisely, PDE, is the only Germanic language which shows Verb Second in a very restricted way in main sentences (and not at all in subordinate clauses). For this reason, PDE can be called a 'residual Verb Second language' (see above).

The following table provides a typology of the different types of Verb Second discussed in this chapter:

Table 11.2. Typology of (Germanic) Verb Second languages

Asymmetric V2	Symmetric V2	Residual V2
main sentences and some subordinate clauses	main sentences and all subordinate clauses	only in some restricted contexts
Swedish, Danish Norwegian, Faroese German, Dutch Afrikaans, Flemish	Icelandic, Yiddish	English

Finally, I would like to briefly draw your attention to another phenomenon, independent of Verb Second, which can be seen if we take another a look at the data discussed above and repeated here:

(17) a. SWE *Eric har [$_{VP}$ läst$_V$ [denne bok]$_O$.]*
 b. DAN *Eric har [$_{VP}$ læst$_V$ [denne bog]$_O$.]*
 c. ICE *Eiríkur hefur [$_{VP}$ lesið$_V$ [þessa bók]$_O$.]*
 d. NHG *Eric hat [$_{VP}$ [dieses Buch]$_O$ gelesen$_V$.]*
 e. DUT *Eric heeft [$_{VP}$ [dit boek]$_O$ gelezen$_V$.]*
 f. PDE *Eric has [$_{VP}$ read$_V$ [this book]$_O$.]*
 g. FRE *Eric a [$_{VP}$ lu$_V$ [ce livre]$_O$.]*

The phenomenon under investigation relates to the verb phrase which I have indicated in the sentences with square brackets. What we are dealing with here is the relative order of the lexical verb and its object. In Swedish, Danish, Icelandic, English, and French the full verb directly precedes the object, for example SWE $[_{VP}$ $[läst]_V$ $[denne\ bok]_O]$. In German and Dutch the lexical verb directly follows the object, for example NHG $[_{VP}$ $[dieses\ Buch]_O$ $[gelesen]_V]$. So we have two types of languages: one where the verb is head-initial, and one where the verb is head-final. If we added all of the languages mentioned here, we would gain the following picture:

Table 11.3. OV and VO languages

VO: $[_{VP}\ V\ O]$	OV: $[_{VP}\ O\ V]$
Swedish, Danish, Icelandic, Norwegian Faroese, English French	German, Dutch Yiddish, Afrikaans Flemish

Verb Second languages can be either head-initial or head-final in the verb phrase. Asymmetric Verb Second languages can also either be OV or VO (German, Swedish), and this applies to symmetric Verb Second languages as well (Icelandic, Yiddish). So there is no correlation between (a special type of) Verb Second and the order of the verb and its object within the verb phrase. Since French as a VO language does not exhibit Verb Second at all, we see that there is also no correlation between OV/VO and Verb Second. Further proof for the latter claim are non-Verb Second languages like Japanese exhibiting OV order.

Syn: 'Tax, did you find parallels to the comparative linguistics of the nineteenth century?'
Tax: 'Definitely. It was quite interesting to see the comparative method applied to the phenomenon of Verb Second across the Germanic languages. It allowed us to view the phenomenon in a broader perspective and it led to generalisations we couldn't have made by looking at just one of these languages.'
Syn: 'I am quite confident that this has become clear throughout the chapter. In the following chapter, we will use these insights and apply the notion of movement to Verb Second, and in more general terms, verb movement.'

Tax: 'To see if you understood what was said above about Verb Second and especially residual Verb Second in English, we provide a number of examples from the BNC that wait for an analysis by you!'
Syn: 'So, 1) take a look at the sentences and identify the finite verb and its position in the main sentence; 2) check if the finite verb is inverted with the subject; and 3) identify and classify the first constituent and try to explain why the case(s) might be instances of residual Verb Second':

(18) a. *'Never in my life have I questioned an appointment', she said, weighing every word.*
   (BNC, H7E 1731)
   b. *Only in this way can opportunities for vertical integration and strategic cooperation between organisations be investigated.*
   (BNC, HHY 661)
   c. *Hardly had I uttered the word – or the phrase signifying it – than I felt within me the need to become what I had been accused of being ...*
   (BNC, A6D 1189)
   d. *Down the stairs came the cat, sullen-eyed.*
   (BNC, AD1 749)

Literature: Most of the studies dealing with Verb Second are generative in nature. The first studies on Verb Second in German and Dutch are Thiersch (1978) and den Besten (1983, 1985). Rizzi (1990) discusses an analysis of Verb Second in PDE and calls it 'residual Verb Second.' In Rizzi (1996) he again deals with this type of Verb Second and postulates the wh-criterion. In Vikner (1995) an analysis of embedded Verb Second as CP-recursion is proposed. Kiparsky (1995) discusses Verb First and Verb Second in Germanic and puts forward the assumption that what Rizzi has called 'residual Verb Second' is actually the original core of the Verb Second system. Rögnvaldsson & Thráinsson's (1990) article discusses embedded Verb Second in Icelandic. The analyses of Cardinaletti and Roberts (2002) and Iatridou and Kroch (1992) uniformly account for Verb Second in main sentences and subordinate clauses in the generative framework. A study dealing with Verb Second in dependency grammar is Osborne (2005).

12 Movement and its application to the syntax of English

In this chapter we will discuss the generative notion of **movement** in more detail. We will take a look at the properties of I(infl) in PDE and other languages and try to account for differences by assuming the presence or absence of (verb) movement.

12.1 Properties of I(nfl)

I would like to start discussing the topic by taking up some of the examples we investigated in the previous chapter:

(1) a. *Eric$_S$ **has**$_{Aux}$ read this book.*
 b. *... because Eric$_S$ **has**$_{Aux}$ read this book.*
 c. *Which book **has**$_{Aux}$ Eric$_S$ read?*
 d. *Never in my life **have**$_{Aux}$ I$_S$ questioned an appointment ...*
 (BNC, H7E 1731)
 e. *Down the stairs **came**$_V$ the cat$_S$, sullen-eyed.*
 (BNC, AD1 749)

As we have seen in previous chapters, typologically English is an SVO language which shows this order quite rigidly in main declarative sentences and in subordinate clauses. This is illustrated with the examples in (1) a. and b. The sentences in c. to d. however deviate from this pattern: in all of these cases the finite verb directly precedes the subject. We can observe this difference and state that subject-verb inversion has taken place. But how can we explain it?

Another case subject to the same phenomenon is illustrated with English and French examples in (2):

(2) a. *Eric **often**$_{Adv}$ meets$_V$ the student from Paris.*
 b. **Eric meets$_V$ **often**$_{Adv}$ the student from Paris.*
 c. **Eric **souvent**$_{Adv}$ rencontre$_V$ l'étudiant de Paris.*
 d. *Eric rencontre$_V$ **souvent**$_{Adv}$ l'étudiant de Paris.*

In English an adverb like *often* must precede the lexical verb as is shown with the contrast between a. and b. In French, the adverb *souvent* (which can be seen as the equivalent of *often*) must precede the lexical verb (see the contrast between c. and d.). So in English we find the order adverb-lexical verb whereas in French we find the order lexical verb-adverb. How can we explain this difference in the position of the finite form of the lexical verb? We can do so by assuming different (unmarked) positions for lexical verbs in a sentence. In the following, we will discuss an analysis that accounts for this difference which is predominantly based on the work by Pollock (1989).

Before we deal with Pollock's analysis in more detail recall that a sentence consists of two parts, the subject and the predicate. The predicate describes the kind of activity that is taking place, and the subject is the entity undergoing this activity. Second, we assume that the verb phrase is layered, which can be nicely illustrated with the following example:

(3) *The linguist meets the student after breakfast.*

Intuitively, we know that the lexical verb stands in a close relation to its argument(s). Put differently, we say that the verb phrase in a sentence supplies the basic thematic roles which make up the proposition. So in our concrete example in (3) we assume that the NP *the linguist* (subject), the NP *the student* (object) and the lexical verb *meet* stand in such a relation, and in a tree representation of this sentence these elements therefore all occur within the VP. In chapter 8 we have said that sentences consist of constituents and that they are built up by putting together or **merging** two constituents. Keeping all of this in mind we build up the structure of the sentence in (3) in the following way: the lexical verb *meet* is a transitive verb which requires an object which is its complement and has the shape of an NP. We first merge *meet* located in the head position of V with its complement (object) *the student*. Then we merge this constituent with a specifier to form the full VP. As noted above the subject and the object are the core elements in the sentence, and in the tree structure they occupy the positions of the specifier and the complement of the VP: the subject in the specifier position and the object in the complement position. The assumption that the subject originates inside of the VP goes back to the end of the 1980s and was called the **VP-internal subject hypothesis** (we'll come back again to the position(s) of the subject and to the assumption that the subject moves from its specifier in VP to the specifier position in IP). The PP *after breakfast* does not stand in such a close relation to the verb; it modifies the action described by the verb and its object but is less central to the activity. Thus, it can be called a circumstant or adjunct (see again chapter 9.2) We assume that as an adverbial (of time) it is adjoined to the VP in the tree structure. In (4) is a tree representation of the VP:

(4)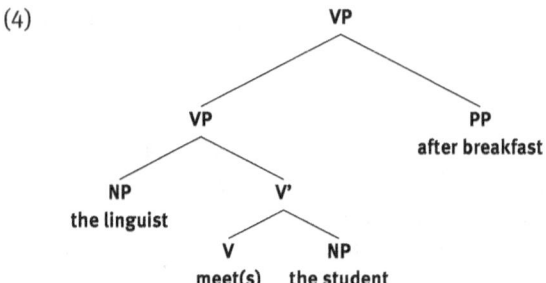

Third, a position for inflection is generally assumed. Examples like those given in (5) speak in favour of such a position:

(5) a. The linguist **will meet** the student after breakfast.
     b. What the linguist **will do** is meet the student after breakfast.
     c. What the linguist **did was** meet the student after breakfast.
     d. **Meet** the student after breakfast, the linguist **did**.

In (5) a. the finite verb *will* marking tense and agreement (present tense, 3rd person singular) is not part of the VP, it occurs to its left. In the so-called 'pseudo-cleft' sentences in b. and c. the finite verbs *will* and *did* are 'dissociated' from the VP, i.e. they occur in the subordinate clause whereas the VP *meet the student after breakfast* occurs in the main sentence (note that *meet* is non-finite!). In addition, the example in c. where the whole VP has been fronted, shows that past tense inflection associated with the lexical verb is marked on the auxiliary in the form *did*. Therefore, it has been assumed that these grammatical properties have an auxiliary-like status, and that the position of the auxiliary not only encodes tense properties of the verb but also dominates person morphology (agreement). This is why tense and agreement inflection are located all in the same position of inflection, or **I(nfl)** for short.

A further question arising is whether the position of inflection determines all of the properties of a sentence. More precisely, the question is if it is justified to say that we have a full functional phrase IP that is headed by I(infl). Many linguists put forward the following examples in favour of this hypothesis:

(6) a. I hope **that** [Susann will dance after lunch].
     b. I hope **for** [Susann to dance after lunch].

(6) a. and b. are two complex sentences consisting of the main clause with the lexical verb *hope* and a complement clause. In a. the complement clause is finite and introduced by the conjunction *that*, and in b. the complement clause is non-finite and

introduced by the conjunction *for*. As a result, in a. *will* is inflected for tense, and in b. *dance* is not inflected. We can say then that the position of inflection also determines whether a sentence is finite or non-finite.

Finally, it can be shown that the position of inflection determines the realisation of the subject:

(7)   a.   *I hope that [**she** will dance after lunch]*.
         b.   *I hope for [**her** to dance after lunch]*.

As you can see, the finiteness or non-finiteness of the subordinate clause determines the form of the pronominal subject: in the finite clause in a. *she* is nominative, and in the non-finite clause in b. *her* is accusative. Further, subjects can sometimes be non-overt (recall what we said in chapter 10.2; for the diachronic perspective see part III, chapter 14). In PDE non-overt subjects can only occur in non-finite clauses:

(8)   a.   *I hope that [**she** will dance after lunch]*.
         b.   **I hope that [will dance after lunch]*.
         c.   *I hope [to dance after lunch]*.

The contrast between (8) a. and b. illustrates that in a finite subordinate clause the subject has to occur overtly, for example as the pronoun *she*. In the non-finite clause in c., however, it can be left out. But we also know that the subject has to be there because *to dance after lunch* refers to the subject *I* in the main sentence (*I hope that I will dance after lunch*).

From these examples, we can conclude the following: a) the properties of a sentence are a function of the features of **I(nfl)**, so I(nfl) heads the sentence; b) the sentence is a projection of I(nfl), IP; c) I(nfl) is the verbal inflectional morphology. It is primarily associated with the verb that heads the VP; d) I(nfl) selects VP with which it forms an intermediate projection, I'. I' combines with the subject of the sentence to form IP, i.e. the sentence. The tree structure representation of a main declarative sentence in PDE thus looks like this:

(9)

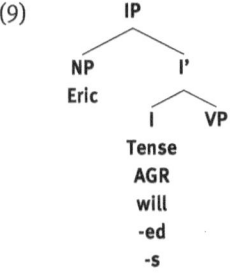

Looking at the structure we can see that sentences are centered around I. I links the subject and the VP in that the properties of I define temporal and/or modal aspects of that relation. If you recall what we have said about the predication relation in chapter 8.1 (the subject and the predicate are the two main parts of a sentence) you will see that the IP is the generative interpretation of a sentence containing exactly this relation.

12.2 Movement as an explanation for cross-linguistic differences

Let's come back to the examples which compare English with French repeated here:

(10) a. Eric **often**$_{Adv}$ meets$_V$ the student from Paris.
  b. *Eric meets$_V$ **often**$_{Adv}$ the student from Paris.
  c. *Eric **souvent**$_{Adv}$ rencontre$_V$ l'étudiant de Paris.
  d. Eric rencontre$_V$ **souvent**$_{Adv}$ l'étudiant de Paris.

From what we have said above, the sentence in a. has the following tree structure representation:

(11)
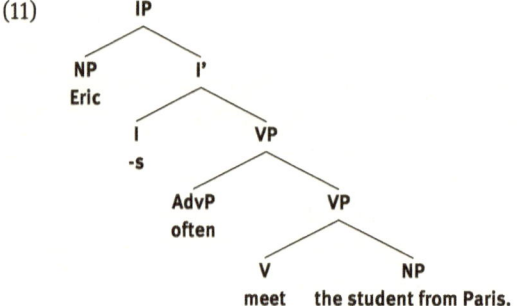

We can observe two things here: first, the inflectional ending -s occurs in I and the verb *meet* it has to attach to occurs in V. Second, the adverb *often* is **left-adjoined** to the VP and occurs between -s and *meet*. Clearly this structure produces an ungrammatical sentence:

(12) *Eric -s **often** meet the student from Paris.

If we directly insert the verb *meet* in I to provide a host for the bound morpheme -s we would gain the following ungrammatical sentence ((10) b. is repeated here):

(13) *Eric meets **often** the student from Paris.

If we apply the same process to French we gain the following grammatical example:

(14) Eric rencontre **souvent** l'étudiant de Paris.

It seems that in French the verb *rencontre* can occur in I and be combined with its inflectional ending *-e* whereas this is not possible in English. How can we explain the problems we ran into in English, and the difference between English and French?

Apart from the operation of merge in generative syntax the operation of **movement** is assumed to explain why it is possible that constituents can occur in positions different from their base positions. Recall that in the GB framework the notion of movement is based on the assumption that the structure of an expression in (any) language can be described at two levels (see again part I, chapter 6): a **deep level** (D-structure) and a **surface level** (S-structure). These two levels are linked by **transformations** which mainly involve moving elements from one position to another. At both levels a number of principles apply: at the deep level, principles that are responsible for the basic organisation of the structure are at work, and at the surface level principles that regulate movement.

The operation of movement can now explain why the sentence in (10) b. (repeated in (13)) is ungrammatical: as you can see, the lexical verb *meets* does not occur directly to the left of its object *the student from Paris* which it does in the grammatical sentence in (10) a.: here *meets* is left-adjacent to its object *the student from Paris*. Rather in (10) b. *meets* occurs to the left of the VP-adjoined adverbial *often*, and this can be interpreted as movement of the verb from its base position within the VP to the I position. But this operation is ruled out in English, lexical verbs cannot move from V to I. In contrast in French, movement of the lexical verb to the I position is obligatory: in (14) the lexical verb *rencontre* occurs to the left of the VP-adjoined adverbial *souvent* and the sentence is grammatical. If the lexical verb occurs in its base position (see (10) c.), the sentence is ungrammatical. So in French the lexical verb has to move to I whereas in English it has to stay in V. The tree structure representation of (14) is given below (the moved element is marked by strikethrough notation):

(15)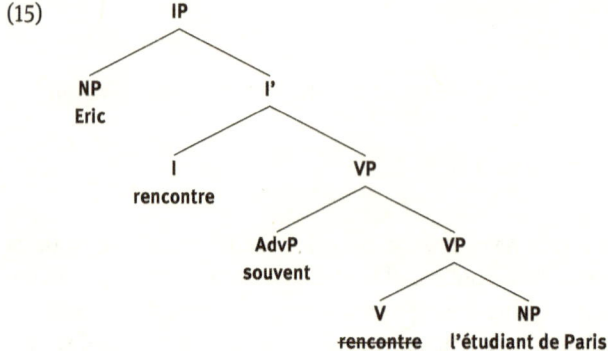

Coming back to the English example in (12) and the question of how to unite the lexical verb with its tense and agreement inflection to obtain a grammatical sentence, in the literature two options have been proposed: either the inflectional suffix in I is lowered to the lexical verb in V, or the lexical verb in V is raised to the inflectional suffix in I. We have already seen that raising is not an option in English. Since I and VP in (11) are on equal footing, both are immediate constituents of I'. Further, since the lexical verb is the head of the core VP it is lower down than the head of I. This is why we say that when I joins V, it lowers onto V (this is what Chomsky proposed in 1957, known as **affix hopping**). In French, the process of raising takes place: the verb in V leaves the VP and moves up to I. By assuming the processes of **lowering** and **raising** we can explain the observed differences between English and French. Note that first of all, lowering is subject to the locality principle (see again part I, chapter 6.2) and second, that the operation of verb raising is the preferred option.

There are cases in English when lowering does not take place. Take a look at the following examples:

(16) a. *Eric will **often** invite the student from Paris.*
 b. *Eric has **often** invited the student from Paris.*
 c. *Eric does **often** invite the student from Paris.*

In all three examples *often* is preceded by auxiliaries (*will*, *has*, and *does*). If the bound inflectional suffix *-s* is associated with an auxiliary, i.e. an auxiliary is inserted in I, the suffix can be attached to a proper host:

(17)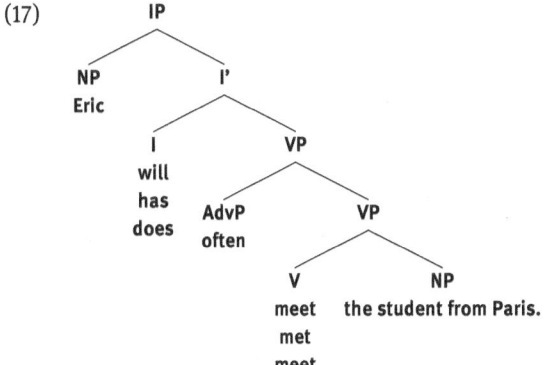

Note that *do* in affirmative declarative sentences is used to add emphatic stress. In chapter 18 of part III you will see that his has not always been the case.

The difference between English and French observed and discussed here has been related to inflectional morphology. First, let's take a look at some verb forms of French:

(18)
Present Tense		Present Perfect			Modality		
je	parle	j'	ai	parlé	je	veux	parler
tu	parles	tu	as	parlé	tu	veux	parler
il/elle	parle	il/elle	a	parlé	il/elle	veut	parler
nous	parlons	nous	avons	parlé	nous	voulons	parler
vous	parlez	vous	avez	parlé	vous	voulez	parler
ils	parlent	ils	ont	parlé	ils	veulent	parler

We see that in French the finite verb has quite a number of different inflectional endings for different person specifications. Compare the French verb forms with the English ones given below:

(19)
Present Tense		Present Perfect			Modality		
I	speak	I	have	spoken	I	will	speak
you	speak	you	have	spoken	you	will	speak
he	speaks	he	has	spoken	he	will	speak
we	speak	we	have	spoken	we	will	speak
you	speak	you	have	spoken	you	will	speak
they	speak	they	have	spoken	they	will	speak

In the Present Tense and the Present Perfect there are very few distinct verb forms, actually only the 3rd person -*s* vs. Ø inflectional ending. In periphrastic forms like *will* + infinitive there is no difference at all between the different forms. Therefore, we say that English has weak verbal inflection whereas French has stronger verbal inflection (even if not all of the graphical inflections are pronounced). It has been suggested that there is a correlation between verbal inflection and movement. In French, which exhibits **strong inflection**, I can attract the lexical verb, i.e. the verb moves to I; in English, which exhibits **weak inflection**, I cannot attract the lexical verb and hence the lexical verb cannot move to I. For further discussion from a diachronic point of view and a refinement of this correlation see part III, chapter 18.

In the remaining part of this chapter we will analyse the first set of data presented right at the beginning of our discussion. For your convenience I repeat the data below:

(20) a. $Eric_S$ has_{Aux} read this book.
 b. ... because $Eric_S$ has_{Aux} read this book.
 c. Which book has_{Aux} $Eric_S$ read?
 d. Never in my life $have_{Aux}$ I_S questioned an appointment ...
 (BNC, H7E 1731)
 e. Down the stairs $came_V$ the cat_S, sullen-eyed.
 (BNC, AD1 749)

The examples in (20) a. and b. exhibit SVO order in a main declarative sentence and a subordinate clause, but the examples in c. to e. show deviations from this order: a sentence-initial constituent is followed by the finite verb and the subject, so subject-verb inversion has taken place. In chapter 11 we have seen that Verb Second languages consistently show this pattern. First, let's take a look at a structure for a main declarative sentence for English:

(21)
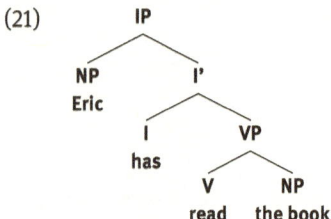

We see that the **linear precedence** of the subject in relation to the verb is hierarchically expressed by **dominance**. In these terms, subject-verb inversion is interpreted as a position of the finite verb that is higher than the position of the subject. In our tree structure above, this would imply a position to the left of *Eric*. The traditional analysis of these structures assumes a CP as highest functional projection in a tree. The C stands for **complementiser** and points to the observation that in Verb Second languages this position can either be occupied by a complementiser (subordinating conjunction) in subordinate clauses or by a finite verb in main declarative sentences.

12.2 Movement as an explanation for cross-linguistic differences — 121

The first constituent in Verb Second sentences occupies the specifier position of CP. The following table serves to illustrate this observation with examples from NHG (the elements in brackets indicate movement):

(22)

CP	C	IP ...	VP
	dass	Eric gestern dieses Buch gelesen	hat
Eric	hat	gestern dieses Buch gelesen	~~hat~~
Dieses Buch	hat	Eric gestern gelesen	~~hat~~
Gestern	hat	Eric dieses Buch gelesen	~~hat~~
	Hat	Eric gestern dieses Buch gelesen	~~hat~~
Welches Buch	hat	Eric gestern gelesen	~~hat~~

We can apply this analysis to the examples in English which show residual Verb Second as well:

(23)

CP	C	IP ...	VP
Which book	has	Eric	~~has~~ read
Which book	did	Eric	~~did~~ read
Which book	will	Eric	~~will~~ read
Never in my life	have	I	~~have~~ questioned an appointment

Obviously, these cases show another type of **verb movement**: movement of the finite verb to the C position. Above, we came to the conclusion that in English lexical verbs cannot move out of V, so the type of verb movement we are dealing with here is **I-to-C movement** of auxiliaries. This type of movement is also found in yes-no questions:

(24) a. Have$_{Aux}$ they$_S$ read this book?
 b. Did$_{Aux}$ they$_S$ read this book?
 c. Will$_{Aux}$ they$_S$ read this book?

In languages like NHG, where lexical verbs can move out of their V position, we talk about **V-to-I-to-C movement** of lexical verbs. What about French then? Take a look at the different positions of the finite verb in the declarative sentence and the yes-no question:

(25) a. Ils$_S$ lisent$_V$ ce livre.
  they read this book
 b. Lisent$_V$ ils$_S$ ce livre?
  read they this book

In (25) a. the subject pronoun *ils* 'they' directly precedes the finite lexical verb *lisent* 'read', yet in b. the order is reversed. Following the analysis of verb movement we have adopted in this chapter, we say that the finite lexical verb has moved from the V position via the I position to the C position:

(26)
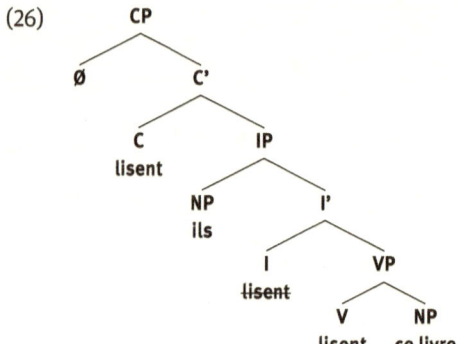

The finite lexical verb *lisent* in brackets in V and I marks the step-by-step movement which is stipulated for this movement operation. For further details I refer you to Haegeman (2001) and the references given below.

Tax: 'Before Syn and I summarise what we have learnt in this chapter, in the following we'll provide some grammatical and ungrammatical examples for English which await your analysis. Recall what we have said about the nature of the verbal morphology and the type of verb movement assumed.'
Syn: 'Are you ready? Okay, so **1)** describe the order of the elements in the sentences by paying special attention of the relative order of the subject and the finite verb; **2)** if you've done that, apply the analysis of verb movement by providing tree structure representations for each of the sentences.'

(27) a. We read this book.
 b. *Read we this book?
 c. Do we read this book?
 d. We are reading this book.
 e. Are we reading this book?
 f. Down the stairs came the cat, sullen-eyed.

Tax: 'So Syn, what have we seen in this chapter?'
Syn: 'We have dealt with the generative notion of verb or head movement. We applied this operation to two contexts by comparing English with French and German: first, the context where a VP-adverb precedes or follows the finite verb, and second, the context where the subject is inverted with the finite verb. We found that the languages under investigation behaved differently in these two contexts. The French data showed that the finite verb preceded the adverb, whereas the English data showed

that the finite verb occurred after the adverb. We said that in French the finite lexical verb moves out of its V position to I because the verbal morphology is strong enough to attract verbs to I. In English this type of movement does not exist because verbal morphology is too weak to attract the finite lexical verb to I. Auxiliaries like *do*, *have*, and modals like *will*, however, can occur in I (i.e. they are inserted in I).'

Tax: 'And then we came back to Verb Second again when we investigated subject-verb inversion which generally occurs in Verb Second sentence. We said that a position higher than the subject position is needed to account for the data. We adopted the analysis for German stating that the first constituent occupies the specifier of C, and the finite verb occupies the C position. In English the residual contexts where Verb Second occurs can be analysed along these lines. Lacking a first constituent in yes-no questions, the specifier position is not filled in these cases, only the finite verb moves to C. Generally, we can conclude that a theoretical notion like verb movement can help us explain the observations we have made by looking at the data for English and the other languages discussed here.'

Syn: 'It seems we have come to the end of part II of this book.'

Tax: 'Yes, and although we have already learnt a lot about grammatical theory and its application to a number of languages, one step is still missing.'

Syn: 'You are right! We still don't know how the phenomena we have come across in PDE have developed in the history of English.'

Tax: 'Fascinating! We shouldn't miss it! Off we go!'

Literature: Introductions to the generative notion of movement are found aplenty, for example in Radford (1997), Radford et al. (1999), Haegeman and Guéron (1999), Haegeman (2001, 2006), and the accessible introduction provided by Sobin (2011). Roberts (1993) investigates differences between instances of verb movement in English and French also adding the diachronic perspective which will become relevant in part III of the book. Concerning analyses of Verb Second as an instance of verb movement see the references in the previous chapter.

Part III: **Diachronic analysis of English syntax**

13 Introduction

In the third part of the book, we will take a look at the sentence structure in older stages of English to get a comprehensive picture of what we have dealt with so far and to better understand why PDE sentence structure is as we find it today. Since the syntax of older stages of English is at least as vast a field as the syntax of PDE, the most prominent phenomena and constructions are selected to make clear differences between PDE and, for example, OE, but also differences between OE and NHG. You will be surprised to see how similar NHG actually is to OE, which I am sure will help you in your learning process.

The first question you might have is: 'What are older stages of English?', I have already mentioned one of them, Old English. It is the first stage of English which is attested in written documents dating from before 1100. If you want to read more about it, I refer you to the classics, Mitchell (1995) and Mitchell and Robinson (2003) (see also the references at the end of chapter 14). Since language is in constant flux, by around 1100, (Old) English had changed so much that linguists (and other scholars from other fields) decided to announce another period, Middle English (ME). This period is somewhere between Old English and more recent periods of English, and that is why it is called 'Middle' English. Its end is dated to 1500, a date which then also marks the beginning of a new period in the history of English, Early Modern English (EModE). This period spans from 1500 to 1700, and it is this period that you probably know most about because Shakespeare is one of, if not the most prominent author of that time. Between EModE and PDE an intermediate step is assumed which is found under the term Modern (British) English, approximately the time between 1700 and 1914. I won't have much to say about this period in this book as there are no dramatic changes on the level of syntax to be found. Finally, PDE is the period of English between 1914 and today. Periodisation is a tricky business, and many authors refrain from giving precise dates. The information I gave is based on the decision of others who are cited below.

In the following, when we talk about Old English, Middle English, Early Modern English, and Present-Day English, we use 'language' as a cover term and are aware of the fact that during all these stages varieties and hence variation existed (and in part II, chapter 10 we have seen this for PDE). In chapter 16, I will say a bit more about that in ME but generally I will use the cover term to point out the most important phenomena in these periods.

Before we start to deal with our syntactic exploration, I am going to give you one example which very nicely illustrates changes from OE, to ME to EModE. As you will see right away, the example is from the bible. Take a look at
Old English (Late West Saxon, ca. 1050)

(1) þa æfter feawa dagum ealle hys þyng gegaderode se gingra sunu 7
 then after few days all his things gathered the younger son and
 ferde wrælice on feorlen ryce ond forspilde þær his æhta, libbende on his
 fared abroad in far-off country and wasted there his goods living in his
 gælsan.
 pride

Middle English (Late 14th-century, South Midlands)

(2) And not aftir many daies whanne alle thingis weren gederid togider the ȝonger sone wente forth in pilgrymage in to a fer cuntre and there he wastide hise goodis in lyuynge lecherously.

Early Modern English (1611)

(3) And not many dayes after, the younger sonne gathered all together, and tooke his iourney int a farre countrey: and there he wasted his substance with riotous liuinng.

What you see right away is that OE looks unfamiliar because of the runic characters it uses for today's <th> and the so-called *ash* found for the /æ/ phoneme. Moreover, there are some diphthongs spelled <ea> or <eo> which we would not expect to find in words like 'all' (*eall*) and 'far' (*feorlen*) today. Also, if you consult the books I recommended to you above, you will find a difference between short and long vowels, indicated by so-called diacritics. This difference is distinctive, meaning that it makes a difference in the meanings of the word. For example the word *ac* meant 'but' and the word *āc* 'oak'. Since we are predominantly interested in the syntax of this time, however, we will leave the levels of phonology and spelling aside (also leaving out these diacritics) and take a look at the morphosyntactic shape and the position of items in a sentence. One striking difference between the OE text and the EModE text is the relative order of the finite verb in the past tense form, *gegaderode* 'gathered', and the subject *se gingra sunu* 'the younger son'. In the OE text the order is finite verb-subject, in the EModE text the order is subject-finite verb. In the ME text we don't know because the passive construction *weren gederid* 'were gathered' is used. We will see that the inversion of the finite verb with subject describes a drastic change between OE and ME times. But next, we will start out with the main properties of sentence structure in OE.

14 Sentence structure of Early English

In this chapter we are going to deal with sentence structure in older stages of English with a focus on OE and ME because they deviate most drastically from PDE.

14.1 Subjects, verbs, and word order in main sentences and subordinate clauses

In chapter 8 of part II we said that according to traditional grammar the sentence is defined in terms of a predication relation between the subject and the predicate. In a sentence from PDE like *The syntactician ponders the problem in her armchair* we get information about the subject, the syntactician, namely that he/she ponders the problem in her armchair. The subject has to be spelled out, otherwise the sentence is ungrammmatical: **ponders the problem in her armchair*. In OE, in some cases, the subject could be left out, which makes it similar to Romance languages like Italian:

(1) ho   mangiato   bene.
     have-1-SG eaten-PART good-ADV

But also in NHG, a sentence like (2) can be uttered without problems (in colloquial, sloppy speech):

(2) Hab   gut   gegessen.
     have-1-SG good-ADV eaten-PART

The non-occurrence of overt subjects depends on the richness of inflectional morphology. NHG, and even more so Italian, are languages which have rich inflectional morphology, the verb endings include grammatical information about person, number, tense, and mood. So just by looking at the verb forms you see right away which grammatical specification we are dealing with (of course, I highly overgeneralised here and left out cases where one form stands for several specifications. For the sake of illustration, we will adopt this simplified description). This is also true for OE. Compare the OE, NHG and Italian verb forms in the paradigm for the verb 'help' in the present tense indicative:
OE and NHG show nearly the same pattern: unique endings for the first, second, and third person, in the plural OE has only one ending for all forms, NHG has the same ending for the first and third person and the *t*-ending for the second person. In languages like Italian we even find a relation where one form corresponds to exactly one grammatical function. The fact that this relation holds in all three languages, albeit

Table 14.1. Verbal inflection of OE, NHG and Italian 'help'

	Old English	New High German	Italian
1-SG	ic help**e**	ich helf**e**	(io) aiut**o**
2-SG	þu hilp**st**	du hilf**st**	(tu) aiut**i**
3-SG	he hilp**þ**	er hilf**t**	(lui) aiut**a**
1-PL	we help**aþ**	wir helf**en**	(noi) aiut**iamo**
2-PL	ge help**aþ**	ihr helf**t**	(voi) aiut**ate**
3-PL	hie help**aþ**	sie helf**en**	(loro) aiut**ano**

to different degrees, explains why an unstressed subject pronoun can be omitted: in Italian person and number can be read off from basically all verb forms, in OE and NHG from some verb forms.

In OE, the phenomenon of null subjects, which is also called **subject-drop** or **expletive pro-drop** in the generative literature (see again part II, chapter 8), occurred with some sets of verbs, for example, weather verbs:

(3) Ða cwom þær micel snaw & swa miclum sniwde swelce micel flys
    then came there heavy snow and so heavily snowed as-if much fleece
    feolle.
    fell
    (Alex:30.11.376)

In PDE, this is no longer possible, we would have to include a subject, in this case *it* as an expletive:

(4) Then heavy snow came and **it** snowed so heavily as if much fleece fell.

In ME, this property is still there to some degree (marked in the example below by Ø), although overt subjects are much more frequent.

(5) Ø hard is to knowe in al poyntis to holde the meene, lyght is hit to faille
    It hard is to know in all points to rule the society easy is it to fail
    '**It** is hard to know in all points (how) to rule the society, and it is easy to fail.'
    (SSecr 130/26, consulted on archive.org)

It also occurs in sentences with a marked topic in initial position as in

(6) as for [Thomas Myller]$_{Topic}$ wyll do nothyng in thys matter.
   as for Thomas Myller   will do nothing in this matter
   'As for Thomas Myller, **he** will do nothing in this matter.'
   (Cely Letters 8.6 in Fischer et al 2000:70)

It has been observed that during the course of the 15th century this construction is used less and less frequently and by 1500 the expletive *it* is the rule.

Note that in coordinations, subjects can generally be deleted, so this is not part of the phenomenon of subject-drop (see also part II, chapter 8.1). Take a look at the following example:

(7) *He stood there and waited for her for hours.*

We would expect to find an overt subject after the coordinating conjunction *and*, and indeed it could be filled in (*He stood there and **he** waited for her for hours*).

Next, we take a look at the predicate of OE sentences, more precisely, at the position of the finite verb. First, we will only discuss those cases where one verb occurs and where the finite verb is identical with the lexical verb. Examples of periphrastic constructions with an auxiliary (finite) and lexical (non-finite) verb will be discussed later. It has been observed that languages with comparatively rich verbal morphology have a freer word order, or to be more precise, a wider range of finite verb-fronting strategies than those without. Thus, we would expect to find more freedom in the placement of the finite verb in OE than in PDE.

In chapter 8 of part II we have also seen that in PDE both main declarative sentences and subordinate clauses exhibit the unmarked order Subject-(finite)Verb-Object, i.e. SVO (recall how we defined 'unmarked' and 'marked' word orders). Note that in the following examples, only the subject, the object, the auxiliary and the lexical verb are marked by indices. Constituents bigger than one word are enclosed in square brackets:

(8) a. *Eric$_S$ plays$_V$ [the piano]$_O$ [every day].*
   b. *Eric$_S$ is$_V$ [quite relaxed]$_{Su-compl}$ because he$_S$ plays$_V$ [the piano]$_O$ [every day].*
   c. *[Every day], Eric$_S$ plays$_V$ [the piano]$_O$.*
   d. *[The piano]$_O$, Eric$_S$ plays$_V$ [every day].*
   e. *Unfortunately, Eric$_S$ plays$_V$ [the piano]$_O$ [every day].*
   f. *Although he$_S$ annoys$_V$ [all members of the family]$_O$, Eric$_S$ plays$_V$ [the piano]$_O$ [every day].*

Regardless of the material added, the ordering SVO is retained (recall that in 8 b. *is quite relaxed* is actually a copular verb followed by the predicate in the form of the participle). If the object occurs in the first position, the order SV is retained. Before we take a look at OE, let's compare the examples in (8) with their NHG equivalents:

(9) a. *Eric$_S$ spielt$_V$ [jeden Tag] Klavier$_O$.*
 b. *Eric$_S$ ist$_V$ [ziemlich entspannt]$_{Su\text{-}compl}$, weil er$_S$ [jeden Tag] Klavier$_O$ spielt$_V$.*
 c. *[Jeden Tag] spielt$_V$ Eric$_S$ Klavier$_O$.*
 d. *Klavier$_O$ spielt$_V$ Eric$_S$ [jeden Tag].*
 e. *Leider spielt$_V$ Eric$_S$ [jeden Tag] Klavier$_O$.*
 f. *Obwohl er$_S$ [alle Familienmitglieder]$_O$ nervt$_V$, spielt$_V$ Eric$_S$ [jeden Tag] Klavier$_O$.*

Obviously, the German patterns are different from those in English: whereas the main declarative sentence in (9) a. and the main clause in b. exhibit the SVO order, the other examples show deviations. In the subordinate clauses in b. and e. we find SOV, and in the main declaratives in c. and d., and the main clause in e. we find VSO order. If the object occurs in first position, the verb also occurs directly after the subject. For NHG, two generalisations can be made: first, in main declaratives fronting of material like adverbials and objects results in the inversion of the subject and the (finite) verb; second, in subordinate clauses the order is SOV. Recall from part II, chapter 11 that this word order pattern of main declaratives has been labelled 'Verb Second' (den Besten, 1983) because the finite verb has to occur in the second position. We said that this is a property of most of today's West Germanic and Scandinavian languages, with the exception of English. In chapter 17 we will take a closer look at its development in the history of English and German.

Next, let's bring in the order of the subject and its predicate in yes/no-questions and wh-questions. Again, first take a look at PDE:

(10) a. *Does$_{AUX}$ Eric$_S$ play$_V$ [the piano]$_O$ [every day]? Yes/No.*
 b. **Plays$_V$ Eric$_S$ [the piano]$_O$ [every day]? Yes/No.*
 c. *When does$_{AUX}$ Eric$_S$ play$_V$ [the piano]$_O$? [Every day].*
 d. *What does$_{AUX}$ Eric$_S$ play$_V$ every day? [The piano]$_O$.*
 e. *Who plays$_V$ [the piano]$_O$ [every day]? Eric$_S$.*

In yes/no-questions ((10) a.), the sentence is introduced by a verb form of the auxiliary *do*, or any other auxiliary depending on the context. What is not possible is to place the inflected lexical verb in first position ((10) b.). The result will be an ungrammatical sentence. If an argument or adjunct of the lexical verb is questioned the respective interrogative pronoun has to occur in the first position and it has to be followed by a

14.1 Subjects, verbs, and word order in main sentences and subordinate clauses — 133

finite form of *do* or another auxiliary ((10) c., d.). The exception are questions introduced by *who* which question the subject of the sentence ((10) e.). Here, the finite form of the lexical verb has to occur.

From what we have said above about rich and weak verbal inflection, we would expect to find differences between PDE and NHG. Take a look at the following examples:

(11) a. *Spielt$_V$ Eric$_S$ [jeden Tag] Klavier$_O$? Ja/Nein.*
      b. *Tut$_{AUX}$ Eric$_S$ [jeden Tag] Klavier$_O$ spielen$_V$? Ja/Nein.*
      c. *Wann spielt$_V$ Eric$_S$ Klavier$_O$? [Jeden Tag].*
      d. *Was spielt$_V$ Eric$_S$ [jeden Tag]? Klavier$_O$.*
      e. *Wer spielt$_V$ [jeden Tag] Klavier$_O$? Eric$_S$.*

Indeed, concerning yes/no-questions, the position of the finite lexical verb differs from PDE: *Spielt* has to occur in first position. The alternative in b. is possible, at least in some dialects, but highly marked. If a different tense form is expressed and a periphrastic construction is needed, then the finite form of the auxiliary occurs in that position. In wh-questions, PDE and NHG differ in that in PDE the auxiliary *do* has to occur again after the interrogative pronoun, whereas in NHG the finite form of the lexical verb can occur. The only context of wh-questions which fully resembles the German pattern is the one introduced by *who* (subject questions).

Based on this data, a third generalisation for NHG can be postulated: in yes/no questions, the finite verb occurs in first position, in wh-questions the finite verb occurs right after the interrogative pronoun.

You will see that the word order patterns in OE resemble those observed in NHG. Take a look at the following examples for main declaratives:

(12) a. *[Se gehæled mann]$_S$ gemette$_V$ [þone Hælend]$_O$ syþþan on þam temple*
         the healed man   found   the lord   then   in the temple
         'The cured man then found the Lord in the temple.'
         (ÆHom_2:276.386)
      b. *[þæt hus]$_O$ hæfdon$_{AUX}$ Romane$_S$ to ðæm anum tacne geworht$_V$...*
         that house had   Romans   to the one sign   made
         'The Romans had made that house to their sole sign.'
         (Or_3:5.59.3.1042)
      c. *Uneaðe mæg$_{AUX}$ mon$_S$ to geleafsuman gesecgan$_V$...*
         Hardly may   man   to faithful   speak
         'Hardly may man speak to the faithful ...'
         (Or_3:9.70.16.1292)
      d. *[On his dagum] sende$_V$ Gregorius$_S$ us fulluht.*
         in his days   sent   Gregory   us christianity
         'In his days, Gregory sent us Christianity.'
         (ChronA,:565.1.207)

e. ne$_{NEG}$ cræwþ$_V$ [se hana]$_S$ todæg ær   þu me ætsæcst.
   not   crows   the cock   today before you me deny
   'The cock will not crow today until you deny me.'
   (Lk_[WSCp]:22.34.5465)

The first generalisation postulated for NHG above holds for OE: whenever elements like adverbials and objects are fronted, the finite verb occurs in front of the subject. What about the second generalisation? Take a look at the following examples:

(13) a. þa   ætstod   se wealdgenga, syþþan   he$_S$ [þas word]$_O$ gehirde$_V$.
        Then stood-still the thief   as soon as he the word   heard
        'As soon as he had heard the word, the thief stood still.'
        (ÆLet_4_[SigeweardZ]:1131.547)
   b. ond he þohte   þæt he$_S$ hi$_O$ gebismrode$_V$.
      and he thought that he them mocked
      'and he thought that he mocked them'.
      (Mart_5_[Kotzor]:Ap3,A.9.509)
   c. On morgen, ða   he aras, he nam þone stan ðe he$_S$ [under hys
      In morning when he rose he took one stone that he   under his
      heafod]$_{Adv}$ lede$_V$.
      head   laid
      'When he rose in the morning, he took the stone that he had laid under his head'.
      (Gen:28.18.1169)
   d. ... ðæt hie$_S$ ryhtne andan$_O$ hæbben$_V$.
      ... that they true   fear   have
      '... that they have true fear.'
      (CP:40.289.16.1898)

As in NHG, in subordinate clauses in OE the finite verb occurs right at the end of the clause preceded by the object(s) or other material like adverbials (of place as in c.). This applies to all types of subordinate clauses (complement clauses, relative clauses, adverbial clauses). Thus, the second generalisation postulated for NHG also holds for OE.

Of course, the picture is much more complicated as there are always exceptions to the rule, for example, pronominal objects can occur right after the subordinating conjunction, here þæt 'that', as illustrated with the example in (14) a. Further, adverbials (here in the form of the PP *on ðære byrig* 'in the town') can occur right at the end of main and subordinate clauses after the finite verb as in b.:

(14) a. þa þa se fiscere   þæt geseah **þæt hine**$_O$ [þa cæmpan]$_S$ woldon
       when the fisherman that saw   **that** him   the warriors   wanted
       niman, ...
       take
       'When the fisherman saw that the warriors wanted to take him...'
       (ApT:51.12.569)
   b. Drihten wæs$_{AUX}$ acenned$_V$ **[on ðære byrig]** þe is gecweden
       Lord   was   brought-forth **in the town** that is called
       Bethleem.
       Bethlehem.
       Lord was born in the town that is called Bethlehem.'
       (ÆCHom_I,_2:192.76.356)

We will come back to the variation that is found in OE concerning the relative order of finite verb and object(s) in chapter 16.

Finally, let's take a look at some data for yes/no-questions and wh-questions in OE which will serve as the basis for answering the question of whether generalisation three made for NHG above is also applicable to this stage of English:

(15) a. þa   cwæð he to þam earman, Wylt$_V$ þu$_S$ beon hal?
       then said he to the poor   wish you be   well
       'Then he said to the poor: Do you wish to be healthy?'
       (ÆHom_2:30.256)
   b. &   cwæð: Eart$_V$ ðu$_S$ Esau, min sunu?
       and said are you Esau, my son
       'and said: Are you Esau, my son?'
       (Gen:27.24.1086)
   c. ða   cwæð heo: Wost$_V$ þu$_S$ þæt þu leorneodes þone creft þe we hatað
       then said she: knowst you that you learnt   the craft that we call
       Geometrica?
       geometry?
       'Then she said: Do you know that you learnt the science that we call geometry?'
       (Solil_1:21.1.268)
   d. Hwæt is$_V$ [se man]$_S$ þe het   þe niman þin bed and gan?
       what is   the man   that command you take your bed and go
       'Who is the man that told you to take your bed and go?'
       (ÆHom_2:47.270)
   e. þa   cwæð se casere him to, Hwi come$_V$ þu$_S$ swa late?
       then said the king him to, why come   you   so late
       'Then the king said to him: Why do you come so late?'
       (ÆHom_8:143.1239)

f. *and cwæð, Hwær lede$_V$ ge$_S$ hine?*
    and said   where lay   you him?
    '... and said: where did you lay him?'
    (ÆHom_6:77.915)

As in NHG, the finite verb in OE is fronted and appears in first position. Depending on the tense form required by the context, finite verb forms of auxiliaries can occur. In wh-questions, the finite form of the lexical verb occurs right after the interrogative pronoun introducing the question. So the result of our short investigation is that the third generalisation postulated for NHG also holds for OE.

In ME, all of the orders described for OE still occur, but their frequency decreases, gradually leading to SVO order as the rule both in main declaratives and subordinate clauses.

First, take a look at some ME examples of main declaratives and try to identify similarities to the patterns described above for OE and NHG:

(16) a. *Marie Magdeleyne$_S$ tooke$_V$ [an alabaustre box of precious oynement]$_O$.*
    Maria Magdalen   took   an alabaster   box of precious ointment
    'Maria Magdalen took an alabaster box for precious ointment.'
    (AELR3,44.540)

 b. *Nu seið$_V$ [sum mann]$_S$: Seal ic luuige ðane euele mann?*
    now says some man: shall I love the evil   man
    'Now some man says: shall I love the evil man?'
    (VICES 1,67.733)

 c. *þanne zayþ$_V$ [oure lhord]$_S$ ine his spelle. 'þou sselt by ine trauayl ine þise*
    then says   our   Lord   in his speech thou sailed by in travel in this
    worlde.
    world
    'Then our Lord says in his speech: you sailed by in travelling this world.'
    (AYENBI,250.2288)

 d. *Ful mykel grace have$_V$ þai$_S$ þat es in þis degre   of lufe, ...*
    full much grace have they that is in this degree of love
    'Much grace they have that is in this degree of love.'
    (ROLLEP,105.684)

These examples show the same word order patterns: SVO if the subject is the first element in the sentence, and VS(O) if a constituent which is not the subject occurs in sentence-initial position. The difference between OE and ME is, that in ME times deviations from the VS(O) pattern occur, i.e. a new pattern arises:

(17) *Thane [the prioure]$_S$ said$_V$ till hym, Gaa.*
then the prior said to him, go
'Then the prior said to him: go!'
(ROLLTR,7.197)

Here, subject-verb inversion does not occur although the sentence is introduced by the temporal adverb *then* which consistently triggered inversion in OE (see chapter 17).

Concerning word order in subordinate clauses, in Early ME (1150–1350) both SOV (old pattern) and SVO (new pattern) are found, sometimes even in one and the same sentence (example (19) from the *Ormulum*).

(18) a. *... þt ich nule$_{AUX}$ þe$_O$ forsaken$_V$.*
    ... that I will-not you forsake
    'that I will not forsake you.'
    (VICES1,67.754)

  b. *... þet ye mahen$_{AUX}$ ane pine$_V$ me$_O$ here.*
    ... that you may at-all torture me here
    '... that you may torture me here at all.'
    (JULIA,102.110)

(19) *Forr þatt I wollde$_{AUX}$ bliþelig þatt all Ennglisshe lede wiþþ ære shollde$_{AUX}$*
    for that I would gladly that all English people with ear should
    lisstenn$_V$ itt$_O$, wiþþ herte shollde$_{AUX}$ itt$_O$ trowwenn$_V$, wiþþ tunge shollde$_{AUX}$
    listen it with heart should it trust with tongue should
    spellenn$_V$ itt$_O$, wiþþ dede shollde$_{AUX}$ itt$_O$ follghenn$_V$.
    spell it, with deed should it follow
    '... because I would wish that all English people should listen with their ears, should trust it with their heart, should spell it with their tongue, should follow it with their deeds.'
    (ORM,DED.L1 13.33)

The variation found in ME marks the word order change within the VP: at this time English develops from an (S)OV to a (S)VO language. That is why in EModE, the order (S)OV hardly exists at all, the odd example can be found sporadically (and maybe only because the reversal of the object *us* and *save* leads to a proper rhyme with *crave*):

(20) *the lorde vs$_O$ both saue$_V$, Albeit in this matter I must your pardon craue, ...*
    (UDALL,L1277.455)

As mentioned above, we will discuss this change in more detail in chapter 16 which is attributed to syntactic variation.

Another quite dramatic change had consequences for the relative order of the subject, the finite verb and the object in main declaratives. In EModE, lexical verbs lost the property to occur in initial position (or second position). Thus, examples like (21) are residues of the OE word order and very hard to find:

(21) *Then come$_V$ you$_S$ in to support the Testimony of Bedloe,*
(OATES,4,72.122)

The unmarked, most frequent word order in main declaratives is SVO as shown in (22) a., exceptions are b. and c. which are, however, still found today. These examples will be discussed in further detail in chapter 17.

(22) a. *The Frenchmen$_S$ fixed$_V$ [their Banners and Standarts]$_O$ with the Banner Royall, ...*
(STOW,594.204)
b. *Not one word says$_V$ Jack$_S$.*
(ARMIN,11.111)
c. *In comes$_V$ [Jack Oates]$_S$, ...*
(ARMIN,11.101)

In EModE times two further changes took place: first, modal auxiliaries like *must, can* or *may* reached their modern status, and second so-called *do*-support became the rule in contexts where formerly the lexical verb could occur in initial position (for a full account I refer you to Lightfoot's seminal work from 1979 and Roberts, 1985). In the literature, it has been suggested that there is a correlation between these two changes and the loss of rich verbal morphology (Roberts, 1993, Vikner, 1997). We will come back to this issue in chapter 18.

What about question formation in post Old English times then? Well, not much has changed in ME as you can see by looking at the following examples:

Yes/no-questions:

(23) a. *Seest$_V$ thou$_S$ not hov Mary Magdalen, ... wassh Iesus feet with*
See you not how Maria Magdalena ... washes Jesus's feet with
teres...?
tears...
'Don't you see how Maria Magdalena ... washes Jesus's feet with tears ...?
(AELR4,19.534)

14.1 Subjects, verbs, and word order in main sentences and subordinate clauses — 139

    b. *and the chelde sayde: 'Edmond, knowyst$_V$ not me?'*
       and the child   said: Edmond, knowst   not me
       And the child said: 'Edmond, don't you know me?'
       (EDMUND,165.46)

The example in b. is especially interesting since the question does not contain an overt subject. We might explain this by saying that the inflectional ending on the verb *know-yst* contains the subject.

Wh-questions:

(24) a. *I praye the, what hatte$_V$ he$_S$?*
        I pray thee, what was-called he
        'I pray you: What was his name?'
        (AELR4,20.582)
    b. *Whi tellest$_V$ tou$_S$ my rygtfulnes, and takeþ my testament by þy mouþte?*
        why tellest thou my rightfulness and taketh my testament by thy mouth
        'Why do you tell my righteousness and take my testament in your mouth?'
        (EARLPS,60.2628)
    c. *Who herd$_V$ it?*
        who heard it
        'Who heard it?'
        (EARLPS,69.3039)
    d. *And thei seiden to hym, Rabi, that is to seie, Maistir, where dwellist$_V$ thou$_S$?*
        and they said   to him, Rabi, that is to say, master, where dwellest thou
        'And they said to him: 'Rabi, that is, Master, where do you dwell?'
        (NTEST,1,20J.81)

Clearly, in yes/no-questions and wh-questions subject-verb inversion still occurred, i.e. the finite lexical verb could still occur in a fronted position and thus still be inverted with the subject (with the exception of questions where the interrogative pronoun is the subject, as we have said above).

In EModE again, not much has changed as you can see from the data given below. The verb forms of the second person singular still show strong inflectional endings and occur at the beginning of yes/no-questions:

Yes/no-questions:

(25) a. *and saide vnto him, Art$_V$ thou$_S$ a master of Israel, and knowest$_V$ not these*
and said unto him, art thou a master of Israel and knowest not these
things?
things
and said to him: 'Aren't you a master of Israel and don't you know these things?'
(AUTHNEW,3,1J.265)

b. *Thynkyst$_V$ thou$_S$ that the worlde is gouernyd by folyshe and by casuall*
Thinkest thou that the world is governed by folish and by casual
chaunces?
chances
'Do you think that the world is governed by foolish and casual chances?'
(BOETHCO,26.132)

Wh-questions:

(26) a. *O yes, who$_S$ knowes$_V$ this woman, who?*
oh yes who knows this woman who
'Oh yes, who knows this woman, who?'
(DELONEY,81.388)

b. *Jack, sayes hee, where lyes$_V$ thy paine$_S$?*
Jack says he where lies thy pain
'Jack, he says, where does your pain lie?'
(ARMIN,13.152)

c. *Iesus saith vnto her, Woman, what haue$_V$ I$_S$ to doe with thee?*
Jesus says unto her woman what have I to do with you
'Jesus says to her: 'Woman, what have I to do with you?'
(AUTHNEW,2,1J.170)

d. *Why baptizest$_V$ thou$_S$ then, if thou be not that Christ, ... ?*
wh baptizest thou then if thou are not that Christ
'Why do you baptise you then, if you are not that Christ, ...?'
(AUTHNEW,1,20J.76)

Concerning the rise of *do*-support, in the corpus which includes texts from between 1500 to 1710, the inflected lexical verb still predominantly occurs in the position directly following the interrogative pronoun (in all three subperiods). This observation shows that the gradual change from the pattern with subject-verb inversion to the pattern with *do*-support has not been completed in EModE times. We will come back to this topic in more detail in chapter 18. The examples provided in (27) are innovative because they show *do*-support:

(27) a. *he said vnto him, Doest$_{AUX}$ thou$_S$ beleeue$_V$ on the Sonne of God?*
(AUTHNEW,9,20J.1308)

b. *Then said I why does$_{AUX}$ thou$_S$ force$_V$ oaths upon Christians contry to thy own knowledge in the gospell times.*
(FOX-E3-P1,98.235)

c. *'What doyst$_{AUX}$ thow gyff$_V$ them?'*
what do   you give them
'What do you give them?'
(MACHYN-E1-P2,85.430)

Before we move on, I would like to summarise our findings: in both OE and NHG the relative order of the subject and the (finite) verb marks sentence type: main declarative sentences are marked by V-S (inversion), subordinate clauses are marked by S-V (non-inversion). There is one construction in OE which nicely demonstrates this:

(28) a. ða   [se Wisdom]$_S$ ða   [þis leoð]$_O$ asungen$_V$ hæfde$_{Aux}$, ða
when the wisdom   then this song   sung   had   then

gesugode$_V$ he $_S$;
became-silent he
'When Wisdom then had sung this song then he became silent.'
(Bo:17.40.5.730)

Compare the equivalent construction in NHG:

(29) *Als [die Weisheit]$_S$ das Lied gesungen$_V$ hatte$_{Aux}$, verstummte$_V$ er$_S$.*

The word order patterns we have discussed so far for OE, PDE and NHG are summarised in the table below ('1st C' stands for 'First constituent'):

Table 14.2. Word order patterns in OE, NHG, and PDE

	main declarative	yes/no question	wh-question	subordinate
OE	[1st C = S]-V-(O)... [1st C]-V-S-(O)...	V-S-(O)...	wh-V-S	S-O-V
NHG	[1st C = S]-V-(O)... [1st C]-V-S-(O)...	V-S-(O)...		S-O-V
PDE	[1st C = S]-V-(O)... [1st C]-S-V-(O)...	Aux-S-(O)...	[wh=S]-V-(O)... wh-Aux-S-(O)...	S-V-O

14.2 Negated sentences

So far, we have talked about sentences without negation, i.e. where the proposition of a sentence is positive. But what do negative sentences in OE and ME look like? Recall the difference between sentence negation and constituent negation and between negative concord and non-negative concord languages (see part II, chapter 8). First of all, sentence negation negates the proposition of a sentence whereas constituent negation negates (only) a constituent in a sentence. Take (again) a look at the following examples:

(30) a. *He did **not** have dinner.*
     b. *He had **no** dinner.*

In (30) a. the proposition of the sentence is negated by *not* which results in the reading 'It is not the case that he had dinner'. Here, negation extends over the entire predicate. In (30) b. the constituent negation *no* negates the constituent to its right, i.e. *dinner* which results in the reading 'It is the case that he had no dinner'. You can clearly see that the scope of *no* is more narrow than that of *not*.

We have seen in part II, chapter 8 that in non-standard varieties of British English, sentence and constituent negation can be combined, so you can hear speakers saying things like:

(31) *He did**n't** have **no** dinner.*

Although two instances of negation occur in this sentence, the contracted form of sentence negation attached to *did* and the constituent negation *no*, the sentence is negated only once: 'It is not the case that he had dinner'. Recall that in Standard English the same sentence (if it occurred) would have a positive interpretation because two realisations of negation in a single sentence give rise to a positive statement. Also recall that languages where different negative expressions combine to express a single logical negation are called negative concord languages, languages like Standard English are non-negative concord languages.

OE was a negative concord language. The element *ne* expressed sentence negation.

(32) a. *He **ne** geseah hine siððan.*
        He not saw   him afterwards.
        'He didn't see him afterwards.'
        (ÆLS_[Book_of_Kings]:296.3879)

b. & þa ðeostru **ne** underfengon þæt foresæde leoht.
and the sad not receive the aforesaid light.
'And the sad people don't receive the aforementioned light.'
(ÆHom_1:35.20)

Ne is often contracted with frequent verbs with a vocalic onset (or *h* or *w*) as for example *nis* (*ne is*) 'is not', *næs* (*ne wæs*) 'was not', *næfde* (*ne hæfde*) 'did not have', *noldon* (*ne woldon*) 'would not'.

(33) a. *Forðæm se wisdom **nis** ufan cumen of hefenum,*
For the wisdom NEG-is from-above come of heaven
'For the wisdom has not come from heaven above.'
(CP:46.347.24.2352)
b. *Be ðæm eft Dryhten cwæð to sumum monnum þe hæfdon ða geðyld,*
Because often Lord says to some men who had the patience
& ***næfdon** ða lufe,*
and NEG-had the love
'Because often the Lord says to some who had the patience but not the love
(CP_[Cotton]:33.222.24.80)
c. *... ðæt he **nolde** witnian his agne suna ða hie agylton,*
that he NEG-wanted punish his own sons when they sinned
'... the he didn't want to punish his own sons when they sinned.'
(CP:17.123.3.826)

Ne could be combined with other elements like *na* 'not (at all)', *nan* 'not one, no', *næfre* 'never' and *naht/noht* (from *nawiht*) 'nothing' which used to be a noun with a preceding constituent negation ('no thing'). The additional negative elements make the sentence more emphatic than it would be with *ne* alone.

(34) & *butan þam Worde **nis** nan þing geworht.*
and without the word NEG-is no thing worked
'and without the Word nothing is created.'
(ÆHom_1:171.103)

Generally, two main patterns emerged:
1) *na/naht/noht* + *ne* + finite verb (predominantly in subordinate clauses) as in (35):

(35) *... þæt God fordemð þa mænn for þa þinge þe **naht nis**,*
that God condemns the man for the thing that not NEG-is
'... that God condemns the people for the thing that is not.'
(Eluc_1_[Warn_45]:1.3)

2) *ne* + finite verb + *na/naht/noht* as in (36):

(36)   &   *for þan*   *hit **nis**   **naht**.*
        and on-that-account it   NEG-is nothing
        'and on that accout it is not.'
        (Eluc_1_[Warn_45]:5.10)

Note that in both examples, the finite verb form of *be* is included in the contracted form *nis*, so the two patterns here are *naht + ne + is* and *ne + is + naht* (this only seems possible for *be*, *have* and modal verbs).

In ME, the status of these two patterns changed. Pattern 2) came to be used more frequently in the function of negation without necessarily conveying emphasis. The negative adverb *naht/noht* acquired a fixed position in this pattern, *ne* + finite verb + *naht/noht* gradually became the regular pattern expressing negation.

Concerning the status of the sentence negation *ne*, in the course of the ME period it more and more often co-occurred with other elements. This can be explained by its properties: it is a so-called light element which was probably unstressed. This is also why it could attach to finite verbs, we have seen above that there are a number of different forms like *nis* etc. Since the other negative elements co-occurring with *ne* were formally and prosodically more prominent, *ne* could be dropped (compare the Modern French negation pattern *ne ... pas* where in speech *ne* is consistently dropped). The following examples illustrate the use of *ne* in ME (in all periods in the corpus): in (37) it occurs on its own:

(37)   a.   *Đe man þe   **ne** haueð rihte bileue on him ...*
              the man who not had   right belief in him.
              'The man who didn't believe in him.'
              (TRINIT,15.169)
       b.   *... þt heo **ne** byð þurh   þt oferswiðen,*
              ... that she not is   through that overpowered
              '... that she is not overpowered through that.'
              (KENTHO,134.25)
       c.   *and þat þis   **ne** was iseyd for a greet priuilegie of special loue*
              and that this not was said   for a great privilege of special love
              'and that this wasn't said for a great privilege of special love.'
              (AELR3,44.535)

In the examples in (38) *ne* plus further negation elements occur in a sentence where *ne* generally precedes the finite verb which is followed by a spelling variant of *not* (*ne-V$_{fin}$-not*):

(38) a. *I **ne** sigge **nacht** þet hi   ne hedden þer   before ine him beliaue;*
       I not say   not   that they not had   there before in him belief
       'I don't say that before they didn't believe in him.'
       (KENTSE,217.82)
   b. *'He þat is not itempted, he **nys**   **not** asaid.'*
       he that is not tempted   he NEG-is not denied
       'He who is not tempted is not denied.'
       (AELR3,27.29)
   c. *... the passage þat Sahaladyn **ne** myghte **not** passen.*
       ... the passage that Saladin   not might not pass
       '... the passage that Saladin might not pass.'
       (MANDEV,22.518)

Contracted forms still exist in ME as the examples below prove:

(39) a. *& how þai **nolde**   nouȝt bene obedient to þe Erche-bisshop of*
       and how they NEG-wanted not   be   obedient to the archbishop of
       Kanterbury.
       Canterbury
       'and how they didn't want to be obedient to the Archbishop of Canterbury.'
       (BRUT3,98.2948)
   b. *for ye shal overcome hem all, whether they wille or **nylle**.*
       for you shall overcome them all whether they want or NEG-want
       'for you shall conquer them all whether they want it or not.'
       (MALORY,13.371)
   c. *I **nel**   neuere haue reste,*
       I NEG-will never have reste
       'I will never rest.'
       (AELR3,30.108)

By the end of the ME period *nat/not* was the obligatory negator, and *ne* occurred only sporadically.

(40) a. *but hit was **not** þe wyll of God,*
       but it was not the will of God
       'but it was not the will of God.'
       (SIEGE,93.719)
   b. *þe clerk wist   **not** wel what he myth sey to hir.*
       the clerk knows not well what he may say to her
       'The clerk doesn't know exactly what he may say to her.'
       (KEMPE,128.2961)

c. *for the Fraynysche parte was **not** alle trewe in hyr comyng.*
   for the French party was not totally true in their coming
   'for the French party wasn't totally loyal in their coming.'
   (GREGOR,177.1145)

In EModE, *not* has established itself as the sole element to express sentence negation, and occurs on its own as shown in the examples below:

(41) a. *... wherin our good will and diligence shall **not** lak, God willing.*
        '... wherein our good will and diligence shall not lack, God willing.'
        (AMBASS-E1-P2,3.2,22.8)
     b. *Jack could **not** endure to bee in the common hall;*
        'Jack couldn't endure to be in the common hall.'
        (ARMIN-E2-H,9.58)
     c. *I do **not** yet know when I shall leave this towne.*
        'I do not yet know when I shall leave this town.'
        (ANHATTON-E3-H,2,212.13)

Nevertheless, some traces of its history can still be found: in (42) a. the OE form *ne* occurs, and in b. negative concord (both examples date to the beginning of the EModE period).

(42) a. *Because for lacke of light, discerne him he **ne** can*
        'Because for the lack of light, discern him, he cannot.'
        (STEVENSO-E1-P2,52.316)
     b. *... that **no** man shuld **not** talke of **no** thynges of the quen.*
        '... that nobody should talk of the matters of the queen.'
        (MACHYN-E1-P1,62.238)

Explanations of why negative concord declined in the course of time are manyfold. One quite prominent assumption is that towards EModE negative concord decreased due to the rise and influence of prescriptive grammars which were based on Classical Latin. In Classical Latin negative concord was disqualified as being illogical because each negative expression is seen as an autonomous logical negation, hence the positive interpretation is a consequence of the logical truth $p \equiv \neg \neg p$. Grammarians of the 18th century commented on this feature of English as being vulgar, ungrammatical, and inappropriate. This might be the reason why in Standard English today, only so-called generic A-quantifiers like *any(thing)* are allowed in the scope of the sentence negator for a negative reading:

(43) a. *He didn't eat **anything**.*
  b. **He didn't eat nothing.*

Recently, quite a number of authors have claimed that the decline of negative concord predates the rise and influence of prescriptive grammars (e.g. Nevalainen, 1998). In his book *Negation in English and other Languages* Jespersen (1917) sees the development of negation as a series of processes which Dahl (1979) later dubbed 'Jespersen's cycle':

> The history of negative expressions in various languages makes us witness the following curious fluctuation: the original negative adverb is first weakened, then found insufficient and therefore strengthened, generally through some additional word, and this in turn may be felt as the negative proper and may then in the course of time be subject to the same development as the original word.
> (Jespersen 1917:4)

In part II, chapter 10 we have seen that in non-standard varieties of PDE negative concord still exists and can be seen as a residue of former times.

Syn: 'So, here we are again!'
Tax: 'Before we summarise the main facts we have some exercises to get you into working with diachronic data.'
Syn: 'Okay, **1)** define the order of the finite verb and the object in each sentence/clause in the examples below':
Old English

(44) a. *and sæde þam Iudeiscum þæt se Hælend hine gehælde.*
    and said the Jews   that the Lord   him healed.
    'and (he) said to Jews that the Lord healed him.'
    (ÆHom_2:53.278)
  b. *He forhogde   ðæt he hit gehierde,*
    he disregarded that he it heard
    'He disregarded that he had heard it.'
    (CP:40.295.16.1948)

Middle English

(45) a. *he heled hem that wounded him,*
    he healed them that wounded him
    'he healed them that wounded him.'
    (AELR4,21.636)
  b. *Lo,   how þis Ladie hard þis holy mans prayour and helped þe Cristen   pepull.*
    behold how this lady heard this holy man's prayer and helped the Christian people
    'See, how this lady heard the prayer of this holy man and helped the Christians.'
    (ROYAL,260.387)

Early Modern English

(46) a. *Chat Bicause thy head is broken, was it I that it broke?*
Chat because your head is broken was it I that it broke
'Chat, because your head is broken, was it I who broke it?'
(STEVENSO-E1-H,54.220)
b. *I saw him when he first came into Church.*
I saw him when he first came into Church.
'I saw him when he first came into church.'
(FARQUHAR-E3-P2,22.101)

Syn: 'And **2)** identify the examples which show negative concord. **3)**, also define the phenomenon and explain the difference between sentence negation and constituent negation. Describe the development of expressing negation in the history of English.'

(47) a. *God ne costnað nænne mann*
god NEG tempt NEG-one man
'God did not tempt any man.'
(ÆCHom_I,_19:330.148.3738)
b. *but his suster fulfilled not his will*
but his sister fulfilled not his will
'but his sister didn't fulfil his will.'
(MANDEV,59.1466)
c. *No, No, reply'd she, I did not mean as you mean,*
No no replied she I did not mean as you mean
"No, no', she replied, 'I did not mean as you mean."
(PENNY-E3-H,160.440)

Tax: 'And, as in the first and second part of the book, we will summarise what we have learnt in this chapter. First, we said that in OE (and partly in ME) subjects could be omitted with certain verbs, for example, weather verbs. This phenomenon is referred to in the (generative) literature as subject-drop or expletive pro-drop. Second, we investigated the position of the finite verb in main declarative sentences, questions, and subordinate clauses. We found that in main declaratives, the finite verb predominantly occurred in the second position. This also applied to *wh*-questions. In *yes/no*-questions, the finite verb occurs in the first position. In subordinate clauses, it is most frequently found in the rightmost position.'

Syn: 'And we also briefly discussed negation. We said that in OE two types of negation must be distinguished: sentence and constituent negation. Sentence negation was expressed by the element *ne* to which further negative elements (for example constituent negations) could be added. In the course of time, *ne* was dropped and *not* became the sentence negation in English.'

Literature: Visser (1973) is a compendium of syntactic constructions from OE to the present day in four volumes. Although today we have corpora to look for structures, it has remained a valuable resource. The reference work for Old English syntax is Mitchell (1995), for a comprehensive introduction to Old English and the Anglo-Saxon culture I refer you to Mitchell (1985) and Mitchell and Robinson (2003).

Mossé (1991) is a comprehensive handbook of ME. The first part deals with all aspects of grammar, the second part is a collection of the most important ME texts. The most comprehensive works on the stages of English are the respective volumes of the *Cambridge History of the English Language*: Hogg (1992) for Old English, Blake (1992) for Middle English, and Lass (1999) for Early Modern English. A more recent introduction to Old English for novice students is Baker (2003), as well as Smith (1991) (for Old English, Middle English, and Early Modern English). Chapter 3 in Hogg and Denison (2008) is an introduction to the history of English syntax in a nutshell. The following three Edinburgh textbooks on the English language provide introductions to Old English, Middle English, and Early Modern English in a nice and accessible way: Hogg (2007), Horobin and Smith (2003) and Nevalainen (2006). A theoretical treatment of several aspects of diachronic syntax in the generative framework is Roberts (2007).

15 Dependency relations in Early English

In part I, chapter 3 we have seen that in medieval times syntax was based on the two key notions of *regimen* 'government' and *congruitas* 'agreement' and that the different cases and relations were categorised and catalogued for pupils learning Latin. Two examples for these relations are repeated here:

(1) *lego   librum*
     read-1-SG book-ACC-SG
     'I am reading a book.'

(2) *homo   gaudet*
     man-NOM-SG rejoice-3-SG
     'A/The man rejoices.'

In part II, chapter 9 we have dealt with the application of these two dependency relations to theoretical models of grammar, in our case generative grammar. In the following, we will first take a look at historical data and then apply the generative notions of government and agreement to these data.

15.1 Agreement and government in Early English

You might have noticed by looking at the examples in the previous chapter that OE did not only have morphological inflection on verbs but also on nominals (the term comprises nouns, pronouns and adjectives) which distinguished grammatical relations.

In the following table, the inflectional paradigms for the demonstrative pronoun *se/þæt/seo* and the nouns *stan* 'stone' (strong, masculine), *þing* 'thing' (strong, long neuter) and *sorg* 'sorrow' (strong, long feminine) are illustrated:
Compare this paradigm with the one for the NHG definite article *der/die/das* and the nouns *Stein* 'stone', *Ding* 'thing', and *Sorge* 'sorrow' and try to find similarities:
By looking at the two paradigms, it is evident again that NHG is quite similar to OE. Both languages morphologically mark case, number and gender. More precisely, both languages have a four-way case system with nominative, accusative, dative, genitive case (in OE instrumental case still occurs, albeit sporadically), a three-way gender system (masculine, feminine, neuter), and a two-way number system (singular, plural). Note however, that OE still shows traces of the Germanic dual system, i.e. first and second person pronouns have the dual forms *wit* 'we two' and *git* 'you two' and they inflect, as the other forms, for case, number, and gender. So in a clause like

Table 15.1. Inflections of the demonstrative pronoun and nouns in OE

		MASCULINE	NEUTER	FEMININE
SG	NOM	se stan	þæt þing	seo sorg
	ACC	þone stan	þæt þing	þa sorg
	GEN	þæs stan**es**	þæs þing**es**	þære sorge
	DAT	þam stane	þam þinge	þære sorge
PL	NOM/ACC	þa stan**as**	þa þing	þa sorg**a**
	GEN	þara stana	þara þinga	þa sorg**a**
	DAT	þam stan**um**	þam þing**um**	þam sorg**um**

Table 15.2. Inflections of the definite determiner and nouns in NHG

		MASCULINE	NEUTER	FEMININE
SG	NOM	der Stein	das Ding	die Sorge
	ACC	den Stein	das Ding	die Sorge
	GEN	des Stein**es**	des Ding**es**	der Sorge
	DAT	dem Stein	dem Ding	der Sorge
PL	NOM/ACC	die Stein**e**	die Ding**e**	die Sorg**en**
	GEN	der Stein**e**	der Ding**e**	der Sorg**en**
	DAT	den Stein**en**	den Ding**en**	den Sorg**en**

(3) ... þonne cume **wit**   to his rice.
 ... then   come we-two to his kingdom
 '... then the two of us come to his kingdom.'
 (ÆLS_[Julian_and_Basilissa]:42.962)

the dual is expressed by the pronoun *wit*. The use of the dual is optional and stresses that exactly two entities are discussed.

You might also have noticed that some forms have the same shape, for example, nouns in the nominative and accusative singular. This can be described as a formal collapse of different, originally separate grammatical functions, which is the result of language change. The term for it is **syncretism**, it is especially apparent in case systems but it generally applies to the loss of all kinds of inflection.

The OE and NHG systems are quite complex, in fact more complex than indicated in the two tables above. There are further distinctions made between strong and weak nouns, long and short stems, athematic nouns etc. Since this chapter serves only as an introduction to the syntax of Early English, I will leave these details aside and refer you to concise grammars of Old English like Mitchell (1985) or Campbell (2003).

Now, let's take a look at some examples from OE for subject-verb agreement and nominal agreement. In the previous chapter we already discussed this type of agreement a bit when we dealt with subject-drop and rich inflection of verbs in OE, (NHG, and Italian). We have seen that finite verbs always distinguish number, and person is distinguished only in the indicative singular, never in the plural (or subjunctive). In the singular past indicative, only the second person is distinguished. These rules apply both to **strong verbs** and **weak verbs**. Now let's take a look at some examples from the corpus (subjects and their verbs are indicated in bold):

Subject-verb agreement for all persons in the present tense indicative:

(4)   a.   *and **ic** **secge** eow forþi ...*
         and I-1-SG say-1-SG you because ...
         'and I tell you because ...'
         (ÆHom_3:34.429)

     b.   *& ... swa swa **ðu** **talest** & **wenest**.*
         and ... so that you-2-SG hope-2-SG and fear
         'and ... so that you hope and fear.'
         (Bede_5:13.430.13.4331)

     c.   *ða **cwæþ** **se Hælend** to þam heardheortum folce*
         then says-3-SG the lord-3-SG to the hard-hearted people
         'then the lord says to the stubborn people'
         (ÆHom_4:31.534)

     d.   *Æt ærestan **we** **lærað**, þæt ...*
         at first we-1-PL teach-1-PL that
         'At first, we teach that ...'
         (LawAf_1:1.2)

     e.   ***Ge** **secgaþ** þæt ...*
         you-2-PL say-2-PL that
         'You say that ...'
         (ÆHom_4:116.585)

     f.   *Gif **hie** þonne **cweðað** þæt þa tida goda wæron, ...*
         if they-3-PL then say-3-PL that the times good were
         'if they then declare that the times were good'
         (Or_5:1.113.17.2367)

Subject-verb agreement for first, and second person singular, and plural in the past tense indicative:

(5)   a.   ***Ic** **sæde** to soðan, ...*
         I-1-SG said-1-SG in truth ...
         'I said truthfully, ...'
         (ÆHom_1:352.189)

b. *for ðam ðe **þu**   me **gehyrdest**;*
   because   you-2-SG me heard-2-SG
   'because you heard me.'
   (Æom_6:91.926)

c. *for þon **hie**   **ondredon** þæt ...*
   forthwith they-3-PL feared-3-PL that ...
   'instantly they feared that ...'
   (Alex:36.10.458)

If we compare the morphological realisation of subject-verb agreement in these examples with the NHG equivalents, again we find similarities: *Ich sage euch ..., ... du hoffst und fürchtest*, etc. Take a look again at Table 14.1 in the previous chapter to find all similarities and differences.

In theoretical, generative terms, recall that subject-verb agreement is a relationship of government since the inflection of the finite clause governs the subject position:

(6)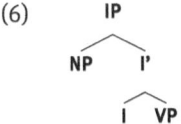

We said that I is a *head* and thus a governor which assigns nominative case to its specifier. Apart from the inflection of the finite clause lexical heads like nouns, verbs, adjectives and prepositions are also governors. We have further seen that the structural notion of government is a local relation defined in terms of **m-command** or **c-command** (if you can't remember the definitions take a quick look again at part II, chapter 9.1!). As you can see in the tree diagram, this condition is adhered to.

The second type of agreement is found between the head noun and its modifiers.

(7)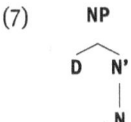

The relevant relation here is the specifier-head relation between the determiner (in the specifier position of NP) and the head N. Since you have become familiar with the examples in chapter 14 above, I would like to use them again for demonstration. Take a look at the following NPs extracted from these examples:

(8) a. *Se   gehæled mann*
       D-NOM-MASC-SG ADJ-PART N-NOM-MASC-SG
       'the healed man'
    b. *se   fiscere*
       D-NOM-MASC-SG N-NOM-MASC-SG
       'the fisherman'
    c. *þæt   hus*
       D-ACC-NEUT-SG N-ACC-NEUT-SG
       'that house'
    d. *þone   Hælend*
       D-ACC-MASC-SG N-ACC-MASC-SG
       'the lord'
    e. *þas   word*
       D-ACC-NEUT-PL N-ACC-NEUT-PL
       'these words'
    f. *þa   cæmpan*
       D-NOM-MASC-PL N-NOM-MASC-PL
       'the warriors'

If you compare these nominal phrases with the different forms given in the paradigm of nominals of OE above, you will see the system behind it. Again, you can compare the OE NPs with their NHG equivalents:

(9) a. *Der   geheilte Mann*
       D-NOM-MASC-SG ADJ-PART N-NOM-MASC-SG
       'the healed man'
    b. *Der   Fischer*
       D-NOM-MASC-SG N-NOM-MASC-SG
       'the fisherman'
    c. *Das   Haus*
       D-ACC-NEUT-SG N-ACC-NEUT-SG
       'that house'
    d. *Den   Heiland*
       D-ACC-MASC-SG N-ACC-MASC-SG
       'the lord'
    e. *Diese   Wörter*
       D-ACC-NEUT-PL N-ACC-NEUT-PL
       'these words'
    f. *Die   Kämpfer*
       D-NOM-MASC-PL N-NOM-MASC-PL
       'the warriors'

In both languages, nouns (and adjectives) can be divided into strong and weak, and as mentioned above, inflect for the grammatical categories of case, number, and gender. The examples from the OE sentences only show masculine and neuter forms, but feminine nouns existed too, of course:

(10) a. *seo sunne*
 D-NOM-FEM-SG N-NOM-FEM-SG
 the sun
 b. *þa modor*
 D-ACC-FEM-SG N-ACC-FEM-SG
 the mother
 c. *þære sæ*
 D-DAT-FEM-SG N-DAT-FEM-SG
 the sea

In theoretical, generative, terms, we have said that in both OE and NHG specifier-head agreement between the determiner and the head noun in an NP is morphologically realised. We have further seen that there is an update of this approach which states that NPs are actually DPs i.e. functional projections headed by the determiner D (see again part II, chapter 9):

(11)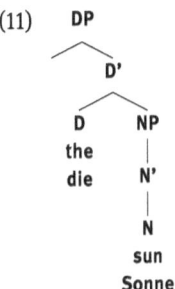

As a consequence, agreement between the determiner and the noun is not established via the spec-head relation but via the head-complement relation (government). So in this framework, agreement is interpreted as government. Since the purpose of this chapter (and this book) is not to provide a detailed analysis of the DP, I refer you to Haegeman and Guéron (1999), and Cook and Newson (2007) for further details on these rather complex theoretical aspects of generative syntax. For the sake of simplicity in the following I will stick to the analysis of NPs as illustrated in (7) above.

Further instances of government are found in PPs and VPs. Prepositions as well as verbs are case assigners: they assign case to the NP they govern. In the two tree diagrams below, you can see both instances of government:

Keep in mind that in OE, just as in NHG, objects precede their verbs, so VPs are **head-final** as you can see in the tree diagram. Also recall that this is an instantiation of the head parameter (see part I, chapter 6.2).

First, take a look at some examples of PPs from the OE sentences above:

(14) a. *on þam   temple*
       in the-DAT-SG temple-DAT-SG
       'in the temple'
    b. *to ðæm   anum   tacne*
       to the-DAT-SG one-DAT-SG sign-DAT-SG
       'to the one sign'
    c. *Æfter þysum   worde*
       after these-DAT-PL word-DAT-PL
       'After these words'

Prepositions like *on* 'on/in', *to* 'to' and *æfter* 'after' assign dative case to the NPs they govern (*þam temple, ðæm anum tacne, þysum worde*). Again, they behave like their NHG equivalents:

(15) a. *in dem   Tempel*
       in the-DAT-SG temple-DAT-SG
       'in the temple'
    b. *zu diesem   einen   Zeichen*
       to this-DAT-SG one-DAT-SG sign-DAT-SG
       'to this one sign'
    c. *nach diesen   Worten*
       after these-DAT-PL word-DAT-PL
       'After these words'

A tree diagram for these PPs would look like this:

(16)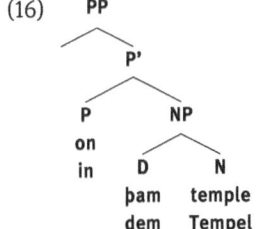

There are, however, other prepositions like *þurh* 'through' which assign accusative case to the NP they govern as exemplified in (17) a. The preposition *on* assigns both dative and accusative case, an example for accusative assignment is b.

(17) a. *þurh* [*þæt halige Word*]$_{ACC}$ *þæs heofonlican Fæder,*
 through that holy word the heavenly father
 'through the holy word of the heavenly father'
 (ÆHom_1:89.57)
 b. *Saga me hwær scyne seo sunne on [niht]*$_{ACC}$.
 say me where shines the sun in night
 'Tell me where the sun shines in the night.'
 (Ad:6.1.15)

The example in a. is also interesting because it contains a genitive phrase *þæs heofonlican Fæder* that is not governed by a preposition at all. Today, as you can see in the translation the preposition *of* is required. In contrast, in NHG *des himmlischen Vaters* in

(18) *durch das heilige Wort*
 through the-D-ACC-NEUT-SG holy-ADJ-ACC-NEUT-SG word-N-ACC-NEUT-SG
 [*des himmlischen Vaters*]$_{GEN}$
 the-D-GEN-MASC-SG heavenly-ADJ-GEN-MASC-SG father-N-GEN-MASC-SG
 'through the holy word of the heavenly father'

is perfectly grammatical as well. So in OE and NHG, inflection for genitive case suffices to express possessive, partitive and descriptive relations whereas in PDE, a preposition (or more precisely the preposition *of*) is required. This development is part of a big change from a synthetic to an analytic language.

In chapter 9.1 of part II we have discussed the notion of government from a synchronic perspective. We have seen that in the GB framework it has been assumed by Chomsky (1986) that a distinction should be made between structural and inherent case. To remind you, **structural case**, i.e. nominative and accusative case, is assigned to the structural position of phrases like NPs and VPs. **Inherent case**, i.e. genitive and dative case, is sensitive to thematic relations which means that this type of case is lexically associated with the governing verb, adjective or preposition. In (14), (15) and (17) we have seen examples for inherent case in NPs and PPs, and further above examples for nominative case which is assigned to the grammatical subject in a certain structural configuration. But what about the VP? Again, I repeat here the examples from above, and concentrate on the lexical verb and its object, *þas word gehirde, hi gebismrode* and *ryhtne andan hæbben*:

(19) a. þa ætstod   se wealdgenga, syþþan   he$_S$ [þas word]$_O$ gehirde$_V$.
Then stood-still the thief   as soon as he   these words heard
'As soon as he had heard these words, the thief stood still.'
(ÆLet_4_[SigeweardZ]:1131.547)
b. ond he þohte   þæt he$_S$ hi$_O$ gebismrode$_V$.
and he thought that he them mocked
'and he thought that he mocked them'.
(Mart_5_[Kotzor]:Ap3,A.9.509)
c. ... ðæt hie$_S$ ryhtne andan$_O$ hæbben$_V$.
... that they true   fear   have
'... that they have true fear.'
(CP:40.289.16.1898)

All three objects—*þas word, hi* and *ryhtne andan*—bear accusative case. It is assigned under government by the verb:

(20)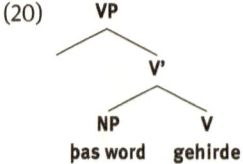

So far we have analysed these syntactic relations in the model of generative grammar which is one type of constituent grammar. In part I, chapter 5.2 and part II, chapter 9.2 we have seen that dependency grammar treats these relations in a different way. Recall that this model is not based on constituents. Rather it is interested in the dependencies between words. Applied to the data discussed above, we may analyse an OE verb phrase and a PP as the following dependency relations:

In (21), we have two relations: between the verb *gehirde* and the noun *word*, and between this noun and the definite determiner *þas*. In (22), again we find two relations: between the preposition *in* and the noun *temple* and between this noun and the definite determiner *temple*. In this way the syntactic relations are definable without referring to the notion of constituency.

In chapter 9 of part II we have also dealt with the question of how to determine structural and inherent case and said that structural case shows neutralisation under passivisation whereas inherent case does not. I will illustrate this with the following two examples from OE with the verb *afliegan* 'to put to flight, expel':

(23) a. *Gregorius **hine**$_{ACC}$ afligde.*
Gregory him put to flight
'Gregory put him to flight.'
(ÆHom_22:624.3676)

b. *Ða wearð [**se god**]$_{NOM}$ afliged of þære fulan anlicnysse.*
then was the god expelled by the foul idol
'Then the god was put to flight by the foul idol.'
(ÆHom_22:593.3653)

The sentence in a. stands in active voice, the object of *afliegan* occurs in the accusative case (*hine*). In b. the sentence stands in passive voice and the accusative case of the active sentence now occurs in nominative case (*se god*). With inherent case things are different, it survives under passivisation (see Fischer et al. 2000):s

(24) a. *Helpað **earmum**$_{DAT}$ 7 **hæfenleasum.**$_{DAT}$*
help poor and needy
'Help the poor and needy'
(WHom:11.197)

b. *Ac **ðæm**$_{DAT}$ mæg beon suiðe hraðe geholpen from his lareowe.*
but that may be very quickly helped by his teacher
'But that may be remedied very quickly by his teacher'
(CP:33.225.22)

Compare with NHG:

(25) a. *Er schlug [den Mann]_{ACC} in die Flucht.*
b. *[Der Mann]_{NOM} wurde (von ihm) in die Flucht geschlagen.*

(26) a. *Er half [den Männern.]_{DAT}*
b. *[Den Männern]_{DAT} wurde (von ihm) geholfen.*

As in OE, in NHG accusative (structural) case is neutralised under passivisation (it occurs as nominative case in the passivised sentence), whereas inherent case (here dative) survives. This is not the case in PDE, and this is why we have passives where the indirect object is promoted to the subject:

(27) a. *He was helped. (*Him was helped)*
b. *He was given the letter. (*Him was given the letter)*

In ME, the OE elaborate inflectional system of both nouns and verbs had been drastically reduced, as you can see from the two tables below:

Table 15.3. Inflections of nouns in ME

		MASCULINE	NEUTER	FEMININE
SG	NOM	ston	þing	sorwe
	ACC	ston	þing	sorwe
	GEN	ston**es**	þing**es**	sorw**es**
	DAT	ston(e)	þing(e)	sorw(e)
PL		stan**es**	þing**es**	sorw**es**

Table 15.4. Verbal inflection of ME 'help'

IND	1-SG	ic/I helpe
	2-SG	þu/thou help**est**/(**es**)
	3-SG	he helpeþ/**es**
	PL	we help**es**/**e(n)**

In the **declension** of the noun, the number of case forms was reduced and grammatical gender was lost. Concerning the verb, an increasing indistinctness of person and mood can be observed. All of the forms were subject to processes of **phonological attrition** and **analogical levelling**. The result of these processes led to a system in which singular nouns have two forms: one for the genitive, the other for all other functions. Pronouns retained three forms: nominative case (*I, he,* etc.), genitive case (*my,* *his*, etc.), and objective case (*he, him*, etc.). The demonstrative article was also affected by these changes and the result by the end of the ME period was the indeclinable *þe* (which is why it was not included in the paradigm for nouns above). *Þat*, which ceased to be used as the grammatical neuter of the demonstrative article, took on more and more of the function of the singular demonstrative for all grammatical genders. In more general terms, the OE system which marked grammatical distinctions (like case) morphologically, developed in ME into a system which marks these distinctions syntactically. What is left is the difference between nominative (subjective) and objective case and stricter rules about where to place constituents functioning as either subject or object(s).

When investigating ME data, it is important to know that due to the loss of the West Saxon written standard, which superimposed OE dialects, a plethora of existing varieties surfaced at that time, so the transitional stage between the old and the new system can be observed quite well. This also means, however, that for almost all words in manuscripts many spelling variants exist because scribes wrote as they spoke. Before we deal with the data from the corpus, I give one example for all verb forms of the verb *helpen* 'help' from the *Middle English Dictionary* (MED online, 2001):

> helpen (v.) Also help, elp, helpi, healpe, heolpe, halpen, hælpan. Forms: sg. 3 helpeth, etc. & holpes & helpþ. sg. 1 & 3 halp, healp, help & holpe, hulpe, huelp & helped; sg. 2 holpe, hulpe & helpedest, holpedest; pl. hulpe(n), holp(e(n)), heolpen, helpen, halp(e), hilpe & helped(en), holpeden; ppl. holp(e(n)), hulpen, help & helped.

By looking at the number of different word forms for *helpen*, you can imagine how hard it is sometimes to identify words. You will, however, get a feeling for ME forms by studying more data.

The changes described above and the evident differences between OE and ME are illustrated with some examples:

Nominal agreement:

(28) a. *[þe þreo furst]*_{NP} *despoylen [þe synful wrecche]*_{NP},
         the three first   disrobed   the sinful wretch
         'the first three undressed the sinful creature.'
         (EDVERN,246.268)
      b. *Y knowe that thou art [a fair wommanן]*_{NP}, ...
         I know that you are a fair woman
         'I know that you are a fair woman.'
         (OTEST,12,1G.421)

As you can see, there are hardly any traces of morphological agreement left between the elements of the three NPs given in bold here.

Concerning verbal inflection, the situation is similar, although in later stages of ME residues of the OE system still can be found:

Verbal inflection:

(29) a. **Y knowe** that thou art a fair womman, ...
I know that you are a fair woman ...
'I know that you are a fair woman ...'
(OTEST,12,1G.421)

b. An hemme, as **þu wost** wel, is þe laste ende of a cloþ;
A hem as you knowest well is the last end of a cloth
'A hem, as you know well, is the end of a cloth.'
(AELR3,34.226)

c. ... how longe that [eny sterre fix] **dwelleth** above the erthe, ...
... how long that any star fix dwells above the earth
'... how long that any fix star remains above the earth.'
(ASTRO,672.C1.320)

d. For so moche water **þei wepten** þat made the forseyd lake.
for so much water they wept that made the forsaid lake
'for so much water they wept that it made the forsaid lake.'
(MANDEV,131.3185)

In these examples, the finite verbs still show morphological marking of the first, second, third person singular and third person plural.

Let's take a look at some examples of structural and inherent case in ME:

Structural case:

(30) a. Lyte Lowys my sone, I **aperceyve** wel by certeyne evydences [thyn
Little Louis my son I perceive well by certain evidences your
abilite] to lerne sciences ...
ability to learn sciences ...
'Little Louis, my son, I notice well by certain signs your ability to learn the sciences ...'
(ASTRO,662.C1.5)

b. And in þe bygynnyng, why þu schalt **preferre** [solitarye lyf] ...
and in the beginning why you shall prefer secluded life
'And in the beginning, why you should prefer a secluded life.'
(AELR3,26.6)

Inherent case:

(31) a. *And gif such temptacioun dure, let **helpe [þy   partye]** streytere*
and if   such temptation   lasts let help   your party   straight
abstinence;
abstinence
and if such tempration lasts let strict abstinence help your party.'
(AELR3,29.83)
b. *And He schal soone **sende þee** help and cunfort vnspeicable, ...*
and he shall soon send   you help and comfort unspeakable
'And he shall send you soon help and inexpressible comfort.'
(HILTON,6.40)

As you can see, formal traces can be found, like the possessive pronoun *thyn* in (30) a. or the pronoun form *þee* marking former dative case in (31) b. The example in (31) a. shows that word order still allowed patterns where the indirect object precedes the subject which occurs sentence final.

As we would expect, in EModE only residues of the once rather elaborate inflectional morphology of OE occur, especially the second person singular ending on verbs can be found:

(32) a. ***thou knowest*** *them well enough.*
you know   them well enough
'You know them well enough.'
(ARMIN,34.150)
b. ***Thou seest*** *then how narrow and strait   that Glory is ...*
you see   then how narow and straight that glory is ...
'You see then how narrow and straight that glory is ...'
(BOETHPR,82.549)
c. ***Thou said'st*** *thy   Lady asked thee, whether he knew of the Business;*
you said   your lady asked you   whether he knew of the business
'You say your lady asked you whether he knew of the business.'
(LISLE,4.116.188)

15.2 Word order within the NP

Finally, I would like to briefly discuss word order within the NP because, as you will see, a number of patterns existed in OE, ME and EModE that you will no longer find today.

In OE, the most frequent order is Determiner-Modifier-Noun, i.e. all modifiers—quantifiers, determiners, demonstrative/possessive pronouns, numerals, adjectives, genitives—precede the NP. Recall the examples from above:

(33) a. *Se   gehæled   mann*
   D-NOM-MASC-SG ADJ-PART N-NOM-MASC-SG
   'the healed man'

   b. *se   fiscere*
   D-NOM-MASC-SG N-NOM-MASC-SG
   'the fisherman'

   c. *þæt   hus*
   D-Sg-ACC-Neut N-Sg-ACC-Neut
   'that house'

However, there are exceptions to the prenominal modification pattern:

(34) a. *elle   Cænt **eastwearde***
   entire Kent eastward
   'all of eastward Kent.'
   (ChronD_[Classen-Harm]:865.1.534)

   b. *his geferan   **ealle***
   his comrades all
   'all of his comrades.'
   (ÆHom_15:33.2155)

   c. *halige weras **manige***
   sacred men many
   'many sacred men.'
   (GDPref_and_4_[C]:12.276.6.4025)

   d. *iong   man **fæger***
   young man fair
   'a fair young man.'
   (Mart_5_[Kotzor]:Au2,B.8.1358)

   e. *Se byrdesta   sceall gyldan ... tyn ambra feðra   &   **berenne***
   The highest-born must pay   ... ten casks feathers and bearskin
   *kyrtel   oððe **yterenne**.*
   garment or   otterskin
   'The highest born must pay ten casks of feathers and bearskin or otterskin garment.'
   (Or_1:1.15.17.262)

Quantifiers and modifiers in -weard, with eall, manig and some other adjectives like fæger 'fair' occur in postnominal position. Postnominal adjectives predominantly occur in coordinations of the type ADJ-N-Conj-ADJ (see the example in e.).
Further, prepositional modifiers and relative clauses always follow the nominal head:

(35) a. *ane boc* **[be cyrclicum   ðeawum]**
one book by ecclesiastical customs
'a book about ecclesiastical customs.'
(ÆCHom_II,_5:49.237.1029)
b. *to þam ylcan campdome*   **[þe   heora fæderas on wæron]**
to the same military-service which their fathers in were
'to the same military service in which their fathers were.'
(ÆLS_[Martin]:31.5990)

In OE, appellatives are often found in combination with a title as in:

(36) *Mercurius,* **se gigant**
Mercurius the giant
'Mercurius, the giant'
(Ad:16.2.40)

As you can see in this example, two nouns or NPs may stand in an appositive relation where one specifies or modifies the other. Similarly, a pronoun can be modified by an appositive NP:

(37) **He** *cwæð,* **se   apostol Paulus**
he said the apostle Paul
'The apostle Paul said ...'
(ChronA_[Plummer]:871.12.809)

Another striking property of OE are genitival modifiers that generally occur after the NP:

(38) a. *Dunecan* **Melcolmes**$_{GEN}$ *cynges*$_{GEN}$ *sunu*$_{NOM}$
Duncan Malcolm's   king's   son
'Duncan, the son of king Malcolm.'
(ChronE_[Plummer]:1093.33.3139)

> b. *þær wearð ofslægen Lucumon* **cynges**$_{GEN}$ **gerefa**$_{NOM}$. & *Wulfheard*
> there were killed Lucomon king's steward and Wulfheard
> ***Friesa**. & Æbbe **Friesa**, & Æðelferð **cynges**$_{GEN}$ **geneat**$_{NOM}$* ...
> Frisian's and Abbe Frisian's and Athelferd king's follower
> 'There, Lucomon, the king's steward, and Wulfheard of the Frisians, and Abbe of the Frisians, and Athelferd, the king's follower, were killed.'

Further, elements of an NP need not occur adjacent to each other, i.e. they may be **discontinuous**. In the example below, the second part of the coordinating AP can occur as postmodifiers separated from the rest of the NP by the subject and the verb:

(39) *Maran cyle ic geseah,* **and wyrsan**
     greater cold I saw and worse
     'I have seen greater and worse frost.'
     (ÆCHom_II,_23:202.106.4491)

In ME the word order patterns within the NP do not differ much from those found in OE. Generally, attributive adjectives are usually found in prenominal position. Postnominal adjectives do exist but they do not resemble the OE pattern illustrated in (34). Instead, we find three patterns that have been attributed to French influence:

(40) a. simple postnominal adjective
         of arte magique 'of magic art'
     b. two or more postnominal adjectives
         thise floryns newe and brighte 'these new and bright florins'
     c. prenominal and postnominal adjective
         with deop dich and dark 'with a deep and dark ditch'

NPs including a title of the form *X of Y* in the genitive could be split:

(41) *þuruh Iulianes*$_{GEN}$ *heste ðe amperur.*
     through Julian's command the emperor
     'by the command of Julian the emperor.'
     (ANCRIW-1,II,109.11)

The loss of this splitting construction may be due to the rise of the so-called **group genitive**:

(42) **The grete god of Loves$_{GEN}$ name.**
the great god of love's   name
'The great god of love's name.'
(Chaucer, *House of Fame*, 1489)

As you can see the genitive ending is added to the last element in the noun phrase containing postmodification (*love's*).

Another possessive construction which started to occur in ME times doesn't show the genitival suffix on the respective noun but as a separate word (*h*)*is* (including all kinds of spelling variants as you can see below):

(43) a. *the kyng **ys** syde;*
the king his side
the king's side
(GREGOR,113.424)
b. *kyng Edwyn **his** nese*
king Edwin his niece
king Edwin's niece
(POLYCH,VI,141.988)

In EModE, a number of patterns are striking: first, a pronoun could function as the head of a noun phrase (see (44) a. and b.); second, determiners and pronouns could co-occur as the examples in (44) c. and d. confirm. Take a look at some examples from Shakespeare's works:

(44) a. *the cruell'st she* (Twelfth Night)
b. *hee of Wales* (Henry IV Part I)
c. *all those his lands* (Hamlet)
d. *of euery these happend accidents* (The Tempest)

None of these patterns can be found in PDE.

Third, three ways to mark possession exist alongside each other. We have seen that the third way, given here, started to emerge in ME times:

(45) a. genitive possessive phrase (*Caesars Funerall*)
b. prepositional construction (*the vices of thy Mistris*)
c. with possessive pronoun *his* (*Mars his heart*)

Today, we are left with two options: a premodifying genitive and a postmodifying prepositional phrase with *of*, the latter of which is sometimes also called the '*of*-genitive'. Sometimes, there really is a choice between the two as in:

(46) a. There were strong objections from *the island's* inhabitants.
     b. There were strong objections from the inhabitants *of the island*.
       (Greenbaum & Quirk: 1990:103)

For the most part, however, one or the other must be selected:

(47) a. I took *father's trousers*.
     b. *I took the trousers *of father*.
     c. I saw the front *of the house*.
     d. *I saw the *house's front*.

It seems that the possibility to use the premodifying genitive depends (among other things) on the semantics of the noun: it must be animate, and not denote personal reference.

 Tax: 'Again, it's time for some exercises: **1)** explain the difference between subject-verb agreement and nominal agreement by using two relevant examples from the chapter; **2)** define the notion of government by explaining one of the examples in (14). **3)** provide a definition for syncretism and identify cases of syncretism by looking again at Table 15.1; **4)** identify subject-verb agreement and nominal agreement in the following data':

(48) a. *Drihten him andwyrde. Ic cume.*
       Lord   him answered. I come.
       'The Lord answered him. I come.'
       (ÆCHom_I,_8:244.90.1457)
     b. *& þonne ge fleoð fram byrig to byrig, ic sende cwealm on eow, & hungor,*
       and when you flee from castle to castle, I send pain on you and hunger
       'and when you flee from town to town I send you pain and hunger'
       (Lev:26.25.3921)
     c. *Ich am he seið as þe pellican þt woneð bi him ane.*
       I am he says as the pelican that lives by him at-any-time
       "I am', he says, 'the pelican that lives by him at any time."
       (ANCRIW-1,II.94.1124)
     d. *and þurh þe sweote smel of þe chese; he bicherreð monie mus to þe stoke.*
       and through the sweet smell of the cheese he beckons many mice to the house
       'and through the sweet smell of the cheese he beckons many mice to the house'
       (LAMBX1,53.686)

Syn: 'And now it's my turn to summarise what we have learnt in this chapter. First, by looking at data from OE and NHG, we observed that grammatical functions are morphologically marked on both nouns and verbs. This means that in both languages we see different types of agreement directly marked on lexical items. We took a look at two of these types by starting out with subject-verb agreement and found proof for this observation. From a theoretical, generative, point of view, we said that subject-verb agreement is also an instance of government because the finite verb governs the subject position in a tree diagram. For the second type of agreement, nominal agreement, we said that the specifier-head relation between the determiner and the head noun in an NP is morphologically realised and that it could also be interpreted as government. Then we discussed further instances of government like government in PPs (where P is the governor) and in VPs (where V is the governor). Concerning VPs, we have seen that the difference between structural and inherent case was made, and we discussed a number of OE examples for both types. Concerning the gradual loss of inflectional endings in the history of English, we found that in ME, endings on nouns and verbs were greatly reduced, which affected subject-verb and nominal agreement. By looking at some examples of EModE, the further erosion of the inflectional system was confirmed. Finally, we briefly discussed word order within the NP and genitival constructions and saw that different patterns occurred in OE, ME, and EModE most of which are no longer found in PDE.'

Literature: All of the traditional reference works recommended in the first chapter deal with the types of agreement and government discussed in this chapter. Allen (1995) is a very interesting work on the loss of case-marking in the history of English. She has also written a number of papers on the genitive, for example Allen (1997) which deals with the origins of the group genitive. Fischer et al. (2000) study the syntax of Early English providing, amongst others, an outline of OE and ME syntax and discussions of morphology and case assignment.

16 Syntactic variation in Early English

In this chapter we will take a closer look at variation in earlier stages of English, and more precisely, syntactic variation within the verb phrase.

16.1 Variation within the verb phrase: OV and VO

In chapter 14 we have already dealt with the relative order of the lexical verb and the object and said that in subordinate clauses, OE was SOV. I also briefly mentioned that things were much more complex and complicated and that deviating patterns existed too. Here, we will survey the order of the object and lexical verb and relate it to another pattern, the possible positions of the auxiliary. We will see that both patterns are connected and that variation in this respect reflects typological changes in grammar (see also part II, chapter 9.2). Let's take a look again at some of the examples from above:

(1) a. þa   ætstod   se wealdgenga, syþþan   he$_S$ [þas word]$_O$ gehirde$_V$.
         Then stood-still the thief   as soon as he these words heard
         'As soon as he had heard these words, the thief stood still.'
         (ÆLet_4_[SigeweardZ]:1131.547)
  b. ond he þohte þæt he$_S$ hi$_O$ gebismrode$_V$.
         and he thought that he them mocked
         'and he thought that he mocked them'.
         (Mart_5_[Kotzor]:Ap3,A.9.509)
  c. … ðæt hie$_S$ ryhtne andan$_O$ hæbben$_V$.
         … that they true   fear   have
         '… that they have true fear.'
         (CP:40.289.16.1898)

From these examples, we could conclude that the object—be it a full phrase or a pronominal object—always precedes the lexical verb (which in all of these cases is also the finite verb). This also seems to apply to subordinate clauses containing both an auxiliary and a lexical verb:

(2) a. þa   he from þam arleasan cyninge [nænige sibbe]$_O$ findan$_V$
         when he from the wicked king   NEG-any friendship find
         meahte.$_{AUX}$.
         might
         '… when he might not find any friendship from the wicked king.'
         (Bede_3:18.234.24.2390)

b. þa   he [ðæt]$_O$ gedon$_V$ hæfde$_{AUX}$, þa   sette he þa reliquias in heora
    when he that done   had   then set he the relics   in their
    cyste, ...
    casket
    'When he had done that, he set the relics in their casket.'
    (Bede_4:33.382.29.3810)

If we compare the order of the object, the lexical verb and the auxiliary in the corresponding examples for NHG, we see again that it resembles OE:

(3) a. ... da er beim bösen König [keine Freundschaft]$_O$ finden$_V$ mochte$_{AUX}$.
     b. Als er das$_O$ getan$_V$ hatte$_{AUX}$, legte er die Reliquien wieder in ihre Schatulle.

Although these word order patterns occurred quite frequently, other patterns could also be found and have to be taken into account. First, objects could follow lexical verbs:

(4) a. &   þa þa he bedypte$_V$ [þæne hlaf]$_O$ he sealde hyne Iudas Scariothe.
         and when he dipped   the   loaf   he sold   him Iudas Iscarioth
         'and when he dipped the bread he surrendered himself to Iudas Iscarioth.'
         (Jn_[WSCp]:13.26.6920)
     b. Ða se geonga mann gehyrde$_V$ [þis word]$_O$ þa   eode he aweg unrot.
         as the young man heard   this word   then went he away grieved
         'When the young man heard this speech he went away grieved.'
         (Mt_[WSCp]:19.22.1294)

In both examples, the accusative object directly follows the finite (lexical) verb, so this is the order we find today in all subordinate clauses. Here, a contrast to NHG arises where VO in this type of clause is completely ungrammatical:

(5) a. *und als er eintauchte$_V$ [das Brot]$_O$ ...
     b. *Als der junge Mann hörte$_V$ [diese Rede]$_O$ ...

Apart from the variation of object-verb and verb-object, there is also variation concerning the position of the auxiliary verb. This type of verb can either surface right at the end of a subordinate clause, i.e. directly after the lexical verb as in the examples in (2), or in a so-called **sentence-medial** position before the lexical verb and object. If these two possibilities are combined with the OV and VO patterns, we would expect to find the following four patterns:

(6) 1. OV-AUX
 2. VO-AUX
 3. AUX-OV
 4. AUX-VO

Let's take a look at some examples from the corpus and see if there is empirical evidence for these patterns:

OV-AUX

(7) a. & þa he þis$_O$ gecweden$_V$ hæfde$_{AUX}$, þa astah ure Drihten on
 and when he this said had then ascended our lord up-to
 heofenas.
 heavens
 'when he had said this then our lord ascended to heaven
 (LS_20_[AssumptMor[BlHom_13]]:149.191.1832)
 b. ... þæt mon [ðissum earde]$_O$ gebeorhgan$_V$ mihte$_{AUX}$ ...
 that man these lands preserve might
 'that man might preserve these lands ...'
 (ChronC_[Rositzke]:1006.34.1416)

AUX-OV

(8) a. ... ðæt Rachel hæfde$_{AUX}$ [ða anlicnyssa]$_O$ forstolen$_V$.
 that Rachel had the idol stolen
 '... that Rachel had stolen the idol.'
 (Gen:31.32.1275)
 b. ... þæt mon hæfde$_{AUX}$ anfiteatrum$_O$ geworht$_V$ æt Hierusalem,...
 that man had amphitheatre made at Jerusalem
 '... that man had made an amphitheatre in Jerusalem.'
 (Or_6:31.150.22.3120)

AUX-VO

(9) a. ... þæt þu mæge$_{AUX}$ læran$_V$ [þone unwisran.]$_O$
 that you may teach the unwiser
 'that you may teach the less educated.'
 (Prov_1_[Cox]:1.59.106)
 b. þæt man sceolde$_{AUX}$ bringcan$_V$ [þone gewundodan cniht$_O$] to him.
 that man should bring the wounded boy to him
 'that someone should bring the wounded boy to him.'
 (GD_2_[C]:11.125.16.1506)

Here, the corpus study reveals a puzzling result: only three of the four patterns are attested, VO-AUX doesn't seem to exist. Well, you could argue that it has to do with the fact that in historical linguistics we have to rely on sparse written data and it is sheer coincidence that the pattern does not occur, or put differently, in a larger corpus the pattern would occur. Although this argument is justified, the observation that the pattern VO-AUX does not occur has been made by a number of experts in the field, particularly Pintzuk (1991, 1999) who was actually the first to discuss and correlate these patterns.

In a number of theoretical approaches to word order and word order change, there is the notion of a basic word order. For example, since the OV word order in OE is most frequent, it can be said that it is the **basic word order**. This implies that orders deviating from OV must be derived. Others believe that the basic word order is the unmarked order and that discourse factors trigger deviations. If we adopt the notion of basic word order, we have two options because a further assumption is that variation is restricted to exactly two options, i.e. **binary parameters** (remember what we have said about the Principle & Parameter approach in part II, chapter 10): either we say OV is the basic word order or VO. In the generative framework, the basic word order is identified as the underlying order from which other orders are derivable. Concerning the variation between object-verb and verb-object observed in OE, we have the following two possible structures for the verb phrase:

The first structure of the verb phrase is **head-initial** because the verbal head precedes its complement (object). The structure in b. is **head-final** because the verbal head follows its complement.

If we postulate OV as the underlying order in OE, deviations from OV are derived by **rightward movement** (of the object). If VO is seen as the underlying order, however, deviations are derived by **leftward movement** (of the object). For both approaches, a number of proponents have sought to prove that they are on the right track, but I won't go into these discussions here. For further reading I recommend Pintzuk and Kroch (1989) who are in favour of the **OV approach**, and Roberts (1997) who is a proponent of the **VO approach** (based on Kayne's (1994) ideas). Before I am going to address a further approach, which sees the synchronic variation found in OE as competition between an OV and a VO grammar, I will come back to the variation found in the position of auxiliaries.

As with OV and VO orders, we have two options: either the auxiliary occurs in a sentence-medial position preceding the verb phrase (12), or it occurs after the verb phrase in a sentence-final position (13):

(12)  (13)

Recall that in generative syntax, the **I(nflectional)** (Infl) position (**T(ense)** position in more current versions of the framework), is filled by the finite verb, thus by the auxiliary in clauses which contain more than one verb. The VO-AUX structure, which does not occur in OE, would look like this:

(14)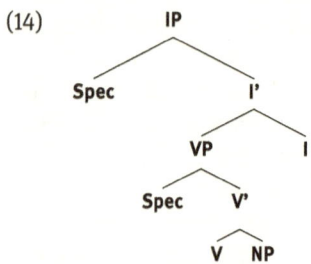

In the works cited above, Pintzuk noted that interestingly, languages which do not show word order variation are either uniformly head-initial or head-final in the IP and VP. Since she did not provide an explanation for the non-occurrence of VO-AUX, she simply stated that a VO phrase cannot co-occur with an Infl-final phrase structure.

An example where both the verb phrase and the inflectional phrase is head-final is NHG. So a sentence like

(15) ... da er beim bösen König [keine Freundschaft]$_O$ finden$_V$ mochte$_{AUX}$.

would have the following structure:

(16)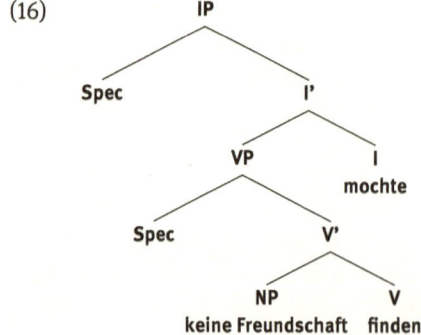

16.1 Variation within the verb phrase: OV and VO

So far, things seem to be quite straightforward: in OE variation occurs between object-verb and verb-object structures, and between auxiliary-verb phrase and verb phrase-auxiliary structures. As you might have guessed, it is even more complicated, i.e. further patterns occur which increase variation.

First, it has been observed that in OE pronominal objects can occur in a position very close to the subject (in generative terms we would say in a high position):

(17) a. ... þæt þa Deniscan him$_O$ ne mehton$_{AUX}$ [þæs ripes]$_O$ forwiernan$_V$.
... that the Danes   them not could   the harvest refuse
'... that the Danes could not refuse them the harvest.'
(ChronA,:896.6.1101)

As you can see, the subordinate clause in (17) contains two objects: *him* as pronominal object in the dative, and a full NP *þæs ripes* in the genitive. Whereas the genitival object occurs directly between the auxiliary and the lexical verb, the pronominal object occurs more to the left, directly after the subject NP. This is a property of pronominal objects that can also be found in cognate languages like NHG:

(18) ... *dass die Dänen ihnen nicht die Ernte verwehren konnten.*

If a base position is assumed for objects, then the question is where its original position was: either in front or after the verb. The same theoretical considerations apply to phenomena that we will discuss in the following.

One pattern which confuses the picture is the occurrence of definite object NPs outside the verb phrase. In the example below, the object is to the left of the sentence negation *ne* and the lexical verb *gecwæð*:

(19) ac he$_S$ [nan word]$_O$ ne gecwæð$_V$.
but he no word   NEG heard
'but he didn't hear any word'
(coaelhom,ÆHom_24:190.3882)

This phenomenon which was dubbed '**scrambling**' by Ross (1967) is a characteristic of the West Germanic languages, therefore it is not surprising that it is also found in NHG:

(20) ... *dass er [das Buch]$_O$ nicht las.*
that he the book   not read.
'that he did not read the book.'

Second, there are cases where the lexical verb immediately follows the auxiliary as in the example b. below. From what we have said and seen above, we would expect the order OV-AUX here (given in a. and reconstructed from b.), but what we (also) find are orders with permutation of the finite and non-finite (lexical) verb: O-AUX-V. In the generative literature, this phenomenon has been called **verb raising**.

(21) a. ... þe æfre on gefeohte his hande afylan$_V$ wolde$_{AUX}$.
... who ever in battle his hands defile wanted
'... whoever wanted to defile his hands in battle.'
b. ... þe æfre on gefeohte his hande wolde$_{AUX}$ afylan$_V$.
... who ever in battle his hands wanted defile
'... whoever wanted to defile his hands in battle.'
(ÆLS_[Maccabees]:857.5405)

There are also cases where the finite verb has permuted with the VP containing the lexical verb and the object. This phenomenon has been called **verb (projection) raising** (for an explanation of these terms, and especially why these processes are seen as instances of raising see van Kemenade, 1987 and Haeberli and Pintzuk, 2006).

(22) a. ... þæt he mehte$_{AUX}$ [$_{VP}$[his feorh]$_O$ generian$_V$].
... that he could his property save
'... that he could save his property.'
(Or_2:5.48.13.927)

If you compare (22) with the examples in (23), you might now be confused because all three examples exhibit the order AUX-OV that we discussed above:

(23) a. ... ðæt Rachel hæfde$_{AUX}$ [ða anlicnyssa]$_O$ forstolen$_V$.
that Rachel had the idol stolen
'... that Rachel had stolen the idol.'
(Gen:31.32.1275)
b. ... þæt mon hæfde$_{AUX}$ anfiteatrum$_O$ geworht$_V$ æt Hierusalem,...
that man had amphitheatre made at Jerusalem
'... that man had made an amphitheatre in Jerusalem.'
(Or_6:31.150.22.3120)

So what is going on? Well, the explanations given are a matter of different theoretical assumptions: in the OV approach a uniform Infl-final base order is assumed, and the only way to explain these data is to say that elements have shifted because obviously the auxiliary (finite verb) does not occur right at the end of the clause as it should.

Therefore, verb (projection) raising has been 'brought on the scene'. However, if you prefer to believe that OV and VO (including Infl-final and Infl-medial) existed alongside each other, then you would state that the pattern AUX-OV is ambiguous, i.e. it can be subject to two interpretations: either the auxiliary really occurs in its sentence-final base position and the verb phrase moved to the right, or it occurs in its sentence-medial base position. Pintzuk, as mentioned above, claimed that there is synchronic variation of OV and VO in OE. In the literature this hypothesis has been given the name **Double Base Hypothesis**. Pintzuk defined a number of criteria to clearly identify true cases of sentence-final and sentence-medial Infl. For her, an example like (24) unambiguously shows the order AUX-OV because the lexical verb is a particle verb (*up adon* 'take up') with the particle occurring in preverbal position which is an indication of its base position.

(24) ... þæt heo wolde$_{AUX}$ [þa baan]$_O$ [up adon]$_V$ þara   Cristes þeowa ...
 ... that she would   the bones   up take   (of)-the Christ's servants ...
 '... that she wanted to take up the bones of Christ's servants.'
 (Bede_4:13.292.5.2942)

Finally, full phrases can occur to the right of the otherwise sentence-final verb as in (25):

(25) ... Drihten wæs acenned on þære byrig þe   is gecweden Bethleem.
 the lord   was born   in the   city   that is called   Bethlehem
 '... the Lord was born in the city called Bethlehem.'
 (ÆCHom_I,_2:192.76.356)

In this example the phrase *on þære byrig þe is gecweden Bethleem* (a PP followed by a relative clause) can occur to the right of the lexical verb *acenned*. This process has been called **extraposition** (to the right of the VP or IP). In other West Germanic languages like NHG we find the same phenomenon. We could either say: 'Der Herr wurde in der Stadt, die Bethlehem heißt, geboren' (no extraposition) or 'Der Herr wurde geboren in der Stadt, die Bethlehem heißt' (extraposition).

Before we move on and take a look at the further development of this instance of syntactic variation, I would like to summarise what we have seen so far: on a descriptive level, variation could be observed concerning a) the relative position of the lexical verb and its object(s) and b) the position of the auxiliary. In this respect, we identified four logically possible word order patterns and found that only three of them actually occur in the data. We have further seen that the different patterns we have come across in the data have been explained with operations like verb (projection) raising and extraposition. I would like to point out again that this applies only if theoretical issues are taken into account, and moreover, only if the data is analysed in a generative framework. In other frameworks, things would look different. Regardless of the framework you choose, you can see the different patterns if you 'just' look at the data and describe it.

16.2 Syntactic variation and grammars in competition

Next, we will test whether the different patterns found in OE times still occur in ME times, restricting ourselves to the variation of OV and VO (in chapter 18 we will come back to the development of the position of auxiliaries). Our assumption is that the variation between OV and VO word order prevails and that there are quantitative changes in the direction of the VO pattern, i.e. more sentences displaying VO than sentences displaying OV, because we know that in the history of English a change from OV to VO has taken place. In these terms, ME has been labelled a transitional stage which nicely shows that language change is going on, actually on all levels of language. But why should ME play this role? Well, partly because of the fact that the dialectal variation prevalent at that time (between 1150 and 1500, to remind you) is directly reflected in ME manuscripts. To understand this, we have to briefly remind ourselves that in OE there was a written standard which no longer existed in ME times, most probably due to the Norman Conquest in 1066. As a result, ME scribes wrote as they spoke and that is why we have evidence for the many dialects that existed at that time. In contrast, the OE West-Saxon standard as a written norm superimposed the dialects that also existed at that time, but since scribes adhered to this standard they often refrained from writing in their own dialect. So ME is the stage in the history of English to learn something about dialectal variation.

Five main dialectal areas are distinguished: southern, Kentish, East Midlands, West Midlands, and northern. These areas resemble the OE ones (which were West Saxon, Kentish, Mercian, and Northumbrian), but since the Mercian Midlands showed so many differences between the eastern and the western parts, these two parts were divided.

Coming back to our phenomenon, variation between OV and VO orders, as expected, we find examples exhibiting both patterns in subordinate clauses (the lexical verb and the object are marked by indices):
Object-verb order:

(26) a. ... þt   ich nule   þe$_O$ forsaken$_V$.
        ... that I   NEG-will you forsake
        '... that I will not forsake you.'
        (JULIA,106.172)

b. ... þat all þe pepull hym$_O$ louet$_V$ and praysyd$_V$ for his meke   leuyng.
   ... that all the people him loved and praised   for his humble living
   '... that all the people loved and praised him for his humble life.'
   (MIRK,12.322)

Verb-object order:

(27) a. ... ðat ic mihte hauen$_V$ [ðat eche lif]$_O$.
       ... that I might have   that each life
       '... that I might have that same life.'
       (VICES1,67.754)
    b. ... þet ye mahen ane   pine$_V$ me$_O$ here.
       ... that you may   at-all torture me   here
       'that you may torture me here at all.'
       (JULIA,102.110)

So it seems that both OV and VO orders were possible in ME. However, the picture is much more complex if we take into account that the different dialects display different degrees of the two options. In their seminal study, Kroch and Taylor (2000) compared findings from a number of ME texts, focussing on differences between the Southeast Midlands and the West Midlands texts. The reason for this choice was that the West Midlands texts seem to behave more innovatively, i.e., they show the VO order to a higher degree, whereas the Southeast Midlands texts behave more conservatively as they show the OE OV order to a higher degree (and therefore less instances of the VO order).

Since the authors wanted to define the base order in the verb phrase, they used the postverbal position of a pronominal object as a criterion for VO order. This assumption is based on the observation that in West Germanic languages, pronouns do not postpose beyond an otherwise final verb which means that when the pronoun occurs after the lexical verb it has not been subject to operations like movement etc.

In Table 16.1, some of the results of Kroch & Taylor's study are given (for the full table see Kroch and Taylor, 2000, 146). As you can see by comparing the percentages of instances of VO orders in the two dialect groups, the differences between the West Midlands texts and the Southeast Midlands texts are quite big: 45% of VO orders in the former group, and only 9% in the latter group. Since it is harder to define OV orders as discussed above for OE, we can (only) say that it does exist to some degree (for a full discussion of possible criteria to define OV I refer you to the paper by Kroch & Taylor). What can be confirmed is that the West Midlands texts are indeed more innovative than the Southeast Midlands texts.

From a more theoretical point of view, we can say that in ME synchronic grammatical variation can be found concerning the order OV and VO between dialects, i.e.

Table 16.1. Position of pronouns in subordinate clauses with auxiliary

	Pre-Verbal (OV)	Post-Verbal (VO)	Post-Verbal %
West Midlands			
Ancrene Riwle	38	36	49%
Katherine Group	46	32	41%
Total WM	84	68	45%
Southeast Midlands			
Trinity Homilies	43	8	16%
Vices and Virtues	78	5	6%
Total SEM	121	13	10%

West Midlands texts show a different grammar from Southeastern Midlands texts. The idea behind this assumption is that this type of syntactic variation involves the use by individual speakers of two grammatical options that are actually not 'allowed' to exist alongside. Above, we have said that in the generative approach, *either* OV *or* VO can exist but not both. If we want to keep this assumption alive still, we must state that the variation we find is diachronically unstable, with the old option (OV) competing with the new one (VO) the latter gradually winning out. This is what Kroch (1989) has called **grammars in competition**, which also implies that at some point in time speakers use both options (just as bilingual speakers do) and drop the old option at the end of the competition process.

The question now is if there is an explanation for this dialectal discrepancy and whether we find further support for our finding, i.e. OV is conservative and occurs more frequently in Southern and Southeastern texts, and VO is innovative and occurs more frequently in Western and Northern texts. It makes sense therefore to include more texts from Northern dialectal areas in our investigation. We will do so by taking a closer look at one very interesting text called *The Ormulum*.

The Ormulum was written by a monk named 'Orm' (the Scandinavian word for 'worm') who lived in the twelfth century in Lincolnshire (East Midlands). At that time, Lincolnshire was part of the area where the Vikings had settled centuries before and where Danish law held sway. The text is an incomplete set of homilies written in very strict iambic metre and in a spelling system that Orm invented himself. He was eager to mark closed syllables by double consonants in a very systematic way, and that is why today we know at least a bit about the vowel quantity at that time. Apart from these aspects, the text contains many Scandinavian loan words and even some Scandinavian syntactic features.

Concerning the syntactic variation discussed so far, in *The Ormulum* we expect to find OV and VO orders in subordinate clauses (with an auxiliary):

Object-verb order:

(28) a. ... *giff þatt he wollde himm$_O$ lokenn$_V$* ...
    ... if   that he would him   protect
    '... provided that he wanted to protect him.'
    (ORM,INTR.L197)

b. ... *swa þatt tu   mihht [Drihhtiness are]$_O$ winnenn$_V$.*
    ... so   that you might Lord's   kindness win
    '... so that you might win the Lord's kindness.'
    (ORM,I,53.513)

Verb-object order:

(29) a. ... *þatt Drihhtin shollde gifenn$_V$ uss$_O$ god   sawless eghesihhþe.*
    ... that Lord   should give   us   good soul's eye-sight
    '... that the Lord shall give us the eyesight of the good soul.'
    (ORM,I,63.567)

b. ... *þurrh   þatt he wollde tolenn$_V$ dæð$_O$ wiþþutenn hise wrihhte &*
    ... through that he would permit   death   without   his fault and
    turrnenn menn till Cristenndom ... & fullhtenn$_V$ hemm$_O$ & clennsenn$_V$
    turn   men till Christendom ... and baptise   them and cleanse
    hemm$_O$ ...
    them
    '... because he wanted to permit death without his fault and turn men to Christendom ... and baptise them and cleanse them.'
    (ORM,I,148.1212)

As mentioned above, there are even clauses with both orders:

(30) *Forr þatt I wollde bliþelig þatt all Ennglisshe lede   wiþþ ære shollde lisstenn$_V$*
    for that I would gladly   that all English   people with ear should listen
    itt$_O$, wiþþ herte shollde itt$_O$ trowwenn$_V$, wiþþ tunge shollde spellenn$_V$ itt$_O$, wiþþ
    it   with heart should it   trust   with tongue should spell   it   with
    dede shollde itt$_O$ follghenn$_V$.
    deed should it   follow
    'because I wished that all English people will hear it, with their hearts should trust it, with their tongues should spell it, with their deeds should follow it.'
    (ORM,DED.L113.33)

If we compare the findings from the East Midlands text *The Ormulum* with those gained by Kroch & Taylor in Table 16.1 for the West Midlands and Southeast Midlands texts, we see right away that the Southeast Midlands texts show significantly fewer VO orders (Table 16.2). The West Midlands texts on the other hand show similar patterns as *the Ormulum*: the *Ancrene Riwle* 49 %, the *Katherine Group* 41 %, and *The Ormulum* (even) 51 % of VO order.

Table 16.2. Comparison of the position of pronouns in subordinate clauses with auxiliary in ME texts

	Pre-Verbal (OV)	Post-Verbal (VO)	Post-Verbal %
West Midlands			
Ancrene Riwle	38	36	49
Katherine Group	46	32	41
East Midlands			
The Ormulum	91	95	51

So *The Ormulum* exhibits the innovative VO word order in about half of all subordinate clauses, and what's more, we have evidence that the speaker/writer Orm used both OV and VO alongside each other in the same clause. In the context of **grammars in competition**, this observation is interpreted in such a way that the author had two different grammars available, which seems plausible in scenarios of intense **language contact**. A good candidate for such a language contact situation in medieval times in England is the contact between speakers of Scandinavian (Old Norse) and English during and after the times of the Viking invasions approximately between the ninth and the tenth centuries (see the comment above on the Danelaw). Some authors have claimed that the innovative VO order derived from the Scandinavian speakers because Old Norse was also VO (see for example Trips, 2002). Thus, the observation that this order is more often found in ME texts which were written in areas occupied by the Scandinavians would corroborate this assumption.

Apart from numerous Scandinavian family names, place names and lexical items of Old Norse origin for example *egg*, *skirt*, *skull*, *give* and *take*, further instances of **grammatical (structural) borrowing** can be found like the third person plural pronouns (PDE *they*, *them*, *their*). Interestingly, whereas the Old Norse forms are most frequently found in Northern dialects, the OE forms *hi(e)*, *him* and *hira* predominantly occur in the Southern dialects. Take a look at the following examples:

North:

(31) **þair** golde and **þaire** tresoure drawes **þam** til dede.
    their gold and their treasure draws them to death
    'Their gold and their treasure draws them to death.'
    (ROLLEP,64.65)

South:

(32) and louye oure uyendes. þet is to zigge **hare** persones. an bidde uor **ham** and
    and love our fiends. that is to say their persons. And pray for them and
    do **ham** guod yef **hy** habbeþ nyede and þou hit migt do.
    do them good if they have need and thou it might do.
    '... and love our enemies, that is to say their people. And pray for them and do them good if they are in need, and you might do it.'
    (AYENBI, 114.2206)

As you can see, the first example is from a text written in a Northern dialect (the text is a part of epistles written by Richard Rolle in the mid fourteenth century), and the forms for the third person pronouns are *þair* 'their' and *þam* 'them' (remember that the scribes at that time wrote as they spoke, which is why we find many different spellings of words). The other example from a Southern (Kentish) text, called *The Ayenbite of Inwyt* ('The Remorse of Conscience'), written by the monk Dan Michel in 1340, shows the OE forms *hare* 'their', *ham* 'them' and *hy* 'they'.

By comparing these examples from different dialectal areas we see that at that time, there were no uniform forms for the third person plural pronouns. In the Northern dialects, all three forms borrowed from Old Norse replaced the Old English ones, and in the Southern dialects, the OE forms remained much longer before they were also gradually replaced by 'they, them, their'. The variation of the old and new forms of the third person plural pronouns in the different Middle English dialects give a good picture of how innovations in the North gradually spread to the South. Since it has been assumed by authors dealing with language contact that grammatical borrowings are an indicator of intense language contact situations (I refer you to Thomason and Kaufman, 1988 and Hickey, 2010), these pieces of evidence taken together seem to speak in favour of language contact induced changes in the ME period. The amalgamation of the two groups—the Anglo-Saxons and the Scandinavians—was facilitated by the cultural similarities between them and by relatively small differences between the two genetically related languages. According to an Icelandic saga of the eleventh century 'there was at that time the same tongue in England as in Norway and Denmark' (Freeborn, 2006, 52).

For other authors (for example Fischer et al., 2000, Roberts, 2007) the change from OV to VO was not induced by language contact between OE speakers and Scandinavian speakers. Rather, they believe that it is a change that was on its way without 'the help from outside'. It has been observed that a number of (S)OV languages have developed into (S)VO languages, whereby the loss of inflections triggering a change from a synthetic to an analytic language might play a significant role (Lightfoot, 2002). From this point of view, the change happens **internal** to language and cannot be explained by **external** factors.

Regardless of whether internal and/or external factors led to this change one very important question is which role language acquisition plays. Recall from part II, chapter 9.2 how acquisition was modelled in the Theory of Principles & Parameters. When parameters are set to certain values according to the PLD children are exposed to they have acquired the grammatical system of their mother tongue(s). But when a language changes we must assume that the grammatical system has also changed. If we believe that the goal of acquisition is to replicate the parental grammar (i.e. the grammar of the previous generation) we will have a hard time explaining change and we will run into the **logical problem of language change**. But if we say that the goal is to approximate the parental grammar we allow for explaining change. Roberts (2007) and others have claimed that sometimes no definite value of a parameter is expressed in the PLD which amounts to say that children acquiring a language have two options then, and they either set the parameter to 0 or to 1, in our concrete case either to OV or VO. The question that arises is how this ambiguity is introduced into the PLD, and one possible answer is language contact, and another the status of the speaker, i.e. the age at the time of acquisition (for a thorough discussion see Roberts, 2007, 230–35).

Now what about the further development of this change? We have said that ME is a transitional stage where, amongst others, the change from OV to VO has taken place. By the end of the ME period, OV orders have almost vanished and VO is the rule. As we would expect then, in EModE, we find the odd example with OV order but by far the most frequent order is VO. I give three examples from the EModE corpus still exhibiting OV order:

(33) a. *When thou thy self [this sentence]$_O$ paste$_V$ of Platos mouth: 'that happy were those common welthes, if eyther wisdom studiers ruld them, or their Rulers wisdom$_O$ imbraced$_V$.'*
'When you yourself passed this sentence from Platos mouth: 'that happy were those wordly riches, if either scholars ruled them, or their rules embraced wisdom."
(BOETHEL-E2-P1,8.18)

b. *Loue like a shadow flies, when substance Loue$_O$ pursues$_V$, Pursuing that that flies, and flying what pursues.*
(SHAKESP-E2-H,46.C2.422)

c. *W=th= intire love and saluts to thyselfe w=th= my daughter, I remaine Thy loveing husband till death us$_O$ part$_V$, Richard Haddock.*
'With entire love and greetings to yourself with my daughter, I remain your loving husband, till death do us part, Richard Haddock.'
(RHADDSR-1670-E3-P2,14.118)

In the first example, which is from Queen Elizabeth I's translation of Boethius's *De Consolatione Philosophiae* (end of 16th century), two sequences of OV occur: *this sentence$_O$ paste$_V$* and *wisdom$_O$ imbraced$_V$*. Since this is a translation from a Latin original we cannot be sure whether the OV orders occurring in the text are due to a direct transfer of the Latin word order in that text. The second example is from Shakespeare (end of the 16th century), and a short glance at the sentence suffices to see that the order of the words has poetical force (that is also why I refrained from translating it), which means that it is quite likely that Shakespeare deliberately flouted the syntactic rules to create poetic effects. The third example (mid/end of the 17th century), which can clearly be seen, is from a letter from husband to wife, and the letter ends with 'till death do us part'. I am sure you have heard this phrase before, which is part of the marriage vow from *The Book of Common Prayer*. The phrase is archaic and fossilised and is witness to an older stage of English.

What these examples then show is that in EModE there are instances of OV order but they do not necessarily reflect productive syntactic rules. In the *British National Corpus* (BNC), I could not find any OV orders apart from those contained in the marriage vow which occurred with a very low frequency. This shows then that there are stages in the history of English (and languages in general) which are more prone to syntactic variation than others. Once a syntactic pattern has developed from A to B via a transitional stage A/B, the new form B is the only option and variation vanishes. Again, much has been written on the topic of the gradualness of change but since this textbook serves as an introduction, I cannot go into detail here. Below, I refer you to the most important works.

Tax: 'Wow, that was interesting! Grammars in competition!'
Syn: 'Before you get carried away I take over and provide the exercises for the readers: **1)** is Old English classified as an OV or a VO language? Identify relevant examples in the text to support your line of argument; **2)** explain the notion of grammars in competition and provide some examples which speak in favour of it; **3)** what are the positions of the auxiliary in OE? Give some examples from the text and describe the word orders found; **4)** describe the position of the lexical verb relative to its object in the OE examples below. Which word orders can be observed and how would you account for them in a theory that assumes one basic word order?'

(34) a. þa   se king þas word geherde, þa   forhtode he þearle swyðe,
          when the king these words heard then feared   he with-all his-might
      'When the king heard these words he feared them with all his might.'
      (LS_28_[Neot]:102.92)

b. ... *hie witon hwæt ic hie lærde.*
    ... they knew what I them taught
    'they knew what I taught them.'
    (HomS_24_[ScraggVerc_1]:38.45)
c. *Đa wæs æfter ðissum þætte Agustinus Breotone ærcebiscop gehalgade twegen biscopas:*
    then was after these that Augustinus Brittany archbishop ordained two bishops
    'Then afterwards Augustinus, the archbishop of Brittany, ordained two bishops.'
    (Bede_2:3.104.12.976)
d. *& hit wæs geworden þa he bletsude hig, he ferde fram him*
    and it was happened when he blessed them he went from him
    'And it occurred that when he blessed them he went from him.'
    (Lk_[WSCp]:24.51.5727)

Tax: 'So what have we learnt in this chapter?'
Syn: 'We have dealt with syntactic variation in the diachrony of English. As an example, variation in the verb phrase, i.e. OV and VO (and V-AUX to AUX-V) word order patterns, were investigated from Old English to the present day. We have seen that variation already existed in OE, but that the perfect time span to look for variation is actually ME because at that time, varieties were not superimposed by a written standard. Furthermore, a change from OV to VO could be observed, and some analyses to deal with this change from a theoretical perspective were discussed. From a generative perspective, the two options available, OV or VO, derive from the notion of binary parameters in generative syntax where one option (gradually) wins out. Concerning an explanation of why this change happened, the standard assumption is that it can either be due to changes internal or external to the system.'
Tax: 'And don't forget to mention that the notion of grammars in competition was introduced which is tightly linked to the assumption that an intense contact situation between Scandinavian speakers and speakers of OE must have existed for a longer period of time.'
Syn: 'Yes, and recently it has been pointed out by several authors that most changes are multifactorial and that to arrive at an adequate explanation one has to take into consideration all of these factors. In the case of the language contact scenario this would mean that possible changes internal to the language must be taken into account as well and vice versa.'

Literature: van Kemenade (1987) is the first theoretical discussion of OE syntax in a generative framework. Kroch (1989) is a seminal paper on the way language changes. He shows that syntactic change is subject to the so-called Constant Rate Effect (which means that the rate of replacement of one grammatical option by another is the same in all contexts in which is occurs). In Pintzuk and Kroch (1989) OE word order in the *Beowulf* is discussed. The authors show that postverbal objects are preceded by a metrical pause which can be taken as an indicator that they are extraposed. Pintzuk (1999) discusses the notion of grammars in competition as an explanation of word order variation in OE. In Trips (2002) the question of whether language contact with Scandinavian led to syntactic borrowing in OE and Early ME is pursued by looking at a number of phenomena peculiar to Scandinavian. Fuß and Trips (2002) try to account for the observation that one of the logically possible four word orders (VO-AUX) does not occur by making use of the grammars in competition model. Pintzuk and Taylor (2006) discuss the loss of OV structures in the history of English by taking a closer look at the properties of the object. Fischer et al. (2000) discuss the change in terms of an internal change as does Roberts (and collaborators) in many of his papers (e.g. Roberts, 1997, Roberts, 2007, Biberauer and Roberts, 2008).

17 Comparative syntax from a diachronic perspective

In this chapter, we will discuss topics of diachronic syntax from a comparative perspective. In chapter 5 we have dealt with the rise of comparative linguistics in the 19th century as a discipline in its own right, with the aim of reconstructing the origins, the developmental history and relationships of and between individual languages on the basis of comparative studies. Here, we will restrict ourselves to comparing a number of languages by looking at the development of one prominent phenomenon—**Verb Second**. We have already touched on this phenomenon in Part II of the book (chapter 11) and in chapter 14.1 of this part of the book, now we will focus on the phenomenon and compare it in the history of English and German.

17.1 Verb Second in Early English

Let's start dealing with the phenomenon by looking again at some of the examples of main declarative sentences from the introductory chapter above:

(1) a. $Eric_S$ $plays_V$ the $piano_O$ [every day].
    b. [Every day], $Eric_S$ $plays_V$ [the piano]$_O$.
    c. [The piano]$_O$, $Eric_S$ $plays_V$ [every day].
    d. Unfortunately, $Eric_S$ $plays_V$ [the piano]$_O$ [every day].

Analyse these examples by counting from left to right in which position the finite verb occurs. What you will find is that in the first sentence the finite verb *plays* occurs in the second position right after *Eric*, whereas in the other examples it occurs in the third position, again right after *Eric*. So, regardless of the material added, the ordering SVO is retained. Before we describe the phenomenon in older stages of English and German, let's compare the examples in (1) with their NHG equivalents:

(2) a. $Eric_S$ $spielt_V$ [jeden Tag] $Klavier_O$.
    b. [Jeden Tag] $spielt_V$ $Eric_S$ $Klavier_O$.
    c. $Klavier_O$ $spielt_V$ $Eric_S$ [jeden Tag].
    d. Leider $spielt_V$ $Eric_S$ [jeden Tag] $Klavier_O$.

If you analyse the data along the same lines as you have done for PDE, you will have found different patterns for NHG: in the first sentence the finite verb *spielt* occurs in second position right after *Eric*, and in the other examples it occurs in second position too, directly following *jeden Tag*, *Klavier* and *leider*. Now if you take a look at the relative order of the subject and finite verb you will see the difference between the two languages (and again recall what we have said in part II, chapter 11: in PDE the order subject-finite verb is retained in all contexts, in NHG only in the first context where the subject is the first constituent do we also find this order; in all other cases the finite verb is inverted with the subject, i.e. finite verb-subject. Below you find a grid that clearly shows that the finite verb occurs in exactly the second position *in all contexts* in NHG, whereas this is not the case in PDE. As you can see, I counted and numbered the constituents from left to right in a merely descriptive fashion leaving aside any theoretical analysis:

Table 17.1. The position of the finite verb in main declarative sentences in PDE and NHG

Position 1	Position 2	Position 3	Position 4	Position 5
Eric$_S$	**plays**$_V$	the piano$_O$	every day$_{Adv}$.	
Eric$_S$	**spielt**$_V$	jeden Tag$_{Adv}$	Klavier$_O$.	
Every day$_{Adv}$	Eric$_S$	plays$_V$	the piano$_O$.	
Jeden Tag$_{Adv}$	**spielt**$_V$	Eric$_S$	Klavier$_O$.	
The piano$_O$	Eric$_S$	plays$_V$	every day$_{Adv}$.	
Klavier$_O$	**spielt**$_V$	Eric$_S$	jeden Tag$_{Adv}$.	
Unfortunately$_{Adv}$	Eric$_S$	plays$_V$	the piano$_O$	every day$_{Adv}$.
Leider$_{Adv}$	**spielt**$_V$	Eric$_S$	jeden Tag$_{Adv}$	Klavier$_O$.

The definition of Verb Second, which was introduced in part II, chapter 11, is taken up here again: in main declarative sentences, the finite verb has to occur in the second position. This rule results in **subject-verb inversion** which can be seen by looking at the PDE and NHG data again: apart from the sentence where the subject is in first position, the finite verb inverts with the subject in all contexts in NHG. In contrast, in PDE subject-verb inversion does not occur (see again part II, chapter 11 for the exceptions to this rule in PDE). In the following, we will see that English and German were quite similar in earlier stages before they developed in different ways.

Let's start with some OE data and see whether it behaves more like PDE or more like NHG:

(3) a. [Se gehæled mann]$_S$ **gemette**$_V$ þone Hælend syþþan on þam temple
    the healed man   found   the lord   then   in the temple
    'The cured man then found the lord in the temple.'
    (ÆHom_2:276.386)

b. [þæt hus]$_O$ **hæfdon**$_{AUX}$ Romane$_S$ to ðæm anum tacne geworht$_V$ ...
    that house had   Romans to the one sign made
    'The Romans had made that house to their sole sign.'
    (Or_3:5.59.3.1042)

c. *Uneaðe*~Adv~ **mæg**~AUX~ *mon*~S~ *to geleafsuman gesecgan*~V~...
    Hardly   may   man to faithful   speak
    'Hardly may man speak to the faithful ...'
    (Or_3:9.70.16.1292)

d. *[On his dagum]*~Adv~ **sende**~V~ *Gregorius*~S~ *us fulluht.*
    in his days   sent   Gregory   us Christianity
    'In his days, Gregory sent us Christianity.'
    (ChronA,:565.1.207)

In the first sentence, the initial constituent is the subject *se gehæled mann* which is directly followed by the finite verb *gemette*. If we compare this sentence with the sentences *Eric plays the piano every day* and *Eric spielt jeden Tag Klavier* OE behaves like both PDE and NHG because obviously they show the same order: subject-finite verb. However, if we take a look at the other examples, differences between OE and PDE emerge: in (4) b. the initial constituent *þæt hus* (object) is directly followed by the finite verb *hæfdon* which has inverted with the subject of the clause. The examples in c. and d. show the same pattern: the initial constituents *uneaðe* (adverb) and *on his dagum* (PP with the function of a temporal adverbial) are directly followed by the finite verbs *mæg* and *sende* which have inverted with the subjects *mon* and *Gregorius* respectively. So OE patterns are exactly like NHG and contrast with PDE, and this implies that English has undergone some changes in the course of time.

What about Old High German (OHG) then? First of all, the period of time labelled OHG is the earliest attested stage in the history of German. As with OE, the same problems arise concerning its periodisation, but it has been said that it can be dated to before 1050 A.D. so you can see that the earliest stages of English and German comprise approximately the same time span. But OE and OHG have much more in common than that, at least from a linguistic perspective. Both languages were highly inflectional, as you can see if you compare the first few lines of the *Lord's Prayer*:

(4) a. *Faeder ure þu þe eart in heofonum, si þin nama gehalgod. Tobecume*
       father our you who is in heaven, be your name hallowed. Come
       þin rice, geweorþe þin will on heofonum swa swa on eorþan.
       your reign, become your will in heaven as on earth.
       (West Saxon)

    b. *Fater unser, thu thar bist in himile, si giheilagot thion namo. queme*
       father our you there are in heaven, be hallowed your name. come
       richi thin, si thin uuilleo, so her in himile ist, so si her in erdu.
       reign your, be your will, so here in heaven is, so be here on earth.
       'Our father in heaven, hallowed be your name. Your kingdom come, your will be done, on earth as in heaven.'
       (Fulda, 850)

In chapters 14 and 15 we have seen that OE and NHG nominals inflect for case, number and gender, and verbs for person, number, tense and mood. This also applies to OHG which can be seen for example by looking at words like *himile*. The noun is directly preceded by the preposition *in* which assigns dative case to it, and this is marked by the inflectional ending *-e*. Similarly, the noun *erdu* has been assigned dative case by *in*. Different forms of the verb 'to be' can be found as well: *bist*, *si* and *ist*. In that respect, OHG resembles both OE and NHG. Since languages which morphologically mark grammatical specifications on words by inflection generally show a freer word order, we would expect to find this property in OHG as well. Thus, placing objects in different positions, for example right at the beginning of a sentence, should be possible. Below, some OHG examples are given, where the finite verb is marked in bold:

(5) a. [Druhtines gheist]$_S$ **ist**$_{AUX}$ sprehhendi$_V$ dhurah mih.
    god's   ghost is   speaking   through me
   'God's spirit speaks through me.'
   (Isidor,213; Robinson 1997:35)

b. [Dhinera uuomba uuwaxsmin]$_O$ **setzu**$_V$ ih$_S$ ubar min hohsetli.
   your   womb's fruit   set   I   over my throne
   'I place the fruit of your womb upon my throne.'
   (Isidor,611;Robinson 1997:9)

c. Dhar$_{Adv}$ **ist**$_{AUX}$ izs$_S$ chiuuisso so zi ernusti araughit$_V$ ...
   there   is   it certainly so to earnest revealed
   'It is certainly so in earnest revealed there.'
   (Isidor,442)

d. [In dhemu nemin cyres] **ist**$_{AUX}$ christ chiuuisso chiforabodot
   in the   name Cyres is   Christ certainly presaged
   'by the use of the name 'Cyres' Christ is certainly presaged.'
   (I 162 in Axel:2007,5)

First of all, the main declarative sentences resemble those of OE and NHG above, in that the first constituents can be a subject in (4) a. (*Druhtines gheist*), an object in b. (*Dhinera uuomba uuwaxsmin*), a locative adverbial in c. (*Dhar*), or a PP with the function of an adverbial of manner in d. (*In dhemu nemin cyres*). In all of these cases, the finite verb occurs in the second position implying subject-verb inversion whenever the subject is not the first constituent. Note that this is true regardless of the type of subject (full NP or pronoun). So it seems that OHG is also a Verb-Second language.

There are other contexts where the finite verb occurs in second position. These contexts are constituent questions introduced by question elements like *hwa* 'who', *hwæt* 'what', *hwelc* 'which' and *hu* 'how' (note that the order of graphemes/phonemes of interrogative pronouns is 'reversed', in OE we have *hw*-elements, in PDE *wh*-

elements). Apart from this context, sentences introduced by the sentence negation *ne* also exhibit Verb-Second. Take a look at the following examples:

(6) a. *Hwæt sculon$_{AUX}$ we$_S$ þæs   nu ma secgan$_V$?*
    what shall   we afterwards now more say
    'What shall we say now more afterwards?'
    (Bede_2:9.132.1.1253)

b. *ne$_{NEG}$ cræwþ$_V$ [se hana]$_S$ todæg ær   þu me ætsæcst.*
    not crows   the cock   today before you me deny
    'The cock will not crow today until you deny me.'
    (Lk_[WSCp]:22.34.5465)

In the first example, the question is introduced by *hwæt* and directly followed by the finite verb *sculon*. Subject-verb inversion occurs between the verb and the subject *we*. In the negation context, the initial constituent is the sentence negation *ne*, directly followed by the finite verb *cræwþ* which in turn is directly followed by the subject *se hana* displaying subject-verb inversion.

We have said above that PDE is not a Verb-Second language because subject-verb inversion does not occur even if a constituent is topicalised, i.e. occurring in the first position of a sentence. Interestingly, the question and the negation context are exceptions to this rule:

(7) a. *What did$_{AUX}$ you say$_V$?*
    b. *Who comes$_V$ with me?*
    c. *[Never in my life] have$_{AUX}$ I seen$_V$ such a thing.*
    d. *[At no time] must$_{AUX}$ this door be left unlocked$_V$.*

In the examples in (7) the finite verb always occupies the second position, i.e. the position directly after a wh-element (*what, who*) or a phrase of negative form or meaning (*never in my life, at no time*). As a conclusion, we can say that in these two contexts PDE resembles OE, in the other Verb-Second contexts PDE deviates from OE. In the literature, these observations have led to the assumption that English lost Verb-Second in the course of time, and that the contexts of question formation and negation are residues of this phenomenon. Below, we will briefly discuss an explanation of this change.

Next, let's turn again to OHG: do we also find Verb Second in question and negation contexts? Take a look at the following examples:

(8) a. /uuvo **gisahi**$_V$ thu$_S$ abrahaman?/
how saw you Abraham
'How can you have seen Abraham?'
(Tatian,451,7)

b. ni$_{NEG}$ **quad**$_V$ ih fon iu allen/
not spoke I of you all
'I haven't spoken of all of you.'
(Tatian,553,21)

The first sentence in (8) a. is introduced by the interrogative element *uuvo* 'how' which is directly followed by the finite verb *gisahi* 'saw'. In b. the initial constituent of the sentence is the negation element *ni* which is directly followed by the finite verb *quad* 'spoke'. If we compare these sentences and many others of that type with those of OE and PDE above, we can say that they show exactly the same order. Since OHG exhibits Verb Second in all the other contexts, like OE, it is also a lexical verb Second language.

In part II, chapter 11, the terms **symmetric Verb Second** and **asymmetric Verb Second** were introduced. Recall that 'symmetric Verb Second' refers to languages which consistently show the phenomenon both in main sentences and subordinate clauses, whereas 'asymmetric Verb Second' refers to those languages which display the phenomenon only in main sentences. A number of Germanic languages were compared and classified according to these two categories. NHG and Dutch for example belong to the class of asymmetric Verb Second languages, and Modern Icelandic and Yiddish belong to the class of symmetric Verb Second languages. In this chapter, we are going to investigate whether OE and OHG are asymmetric Verb Second languages or not. To do that, we will take a look at some data displaying subordination:

(9) a. forþon þe hie wiston [þæt **[on hire**$_{PP}$**]** **eardode**$_V$ se heofonlica cyning,]
because they knew that in her dwelled the heavenly king
'... because they knew that in her the heavenly king dwelled.'
(HomU_18_[BlHom_1]:11.148.135)

b. ða sædon hig [þæt **þær**$_{Adv}$ **ferde**$_V$ se Nazareniscea hælend.]
Then said they that there went the Nazarene saviour
'Then they said that the Nazarene saviour went there.'
(Lk_[WSCp]:18.37.5163)

c. ... þonne hie wenaþ [ðæt hie$_S$ ryhtne andan$_O$ **hæbben**$_V$.]
... then they believe that they true fear have
'... then they believe that they have true fear.'
(CP:40.289.16.1898)

(10) *In dhesemu quihide ni   bluchisoe eoman, [ni **dhiz sii**$_V$ chiuuisso dher ander*
     in this   saying NEG doubts   someone that this be certain   the other
     heit godes]
     form of-god
     'In this saying no one should doubt that this is certainly the second form of God.'
     (Isidor,197; Robinson 1997:62f)

In the OE examples in (9) and the OHG example in (10), *that*-complementation is indicated by square brackets. In the OE example in a. the first constituent is the PP *on hire* directly followed by the finite verb *eardode*, and in the example in b. the first constituent is the locative adverbial *þær* directly followed by the finite verb *ferde*. In both cases, the subject follows the finite verb (*se heofonlica cyning* in a. and *se Nazareniscea hælend* in b.). If you compare the ordering of elements in these (subordinate) clauses with those above in main sentences, you will come to the conclusion that Verb Second can occur in subordinate clauses too: a constituent which is not the subject can occur in the first position (directly after the complementiser *þæt*), a finite verb directly follows the first constituent in second position, and the subject of the clause is inverted with the finite verb and thus occurs in third position. Note that this is only possible in a restricted set of clauses, actually only in clauses which are complements of **verba dicendi**, i.e. verbs of saying, or so-called bridge verbs (see also part II, chapter 11) like *say* or *know* (for further exceptions see the recommended literature below). The example in c. demonstrates that Verb Second is possible but not required in these clauses. Here the finite verb occurs right at the end of the subordinate clause.

In OHG, the same holds true: the first constituent in (10) is followed by the finite verb *sii* which in turn is followed by the subject *dher ander heit godes* (note that here the finite verb and the subject are not adjacent, the adverb *chiuuisso* intervenes).

Before we briefly deal with exceptions to the Verb Second rule, I am going to summarise what we have seen so far in this chapter: by comparing older stages of English and German with PDE and NHG, we have seen that both OE and OHG resemble NHG much more than PDE: a constituent which is not the subject can occur in the first position and is followed by the finite verb. The finite verb in turn precedes the subject, i.e. it inverts with the subject in these cases (the unmarked case is when the subject precedes the finite verb). This ordering of constituents quite frequently occurs in main declarative sentences and has been labelled Verb Second. Further, this ordering can also occur in subordinate clauses although in a restricted sense: if the verb of the main sentence is a *verbum dicendi*, or bridge verb, it may trigger Verb Second in its complement clause. Since this is not consistently the case, the type of Verb Second we find in OE and OHG is asymmetric Verb Second.

Next, we will turn to a systematic exception to the Verb Second rule which has something to do with the nature of subjects and is found in both OE and OHG.

First, take a look at the following OE examples and focus on the relative order of finite verb and subject (given in bold): by now you should be familiar with these word order patterns:

(11) a. [ðone lichoman]$_O$ **gesohte**$_V$ [sum deaf man ond feþeleas]$_S$.
   the body sought some deaf man and crippled
   'Some deaf and crippled man looked out for the body.'
   (Mart_5_[Kotzor]:Se5,B.8.1657)
   b. [ðæt]$_O$ **he**$_S$ **dyde**$_V$ on Sigeberhtes dagum þæs cyninges.
   that he did in Sigberth's days the king's
   'That he did in king Sigberth's days.'
   (Mart_5_[Kotzor]:Ja16,B.18.115)
   c. On ðam dæge **worhte**$_V$ **God**$_S$ [leoht & merigen. & æfen]$_O$:
   on this day created God light and morning and evening
   'On this day, God created light, morning and evening.'
   (ÆCHom_I,_6:229.150.1148)
   d. þurh his wisdom **he**$_S$ **geworhte**$_V$ [ealle þing]$_O$.
   through his wisdom he created all things
   'Through his wisdom, he created all things.'
   (ÆCHom_I,_1:179.16.18)

The examples in (11) a. and c. exhibit the Verb Second pattern we have discussed above: a non-subject consituent in first position is followed by the finite verb, which in turn is followed by the subject of the sentence. Now, what about the examples in b. and d.? Here, the non-subject consituent in first position is followed by the subject, which in turn is followed by the finite verb of the sentence, so subject-verb inversion has not taken place. If you take a very good look, you see that the types of subjects occurring in the sentences in (11) differ; in a. and c. they are full phrases, and in b. and d. pronouns. A systematic difference arises: whenever the subject is a full phrase, subject-verb inversion occurs and the Verb Second pattern is triggered; whenever the subject is a pronoun, subject-verb inversion does not occur and **Verb Third** is the result. Now take a look at OHG:

(12) a. [In dhemu nemin cyres] **ist**$_{AUX}$ **christ**$_S$ chiuuisso chiforabodot
   in the name Cyres is Christ certainly presaged
   'by the use of the name 'Cyres' Christ is certainly presaged.'
   (I 162 in Axel:2007,5)

b. [Erino portun]$_O$ **ih$_S$ firchnissu$_V$,** iisnine grindila firbrihu endi [dhiu
   bronze gates I shatter iron locks smash-1-SG and the
   chiborgonun hort] **dhir$_O$ ghibu$_V$.**
   hidden treasure you give-1-SG
   'I shatter bronze gates, I smash iron locks and I give you the hidden treasure.'
   (Isidor, 157;Robinson 1997:17)

c. [Dhinera uuomba uuwaxsmin]$_O$ **setzu$_V$ ih$_S$** ubar min hohsetli.
   your womb's fruit set I over my throne
   'I place the fruit of your womb upon my throne.'
   (Isidor,611;Robinson 1997:9)

If the subject is a full phrase as in (12) a. Verb Second occurs, but if the subject is a pronoun the picture is not so clear: in b. it intervenes between the first constituent of the sentence and the finite verb, and the result is Verb Third, but in c. Verb Second occurs although the subject is a pronoun. So OHG does not exactly have the same properties as OE. Also note that in the example in b. the finite verb form *ghibu* bears verbal inflection which is strong enough to express the subject (that is why no extra subject occurs and why the verb forms are glossed 'smash-1-SG' etc.). Further, it can be seen that object pronouns can also trigger Verb Third: in the coordinated clause *endi [dhiu chiborgonun hort]* **dhir$_O$ ghibu$_V$**, the object pronoun *dhir* 'you' intervenes between the first constituent and the finite verb form *ghibu* which includes the subject. The example below shows that OE object pronouns have the same potential, they can also intervene between the first constituent and subject:

(13) [þin agen geleafa] **þe$_O$ hæfþ$_{AUX}$** gehæledne$_V$.
    your own faith you has healed
    'Your own faith has healed you.'
    (HomS_8_[BlHom_2]:15.24.201)

Matters are different in some special contexts which today trigger Verb Second in English, i.e. *wh*-questions and negation contexts (the examples below for OE and OHG were already discussed above and are repeated here):

(14) a. Hwæt **is$_V$ [se man]$_S$** þe het þe niman þin bed and gan?
       what is the man that command you take your bed and go
       'Who is the man that told you to take your bed and go?'
       (ÆHom_2:47.270)

   b. þa cwæð se casere him to, Hwi **come$_V$ þu$_S$** swa late?
      then said the king him to, why come you so late
      'Then the king said to him: Why do you come so late?'
      (ÆHom_8:143.1239)

c. Ne **meaht**_{AUX} þu deman_V Gallia biscopas buton heora agenre
    not might   you judge   Gaul's bishops but   their own
    aldorlicnesse,
    authority
    'You might not judge the Gaul's bishops but their own authority.'
    (Bede_1:16.74.5.679)
    ne_{NEG} **cræwþ**_V [se hana]_S todæg ær   þu me ætsæcst.
    not   crows   the cock   today before you me deny
    'The cock will not crow today until you deny me.'
    (Lk_[WSCp]:22.34.5465)

As you can clearly see, in these contexts no contrast between subjects as full phrases and pronouns occur: regardless of their status, the subjects of these sentences are in a position directly following the question word and the finite verb. The same applies to sentences introduced by a negation element.

In OHG, subject pronouns in these contexts do not cause a violation of Verb Second either: as in OE above, they occur directly after the question and negation word, and the finite verb:

(15) a. /uuvo **gisahi**_V **thu**_S abrahaman?/
         how   saw   you   Abraham
         'How can you have seen Abraham?'
         (Tatian,451,7)
     b. ni_{NEG} **quad**_V **ih**_S fon iu   allen/
         not   spoke I   of you all
         'I haven't spoken of all of you.'
         (Tatian,553,21)

Another context which does not exhibit violation of the Verb Second pattern are sentences with the initial temporal adverb þa/þonne 'then' and nu 'now':

(16) a. þonne **afylde**_V **he**_S symle   hys fynd
         then   defiled   he   continually his fiend
         'Then he continually defiled his enemy.'
         (Mart_2.1_[Herzfeld-Kotzor]:Ju25,A.18.28)
     b. Nu **cweðe**_V **ge**_S, þæt ge ne magon beon butan wimmannes þenungum.
         now say   you   that you not may be   but   women's   attendants
         'Now you say that you may not be all but women's attendants.'
         (ÆLet_1_[Wulfsige_Xa]:15.16)

The same seems to apply to OHG:

(17) /[noh] nu **niarsteig**$_V$ **ih**$_S$/ zi minemo fater/
yet now NEG-ascended I to my father
'I am not yet ascended to my Father.'
(T 665,24 in Axel 2007:248)

We will see below that this context was one of the first contexts exhibiting **synchronic variation** between Verb Second and Verb Third orders in ME times, which can be analysed as an indicator of the gradual loss of the phenomenon.

Although NHG is a Verb Second language, the status of pronominal subjects and objects are different from OE and OHG. First, regardless of the type of subject, it systematically occurs under the conditions discussed above:

(18) a. [Bronzene Pforten]$_O$ **zerschmetterte**$_V$ [der **Mann**$_S$] und fand den verborgenen Schatz.
b. [Bronzene Pforten]$_O$ **zerschmetterte**$_V$ [er$_S$] und fand den verborgenen Schatz.
'The man/he shattered bronze gates and found the hidden treasure.'

Second, object pronouns cannot violate Verb Second:

(19) a. *[Dein eigener Glaube]$_S$ **dich**$_O$ geheilt hat.
b. [Dein eigener Glaube]$_S$ **hat**$_V$ **dich**$_O$ geheilt.
'Your own faith has healed you.'
c. *Ich fand den verborgenen Schatz und **dir**$_O$ ich ihn **gebe**$_V$.
d. Ich fand den verborgenen Schatz und ich **gebe**$_V$ ihn **dir**$_O$.
'I found the hidden treasure and I give it to you.'

The ungrammatical sentences violate the Verb Second pattern because the pronominal object intervenes between the first constituent and the finite verb. In the grammatical sentences, the finite verb occurs in second position and is followed by the object(s).

The Verb Second and **Verb Third** patterns discussed so far are summarised schematically in Table 17.2 (note that 'XP' stands for 'any constituent which is not the subject').

In the final part of this chapter, we will deal with the further development of Verb Second, i.e. its loss in the course of time. You will see that the status of subjects will play an important role in this process.

Table 17.2. Verb Second and Verb Third patterns in OE and OHG

Main sentence	Position 1	Position 2	Position 3
	XP	V_{fin}	full subject
	XP	subject pronoun	V_{fin} (variation in OHG)
	wh/NEG/þa/nu	V_{fin}	full subject/pronoun
Subordinate clause	**Position 1**	**Position 2**	**Position 3**
bridge verb + complementiser	XP	V_{fin}	subject

17.2 Loss of Verb Second in English

In chapter 16 the dialectal situation in ME times was introduced, and it was said that concerning the absence/presence of OV and VO orders, dialects behaved quite differently. The southern texts investigated exhibited more OV orders and seemed to behave more conservatively (following OE patterns) whereas the northern texts behaved more innovatively by exhibiting more instances of VO orders. In this chapter, we would like to see if this variation across dialects can also be found for the Verb Second phenomenon. So the prediction is that southern texts behave like OE texts showing all the Verb Second patterns discussed above, and the northern texts behave in a more innovative way showing violations of Verb Second.

In the following, I will concentrate on two texts to illustrate differences as clearly as possible: I will compare one southern text written in Kent with one northern text written in West Yorkshire. The first text is the *Ayenbite of Inwyt* (which can be translated into 'The remorse of conscience') which was written by a monk called Dan Michel in 1340. The text is a direct translation of the French work *La somme le roi* by Friar Laurent in 1279. The second text is *The Northern Prose Rule of St. Benet* which was written in about 1425 and is said to be the first northern prose document. In the following, we will take a look at all of the Verb Second contexts we have extensively discussed above for OE (we restrict ourselves however to main declaratives).
Let's start with the southern text:

(20) a. *[þis article]$_O$ zette$_V$ [saynte peter]$_S$.*
       this article   set   Saint   Peter
       'This article Saint Peter ordained.'
       (AYENBI,12.151)

b. [To þise zeue digtinges]$_{PP}$ / **belongeþ**$_V$ [alle þe zennes]$_S$ / þet byþ
to these seven divisions belong all the sins that are
y-bore of prede.
born of pride
'To these seven division all the sins belong that are caused by pride.'
(AYENBI,17.255)

c. Efterward$_{Adv}$ / **comþ**$_V$ **sleuþe**$_S$.
afterwards comes sloth
'Afterwards sloth comes.'
(AYENBI,32.532)

d. [of þisen]$_{PP}$ / **we**$_S$ **habbeþ**$_{AUX}$ yspeke$_V$ aboue.
of these we have spoken above
'We have spoken of these above.'
(AYENBI,44.748)

The first three examples (20) are those which unambiguously exhibit Verb Second in main declaratives since they are introduced by an object, a PP and a temporal adverbial. All of them display a full phrase as subject and subject-verb inversion. The example in d. exhibits the violation of Verb Second: as in OE, the subject pronoun (*we*) intervenes between the first constituent (the PP *of þisen* and the finite verb *habbeþ*). The contexts where Verb Second is never violated are constituent questions and negative sentences. Concerning the other contexts like sentences introduced by *þa/þanne*, *nu* etc. the gradual loss of Verb Second is observable: compare (21) b. and c:

(21) a. and acseþ. 'And **huer is**$_V$ nou [þe ilke dyaþ]$_S$. and huanne ssel$_{AUX}$ he$_S$
and asks and where is now the same death and when shall he
come$_V$?'
come
'and asks: 'And where is the same death now? And when shall he come?"
(AYENBI,264.2534)

b. **þanne is**$_V$ **he**$_S$ / of þe kende / of þe baselycoc.
then is he of the kind of the basilisk
'Then he is of the kind of the basilisk.'
(AYENBI,28.434)

c. **þanne he playþ** ate des.
then he plays at dice
'Then he plays dice.'
(AYENBI,51.905)

The context with *þa/þanne* as first constituent displays variation between Verb Second and Verb Third with a pronominal subject. In Table 17.3 which provides the results of

Kroch & Taylor's (1997) study on Verb Second in the *Ayenbite of Inwyt* this tendency is evident:

Table 17.3. Verb Second in the Ayenbite of Inwyt (Kroch & Taylor 1997:312)

preposed element	NP subjects			pronoun subjects		
	number inverted	number uninverted	% inverted	number inverted	number uninverted	% inverted
NP complement	14	3	82	1	11	08
PP complement	2	0	100	0	1	00
ADJ. complement	5	0	100	0	1	00
than	4	12	25	7	5	58
nou	1	0	100	7	7	50
PP adjunct	5	9	36	1	30	03
any other adverb	19	15	56	5	52	10

If you compare the figures in the table you see that in almost all contexts subject-verb inversion occurs if the subject is a full phrase. The exceptions are adjuncts and adverbs (including 'then'). Whenever the subject is a pronoun, subject-verb inversion is much less likely to occur except in sentences introduced by *than*, *nou* and some other adverbs where we find lower rates of inversion. Overall, however, this text preserved the OE Verb Second pattern quite well.

Let's compare this finding to the data from the northern text:

(22) a. *Glutunie$_O$ luue$_V$ þai$_S$.*
gluttony love they
'They love gluttony.'
(BENRUL,4.116)

b. *[In þis sentence]$_{PP}$ mustirs$_V$ [sain benet]$_S$ us hu we sal lede ure lif,*
in this sentence musters saint benet us how we shall lead our life
'In this sentence Saint Benet tells us how we shall lead our lives.'
(BENRUL,2.37)

c. *þus$_{Adv}$ kennis$_V$ [ure lauerd]$_S$ us his werkis, at folu his cumandementis.*
thus teaches our lord us his works to follow his commandments
'Thus, our lord teaches us his works to follow his commandments.'
(BENRUL,3.67)

d. *Now$_{Adv}$ haue$_{AUX}$ we$_S$ deuisid$_V$ þe ordir of þe salmis on þe niht, at*
now have we devised the order of the psalms in the night, at
matins.
matins
'Now we have devised the order of the psalms in the night and at matins.'
(BENRUL,18.617)

e. *þan*~Adv~ **prai**~V~ **we**~S~ *þus:* 'Lauerd, þu   for-giue vs ure sinnis, ...'
   then   pray   we   thus   lord   thou forgive us our sins
   'Then we pray thus: 'Lord, forgive us our sins ..."
   (BENRUL,19.638)

The examples in (22) exhibit consistent Verb Second, i.e., subject-verb inversion in all contexts. Strikingly, inversion is also found in contexts with sentence-initial *þan* and *now*. This finding stands in clear contrast to the findings from the southern text. If we take a look at other constituents in initial position, like PP adjuncts, we do find some instances of uninverted pronominal subjects as you can see below:

(23) a. *[By-tuix þalde]*~PP-ADJ~ **þai**~S~ **sal**~AUX~ *lie*~V~.
        between the-old   they   shall   lie
        'They shall lie between the old.'
        (BENRUL,20.701)

    b. *[Yef þai ete at midday]*~PP-ADJ~, **sho**~S~ **salle**~AUX~ *ete*~V~ *at noon*;
        if they eat at midday   she   shall   eat   at noon
        'If they eat at midday, she shall eat at noon.'
        (BENRUL,21.724)

However, these cases are rather rare, and a look at the table below confirms this:

Table 17.4. Verb Second in the Northern Prose Rule of St. Benet (Kroch & Taylor 1997:313)

	NP subjects			pronoun subjects		
preposed element	number inverted	number uninverted	% inverted	number inverted	number uninverted	% inverted
NP complement	7	0	100	58	3	95
PP complement	18	0	100	10	0	100
ADJ. complement	1	0	100	4	2	67
then	15	0	100	28	1	97
now	–	–	–	2	0	100
PP adjunct	42	5	89	73	7	91
any other adverb	25	1	96	51	5	91

So, by looking at Verb Second data from these two texts from different dialectal regions, synchronic variation in ME times can be observed. If we included texts from other regions like the East and the West Midlands we would even get a more diverse picture. The synchronic variation observed implies that a change is going on here, one that leads from the OE Verb Second grammar to the gradual loss of this property. But if this property is lost, why is the northern text even more consistent in displaying

Verb Second? One explanation suggested to explain this empirical observation is that again, it might have to do with Scandinavian (Old Norse) influence on English. Since other grammatical features seem to have been borrowed, this aspect could have been borrowed too. More precisely, in the literature it has been assumed that Old Norse Verb Second was more consistent and systematic than OE Verb Second. This means that regardless of the status of the subject, the finite verb always had to occur in second position, which is exactly the state of affairs we find today in NHG. Since it was the region of the Danelaw including northern and north eastern dialectal areas, where the Scandinavians predominantly settled back then due to this language contact situation, their version of Verb Second was borrowed by the English speakers in this region. These assumptions can then explain the dialectal difference between Verb Second in the northern text, which is more consistent, and Verb Second in the southern text, which is less consistent as the OE pattern was. However, another question related to this line of argument is why English lost Verb Second in the end. After all, languages like NHG and the Modern Scandinavian languages, which all display consistent Verb Second, have not lost this property. A satisfying answer has not been proposed so far, but some say that English lost the ability of verbs to appear in the second position in the clause for system internal reasons. In the next chapter, we will deal with this property from a more theoretical point of view when we discuss verb movement.

Instances of Verb Second still occur after the ME period, as the examples of EModE given below demonstrate:

(24) a. Then **sayd**$_V$ **they**$_S$ vnto him: what arte thou that we maye geve an answer to them that sent vs.
'Then they said to him: who are you that we may give and answer to them that sent us.'
(TYNDNEW-E1-H,1,20J.44)

b. Than **sayed**$_V$ *[my lord cheffe justyes]*$_S$ unto me, "Syr, whate make yow here?
'Then my overlord said to me, 'Syr, why are you here?"
(MOWNTAYNE-E1-H,206.171)

c. Thus **passed**$_V$ **they**$_S$ this night, after having received from the slaves all imaginable respect and obedience.
'Thus they passed this night, after having received from the slaves all imaginable respect and obedience.'
(BEHN-E3-H,189.144)

In the corpus, most instances of main declaratives with Verb Second occur in the first subperiod, i.e. from 1500 to 1569, but as you can see from the examples above, the pattern still occurs at the end of the EModE period (indicated by E3) around about

1660. The pattern however becomes more and more restricted to some contexts, in the examples it occurs when the first constituent is an adverb(ial).

Even in the corpus of Modern British English (1700–1910) instances of Verb Second appear:

(25) a. *[Some Days after]*, **came**$_V$ *[the Cacique, or petty Prince of those People]*$_S$, *clad in Skins, follow'd by many of his People naked, but painted, some white, some black, and some with other Colours.*
'Some days after, the Cacique, or petty prince of those people came, clothed in skins, followed by many of his people naked, but painted, some white, some black, and some with other colours.'
(COOKE-1712,1,433.210)
b. *'I see it',* **replied**$_V$ **Sam**$_S$, *with a placid nod of the head.*
'I see it', Sam replied, with a placid nod of the head.
(DICKENS-1837,546.44)
c. *'Like it, or dislike it',* **said**$_V$ *[a vigorous teacher]*$_S$ *once to a class of boys in my presence.*
''Like it or dislike it', a vigorous teacher once said to a class of boys in my presence.'
(BENSON-1908,42.75)

As above, it is restricted to some contexts, either to sentences introduced by an adverbial or directly after a part of direct speech. The latter is actually still found in novels as example (26) a. shows. The example in b. where the main declarative is introduced by the temporal adverb *then* and followed by the archaic forms of the verb *be* and the second person singular pronoun *you* reflect a period of time where in this context, Verb Second was still possible. In c. a PP with the function of a locative adverbial is the first constituent, followed by the finite verb and the subject. In the literature, this pattern is called **locative inversion**.

Apart from these very rare instances of the pattern, and in the contexts of *wh*-questions and negative sentences, it has vanished from today's English.

(26) a. *'Last time we did this you were a kitten',* **said**$_V$ **Marina**$_S$. *'Are you growing up?'*
(BNC, A0L 2773–4, sample from prose fiction *Jay loves Lucy*, 1993)
b. *Then* **art**$_V$ **thou**$_S$ *modest, and the wine grows bold ...*
(BNC CFF 668, sample from the book *Alternative saints*, 1989)
c. *[Down the stairs]* **came**$_V$ *[the cat]*$_S$, *sullen-eyed.*
(BNC AD1 749, sample from the book *Ladies and Gentlemen*, 1968)

Syn: 'Now let's see if you have understood what a Verb Second language is. Here are your tasks: **1)** are both OE and OHG Verb Second languages? If so, which examples in the text clearly and unambiguously demonstrate this? Identify these examples and describe the word order found; **2)** in ME, two different types of Verb Second occur. In which varieties do they occur and which explanation is given in the text? **3)** describe the Verb Second patterns illustrated with the examples below. Which examples display deviations and how can they be accounted for?'

Old English

(27) a. *Wel wiste Crist   hwæt he don wolde.*
     wel knew Christ what he don wanted
     'Christ knew well what he wanted to do.'
     (ÆCHom_I,_12:276.45.2222)
   b. *Ðæt he dyde on Sigeberhtes dagum þæs cyninges.*
     That he did in Sigeberhtes days   the kings
     'That he did in the days of King Sigeberth.'
     (Mart_5_[Kotzor]:Ja16,B.18.115)
   c. *Him andwyrde se bisceop, Forgeafe God ælmihtig þæt ðu fyligdest wysdome;*
     Him answered the bishop, 'Forgave God almighty, that you followed wisdom'
     'The bishop answered him, 'May God Almighty forgive you that you followed wisdom.'
     (ÆLS_[Basil]:210.588)

(28) a. *þe tresur   of god er þai.*
     the treasure of God are they
     'They are the treasure of God.'
     (BENRUL,7.199)
   b. *þan seid ich, Se!*
     than said I   see
     'Then I said: 'See!''
     (EARLPS,48.2093)
   c. *In þis ȝere regneth Darius, þe vii   kyng in Perse,*
     in this year reigned Darius the seven king in Persia
     In this year Darius VII, king of Persia, reigned.
     (CAPCHR,40.272)
   d. *þan þei left her childe in Pruce wyth her frendys,*
     then they left her child in Pruce with her friends
     'Then they left her child in Pruce with her friends.'
     (KEMPE,225.3636)

Tax: 'Now, what have we learnt in this chapter?'
Syn: 'First, we wanted to know whether OE and OHG were Verb Second languages. This was confirmed by looking at main declaratives with a non-subject in initial position followed by the finite verb and the subject. We found that in this respect, both languages behaved quite similarly to NHG and quite

dissimilarly to PDE. As concerns the question of whether OE and OHG were symmetric or asymmetric Verb Second languages, we came to the conclusion that in subordinate clauses Verb Second occurs in a restricted set of clauses, namely those which are complements of *verba dicendi*, and therefore both languages are asymmetric Verb Second languages.'

Tax: 'And we observed an exception to the Verb Second rule which was triggered by the status of the subject: whenever it was a subject pronoun it intervened between the first constituent and the finite verb resulting in Verb Third. Although both OE and OHG showed examples adhering to this rule, we have seen that in OHG there is variation, i.e. sometimes Verb Second occurs, sometimes Verb Third occurs. Compared with OE, NHG behaves differently in this respect because Verb Second consistently occurs, regardless of the status of the subject.'

Syn: 'Right. And finally, we dealt with the development of Verb Second knowing that PDE is no longer a language with this property. In ME, we investigated a northern and a southern text and found that there were clear differences between the two. The southern text was quite similar to the OE Verb Second pattern because, in most cases where the subject was a pronoun, there was no inversion of the finite verb and the subject. In the northern text, however, in this context Verb Second also occurred quite systematically and therefore behaved rather like NHG and other Modern Germanic languages. We briefly discussed how we could explain this difference and said that one possibility was to assume language contact with the Scandinavians which led to the borrowing of consistent Verb Second in the northern dialects. Finally, we saw that until PDE, residues of Verb Second occur but restricted to a small set of contexts, namely, in *wh*-questions, negative sentences, in quotations from older texts like e.g. the Bible, and after direct speech.'

Literature: den Besten (1983) is one of the first papers which defines Verb Second as movement to the C position. In Vikner (1995) verb movement and transitive expletive constructions are discussed. This includes a discussion on Germanic languages possessing (a)symmetric Verb Second. A CP-recursion analysis for embedded Verb Second languages is proposed. In Rizzi (1990) the term 'Residual Verb Second' is suggested for the first time, and commented on in Kiparsky (1995). Kroch and Taylor (1997) was discussed in length above. The paper explains the loss of Verb Second in ME times by assuming language contact between Northern and Southern dialects (whereby the Northern dialects may have been influenced by Scandinavian). Kroch et al. (2000) is a case study of Verb Second in ME and pursues the question of whether language contact with Scandinavian can be seen as a cause for this change. Haeberli (2002) discusses a possible correlation between inflectional morphology and the loss of Verb Second in English. In Trips and Fuss (2009) one Verb Second context—sentence-initial *þa* in OE—is investigated. The traditional analysis of this context as operator context is called into question and a new analysis where the adverb has anaphoric/deictic properties is proposed. Axel (2007) is a comprehensive work on verb placement and Verb Second in OHG. In Santorini (1995) two types of Verb Second in Yiddish are discussed.

18 Syntactic movement in the history of English

In this chapter, we will take a more theoretical standpoint and interpret the data we have come across so far (and some new data as well) in a theoretical framework which assumes **movement**. As you might have already guessed, this framework is generative grammar. Reading the chapters 6 of part I and 12 of part II you already have the necessary background knowledge to understand why a notion like movement can be very helpful in explaining language data, or why the assumption of the presence or absence of movement can explain differences between languages.

18.1 Loss of verb movement

We will address these aspects by looking at examples from OE and PDE. Try to analyse the structure of the following example that you are hopefully familiar with by now, by focussing particularly on the relative order of the finite verb and the subject:

(1) [On his dagum]$_{Adv}$ **sende**$_V$ Gregorius$_S$ us fulluht.
    in his days   sent   Gregory   us Christianity
    'In his days, **Gregory sent** us Christianity.'
    (ChronA,:565.1.207)

In OE, the finite verb *sende* is inverted with the subject *Gregorius*, i.e. subject-verb inversion occurs in this sentence. This is not surprising since it is a case of Verb Second. In the translation of PDE however, the finite verb *sent* is not inverted with the subject *Gregory*, i.e. subject-verb inversion does not occur. If we added further OE examples exhibiting Verb Second we would find the same pattern: subject-verb inversion whenever the initial constituent is a non-subject, and no inversion in the translation of PDE. But what about these examples?

(2) a. Hwæt **sculon**$_{AUX}$ **we**$_S$ þæs   nu ma secgan$_V$?
       what shall   we   afterwards now more say
       'What **shall we** say now more afterwards?'
       (Bede_2:9.132.1.1253)
    b. and cwæð, Hwær **lede**$_V$ **ge**$_S$ hine?
       and said   where lay   you   him?
       '... and said: where **did you** lay him?'
       (ÆHom_6:77.915)

In the question context in OE, we see that subject-verb inversion occurs as well: in the example in (2) a. the finite verb *sculon* precedes the subject pronoun *we*, and in b. the finite verb *lede* precedes the subject *ge*. But what about PDE? The translation of the OE example in a. has the same order: *wh*-element-V$_{fin}$-subject pronoun. In b. however, a form of *do* is inserted which inverts with the subject. The lexical verb *lay* occurs in the infinitive after the subject pronoun: *wh*-element-V$_{fin}$(*do*)-subject pronoun-Vnonfinite-object.

Also recall that in OE subordinate clauses, the finite (lexical) verb most frequently occurred right at the end of (subordinate) clauses following the object, and not in the second position (for exceptions see chapter 14 above):

(3) ond he þohte   þæt he$_S$ **hi$_O$ gebismrode$_V$.**
and he thought that he them mocked
'and he thought that he **mocked them**'.
(Mart_5_[Kotzor]:Ap3,A.9.509)

Concerning the position of the finite (lexical) verb in main declaratives (Verb Second) and subordinate clauses we can see differences between OE and PDE. Now take a look at some further examples:

(4) a. *Moyses him **abæd oft**   miltsunge.*
Moses him bid   often pardon
'Moses **often asked** him to have mercy.'
(ÆHom_1:228.128)
b. *Ure Drihten **sæde oft**   swiðe digle   bigspell;*
our lord   said often very obscure examples
'Our Lord **often gave** very obscure examples.'
(ÆHom_3:1.397)
c. *Soðlice   se halga wer Benedictus ne **aras na** fram his rædingce,*
Certainly the holy man Benedictus not arose not from his reading
'Certainly, Benedict, the holy man, did **not rise** from his lessons.'
(GD_2_[C]:31.164.22.1978)

What is of interest here for us is the relative order of the finite (lexical) verb and VP adverbs like *oft* 'often' or the negative adverb *na* 'not (at all)'. In example (4) a. the finite lexical verb *abæd* directly precedes the adverb *oft* 'often', and in the b. example we have the same state of affairs between *sæde* 'said' and *oft*. In c. the pattern is similar, here the finite lexical verb *aras* 'rose' directly precedes the negative adverb *na* 'not (at all)'. If you compare the OE version with the PDE version, you will see that in the first two cases with *often*, the order is reversed, whereas in PDE in the c. case, the past tense form of the auxiliary *do* occurs which is directly followed by the negation *not* and the lexical verb in the infinitive (*rise*). So it seems that we have two inversion patterns in OE which we don't have in PDE. I have summarised these patterns in the table below:

Table 18.1. Inversion patterns in OE and PDE

1. Relative order S-V_{fin} (Verb Second)				S-V inversion
OE	XP	V_{fin}	subject	yes
PDE	XP	subject	V_{fin}	no
OE	*wh*-element *neg*-element	V_{fin}	subject	yes
PDE	*wh*-element *neg*-element	V_{fin}(Aux)	subject	with Aux
2. Relative order V_{fin}-adverb (VP-adverb-verb inversion)				S-V inversion
OE	subject	V_{fin}	*oft*	yes
PDE	subject	*often*	V_{fin}	no
OE	subject	V_{fin}	*na/ne*	yes
PDE	subject	*not*	V_{fin}	no

The first pattern can be described as subject-verb inversion in main declaratives, i.e. in Verb Second contexts. In OE the finite verb occurs in second position, it can either be the lexical verb or an auxiliary. In contrast, PDE does not allow the finite lexical verb to be inverted with the subject (no V2). In contexts with a wh-element (or a negative element) in first position both OE and PDE show the same order: in OE general inversion of the finite verb with the subject, in PDE inversion of the finite form of an auxiliary with the subject.

For the moment, the second pattern can be described as **VP-adverb-verb inversion**, which is not restricted to sentence type. In OE, the finite verb inverts with the adverb and can be a lexical verb. In PDE, the inversion of VP-adverb and finite lexical verb is not possible. These are the empirical facts. Next, we are going to analyse these facts in the generative framework by saying that the occurrence of subject-verb and VP-adverb-verb inversion can be explained by verb movement.

Recall that the notion of movement is based on the assumption that the structure of an expression in (any) language can be described at two levels (recall what was said about the **Theory of Government & Binding** in part I, chapter 6, see also part II, chapter 12): a deep level (**D-structure**) and a surface level (**S-structure**). These two levels are linked by **transformations** which mainly involve moving elements from one position to another. At both levels a number of principles apply: at the deep level, these are principles that are responsible for the basic organisation of the structure, and at the surface level principles apply that regulate movement. Here, we will leave aside the further development of movement into the much more general concept of **Move** α which states 'move any element anywhere' (for checking reasons). For details I refer you to the works cited below.

Although different types of movement are distinguished, we will focus on one type which directly involves verbs, i.e. head movement (movement of a head of a phrase rather than a whole phrase). We will see that in OE the movement of lexical verbs to a functional head is possible whereas in PDE it is not. To illustrate this type of movement in a structure, we will use the following tree diagram:

(5)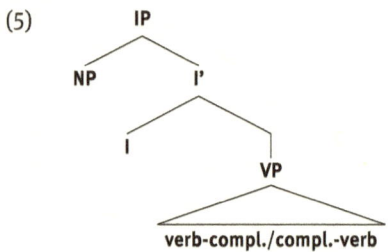

Take a look again at the differences between OE and PDE:

(6) a. OE: He asked **often** about her job.
 PDE: He **often** asked about her job.
 b. OE: He rose **not**.
 PDE: He did **not** rise.

Let's assume that the adverbs *oft/often* and *na/not* have about the same properties and therefore occur in the same position in a sentence (see Pollock, 1989 for similar assumptions based on contrasts between English and French and part II, chapter 12). I indicated this by aligning these elements. It has also been said that these elements mark the left edge of the VP, so if an element appears to the left of them, we know that it is outside the VP. What you immediately see now is that the different orders observed between OE and PDE result from different positions of the lexical verb: in OE to the left of the adverbs, in PDE to the right. Moreover, in the example with negation in PDE, the past tense form of *do* occurs in the same position as the OE past tense form *rose*, and the PDE infinitive form *rise* occurs right after *not*, just as in the example above with *asked* occurring right after *often*. In generative terms, we say that in OE the finite form of lexical verbs occur higher (in the tree) than in PDE. This difference is illustrated with the following trees:

(7)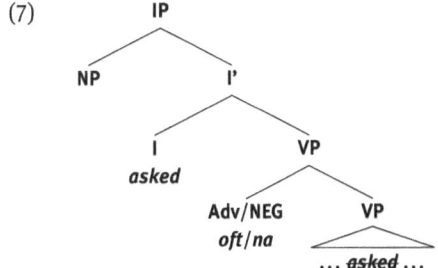

As the tree in (7) shows, in OE the lexical verb can move to a higher position; it is assumed that it moves to the functional head I (remember that I stands for Inflection), since it is the position where 'inflectional' information about Tense and Agreement is located (as discussed in part II of the book, this position is often called T(ense)). This instance of verb movement is also called V-to-I (or V-to-T) movement.

(8)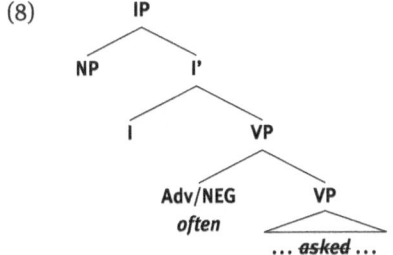

In contrast, in PDE the finite lexical verb cannot move to this position and has to stay down in V, i.e. within the VP. However, the lexical verb is finite bearing inflections of tense and agreement which means that it must get together somehow with I, even though it does not leave the VP. As mentioned in part II, chapter 12.2, to resolve this theoretical problem Chomsky (1957) proposed a process called affix hopping whereby inflections move down to the verb. Note that it involves rightward and downward movement which is quite unusual and violates a number of principles (for further details I refer you to Chomsky's work itself and Cook and Newson (2007)).

What about the example where in PDE the auxiliary *do* occurs? Since the auxiliary occurs to the left of *not*, it must be in a higher position than the V-position. Take a look at the following tree:

(9)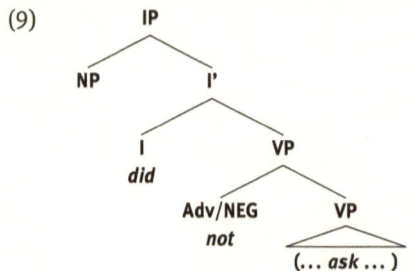

You can see that *did* is inserted in the I position because the lexical verb *ask* is stuck inside the VP. Since the auxiliary *do* carries all the 'inflectional' information here, the lexical verb is in the infinitive. As a first result we can say that in OE finite lexical verbs can move from V to I whereas in PDE this is not possible. Auxiliaries like *do* occur in I (we will come back to this point below).

But what about sentences lacking adverbs of this type? For illustration purposes let's use the OE example from above without the adverb *oft*:

(10) *Ure Drihten **sæde** swiðe digle   bigspell;*
 our lord   said very obscure examples
 'Our Lord **gave** very obscure examples.' (ÆHom_3:1.397)

Due to the properties of lexical verbs in OE, i.e. due to their rather rich morphological inflection, we assume that they always move from V to I. In sentences where the left periphery of the VP is marked by VP-adverbs we can 'see' this directly, in sentences lacking these adverbs we cannot. But since we know that in OE lexical verbs have this property, we would say that the finite verb *sæde* has moved from V to I, and this applies to all other sentences.

Another instance of verb movement operates on Verb Second sentences. We said that in these cases subject-verb inversion occurs. Since the subject of a sentence is assumed to be located in the specifier of IP, inversion implies that the finite verb occurs higher than the subject, or in more descriptive terms, to the left of it. To explain these structures, another functional projection, the C(omplementiser) Phrase, is added:

(11)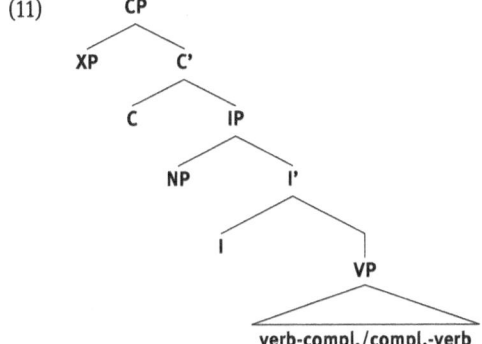

In OE Verb Second structures, the initial constituent occupies the position in the specifier of CP, and the finite lexical verb occurs in C. It is assumed that it moves from V to I to C. This is illustrated in the tree below:

(12)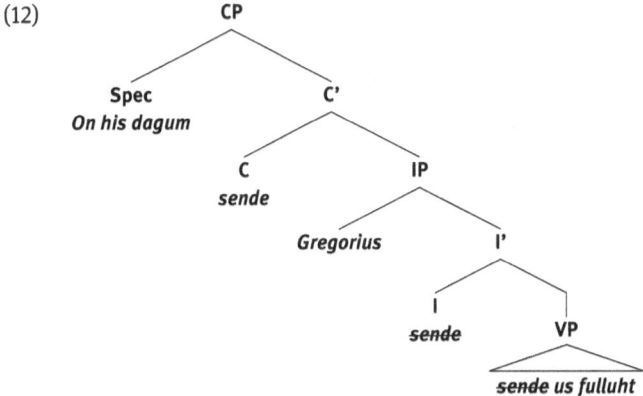

For OHG the same applies, so all the examples we discussed in chapter 17 would have tree structures like (12). Recall that OE was similar to NHG in a number of respects, for example word order. Thus, the translation of the OE sentence above into NHG would be: *In diesen Tagen sandte Gregorius uns den christlichen Glauben.*

We said above that verb movement is head movement, which simply means that a finite (lexical) verb moves from the head V position to the head I position of IP, and, in the case of Verb Second, to the head C position of CP. So if verb movement is possible, it happens in small steps from one head position to another head position. Because of that it has been said that both V-to-I movement and I-to-C movement are **local operations**. Travis (1984) and others have claimed that this 'behaviour' of verbs is not accidental but rather subject to some principle of UG. She called it the **Head Movement Constraint** which states that a head can only move from the head position in one phrase to the head position in the immediately containing phrase in the structure. I leave it to you to verify this constraint by looking again at the structures we have discussed so far in this chapter.

In PDE, lexical verbs cannot undergo verb movement, and as a result, subject-verb inversion does not occur and the equivalent sentences do not display Verb Second. Instead, the lexical verb remains in V. In questions, things are different: in both OE and PDE the finite verb occurs in the C position and the *wh*-element in the specifier of CP. Whereas in OE finite lexical verbs and auxiliaries are located in C, in PDE only auxiliaries can occupy this position; lexical verbs have to stay in V. So only auxiliaries can undergo I-to-C movement in these cases. Take a look at the following trees and check if you have understood the analysis of these sentences.

(13)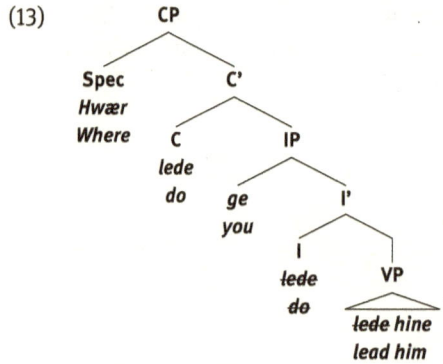

(14)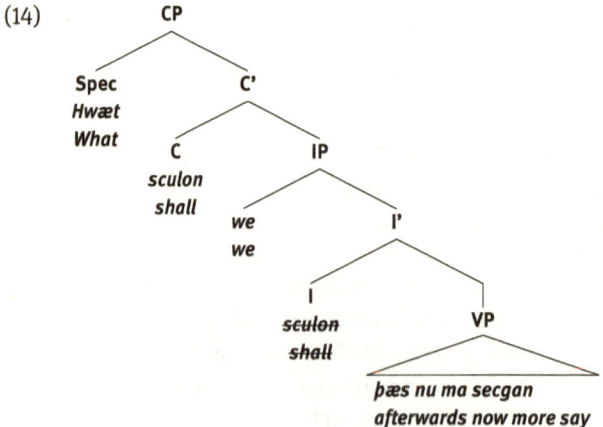

In the tree in (14) OE *sculon* and its PDE equivalent *shall* seem to have the same properties, i.e. they are auxiliaries and undergo movement from I-to-C. This is only partly correct because *sculon*, the predecessor of today's *shall*, actually used to be a lexical verb in OE and ME times. We can see that by looking at its lexical semantics: according to the OED it carried meanings like 'owe money or allegiance to somebody', which shows that it used to be a (di)transitive verb requiring one or more complements. This can be seen by looking at the following examples cited in the OED:

(15) a. *Seþe* **sculde** *him undred denera.*
    He (who) owed   him hundred dinarii
    'He (who) owed him a hundred dinarii.'
    (c975,Rushw.Gosp.Matt.xviii.28)
  b. *Be the fayth ic* **schal** *to God.*
    By the faith I owe to God
    'By the faith I owe God.'
    (c1325,Poem temp.Edw.II(Percy Soc.)xxxiv)

Other verbs like OE *willan*, *magan*, *cunnan* and *motan*, which are translated into PDE as the modals *will*, *may*, *can* and *must* had the same properties as *sculan*, i.e. they all behaved like lexical verbs in OE and ME times. The main characteristics of lexical verbs are that they have full person-number paradigms (exhibiting subject-verb agreement), they may take objects, they can occur adjacent to each other in series, and in infinitives and gerunds. Moreover, in OE they could occur in sentence-final position like other lexical verbs. I give some further examples from the OED here which confirm these facts:

(16) a. *Ne drincð nan man eald win, &* **wylle** *sona þæt niwe.*
    not drinks no man old   wine and wants soon the new
    'No man drinks old wine and immediately wants to have the new one.'
    (c1000,West Saxon Gospels: Luke (Corpus Cambr.)v.39)
  b. *Ðeos wyrt ...* **mæg** *wiðmanega untrumnyssa.*
    this herb ... avails against-many illnesses
    'This herb ... helps against many illnesses.'
    (OE,tr.Pseudo-Apuleius Herbarium (Vitell.),(1984) clxxi.214)
  c. *Ne* **can** *ic eow.*
    not know I you
    'I don't know you.'
    (c1000,West Saxon Gospels: Matt. (Corpus Cambr.) xxv. 12
  d. *Hie ... eft wæron biddende þæt Metellus to Rome* **moste**.
    they ... often were bidding   that Metellus to Rome wished
    'They ... were often asking if Metellus might be permitted to go to Rome.'
    (eOE,tr.Orosius Hist.(BL Add.)v.ix.123)

18.2 The rise of modals and *do*-support

Lightfoot (1979, 1991) was one of the first to deal with syntactic change within the generative framework and especially with the development of **modals** in the history of English. In all the Germanic languages a set of verbs occurs with properties that set them apart from other verbs. They are the so-called **preterite-present verbs** because at one point their preterite forms were reanalysed as present tense forms. Evidence for this change is the fact that these verbs do not exhibit third person singular forms. Compare the following examples:

(17) a. *gif heo **sceal** to heofonum fleogan.*
　　　if she oblige to heaven 　　fly
　　　'I she shall fly to heaven.'
　　　(Ad:27.1.64)

　　b. *& fela ðinga, ðe ic nu genæmnian ne **can**, ...*
　　　and many things that I now address　　not know
　　　'and many things that I cannot address now.'
　　　(LawGer:17.30)

　　c. *þa **cwæþ** se engel to hire, Se Halga Gast **cymeþ** ufon　　on þe,*
　　　then says the angel to her the holy ghost comes from-above on you
　　　'Then the angel says to her: 'The Holy Ghost comes down on you from above."
　　　(HomU_18_[BlHom_1]:7.75.77)

In the examples above, both the third person singular present tense forms *sceal* and *can* lack the inflectional marker *-eþ/-es* which occur on lexical verbs as in *cwæþ* and *cymeþ* (also compare PDG: *Er singt ein Lied* 'He sings a song' vs. *Er kann singen* 'He can sing a song.'). Lightfoot suggests that morphological peculiarities like these were responsible for the changes that affected this set of verbs.

Lightfoot states that the OE **premodals** given above were subject to **reanalysis** which can be seen by the fact that in the course of time, they lost the properties of lexical verbs and developed into auxiliaries. More precisely, they lost their ability to take objects and they became inflectionally distinct after the loss of other preterite-present verbs (like *dugan* 'be capable of', *þurfan* 'be under an obligation'; see the PDG equivalents *taugen* and *dürfen*). Further, their present and past tenses became non-temporal in certain senses due to the loss of the subjunctive mood, and they were never followed by the infinitive marker *to*. The reanalysis consisted of **recategorisation**: the OE premodals were categorised in the lexicon as verbs but came to be recategorised as grammatical/functional verbs (auxiliaries), or as Lightfoot puts it: 'INFL markers' (1991:142). As a result, they came to be base generated under I (**I-insertion**) and could thus no longer undergo verb movement from V to I. Since *do* also developed from being a lexical verb to becoming an auxiliary (so-called 'dummy do'), the I position became a position for a subclass of verbs (lacking verbal properties). In the course of time, all lexical verbs of English lost the property to raise from V to I (note that today the modals have the status of auxiliaries only whereas *do* can function both as an auxiliary and lexical verb). One explanation for the latter change was put forward by Vikner who formulated the following condition on verb raising:

> An SVO language has V-to-I movement if and only if person morphology is found in all tenses. (Vikner, 1995, 200)

What this means is that the loss of inflectional morphology in English might have led to the loss of verb movement. We have already seen that in ME the loss of inflectional morphology is well under way but not completed. Thus, we expect to find instances of verb movement at that time, and indeed regarding Verb Second, we did find quite a number of sentences which displayed V-to-I-to-C movement. Concerning the rise of modals, there is agreement in the literature that by the sixteenth century this change must have been completed. The same seems to apply to the rise of *do*-support. As for lexical verbs, by the late-seventeenth century, changes in their distributional behaviour reflects the loss of their ability to move to I.

Although we have seen that Verb Second still existed in ME, we haven't taken a look at V-to-I movement which we will do now by investigating some data from the corpora. From the line of argument we pursued above, we expect lexical verbs to occur in a position to the left of the negation element and adverbs, i.e. outside the VP, as long as V-to-I movement exists (as a rule).

The following examples give evidence for V-to-I movement (for all ME periods in the corpus, i.e. from 1150 to 1500):

(18) a. ðane þu ne **luuest$_V$ noht** þe seluen?
    then you not lovest   not   thee selve
    '... than you don't love yourself.'
    (VICES1,37.447)

b. and ber vp hand, leg or foot, þat þey **hange$_V$ not** doun so pitously,
    and bear up hand, leg or foot that they hang   not down so piteously
    '... and hold up your hand, leg or foot that they don't hang down so piteously.'
    (AELR3,49.741)

c. þus don men þat stondon in science and **worche$_V$ not** aftur by þes
    thus do men that stand   in science and work   not after by this
    science.
    science
    'Thus do men that stand in science and do not obey this science.'
    (WYCSER,590.3802)

    d. *But wayte ye* **make$_V$ not** *many questions with her nor her men,*
       but wait you make not many questions with her nor her men
       '… but wait: 'You don't call into question much concerning her or her men.'
       (MALORY,4.81)

    e. *But lordes & knyghtes & othere noble & worthi men þat* **conne$_V$**
       But lords and knights and other noble and worthy men that can
       not *latyn but lityll*
       not Latin but little
       'But lords, and knights, and other noble and worthy men that know but little Latin …'
       (MANDEV,4.40)

All of the examples in (18) have the finite verb directly preceding the negation element *not*. The example in e. nicely shows the use of *conne* 'can' as a lexical verb: here, it means 'know (Latin)'. In PDE instead we would find *can speak Latin* where the meaning of *can* would express modality ('I am able to speak Latin').

A number of examples in the ME corpus prove that V-to-I movement no longer occurred in a systematic fashion although the examples I found are still quite rare. Take a look yourself:

(19) a. … *3if þou hit* **not fordo$_V$**.
         if thou it not fordo
      'if you don't destroy it.'
      (EDVERN,242.102)

    b. … *þat Seint Ruffus* **not be-gan$_V$** *þis ordr, but þat he reformed þis ordre.*
         that Saint Rufus not began this order but that he reformed this order
      '… that Saint Rufus didn't begin this order but that he reformed this order.'
      (CAPSER,147.42)

    c. … *þat he by his manhede* **doþ$_V$ not** *such þing, whan he by þis kynde*
         that he by his manhood does not such thing, when he by this kind
      doþ$_V$ not *pryncipally þis þing.*
      does not principally this thing
      '… that he by his incarnation as man doesn't do such a thing, when he by nature doesn't principally do this thing.'
      (WYCSER,419.3475)

d. ... *that thei **do**$_{AUX}$ **not synne**$_V$ aȝens the Lord, and wraththe either*
    that they do   not sin   against the lord and rage   or
*veniaunce **come**$_V$ **not** on ȝow, and on ȝoure britheren;*
vengeance comes not on you and on your brethren
'... that they don't sin against the lord, and neither rage nor vengeance comes on you and your brethren.'
(PURVEY,I,23.1111)

The examples in (19) a. and b. show that V-to-I movement has not taken place. The two instances of *do* in c. illustrate that it still has lexical verb character since it occurs with an object (*such þing/þis þing*). The example in d., which is from a text from the end of the 14th century, is a case where *do* has the function of an auxiliary. It was the only case I found in the corpus. Note also that in the second conjunct, the order 'lexical verb-*not*' occurs again.

Apart from these examples we find the use of modals as auxiliaries:

(20) *For which thou **mayst**$_{AUX}$ **not drede**$_V$ be no manere that alle the thinges that*
    for which thou may   not dread by no manner that all the things that
ben anywhere, ...
be anywhere
'for which you may not dread by no means that all the things that are anywhere ...'
(BOETH,436.C1.310)

In (20) the ME modal form *mayst* directly precedes *not* which is followed by the lexical verb *drede* 'dread'. This looks like the modern use of modals; in this context it does not have the status of a lexical verb.

Interestingly, in the EModE corpus V-to-I movement still occurs with a moderate frequency (in all subperiods, i.e. from 1500–1710). Below I give some examples:

(21) a. *... that they **know**$_V$ **not** of, nor will not be conselled therto.*
    '... that they don't know, nor will be counselled in that respect.'
    (APLUMPT-E1-H,168.15)
b. *... and still Jack **forgat**$_V$ **not** the pie, ...*
    '... and still Jack didn't forget the pie, ...'
    (ARMIN-E2-H,13.148)
c. *that he struck an awe and reverence, even into those that **knew**$_V$ **not** his quality;*
    '... that he caused awe and reverence, even in those that didn't know his quality.'
    (BEHN-E3-P1,152.81)

It seems that at that time this movement operation becomes more and more restricted to a number of verbs, for example *know*.

There are some cases where the lexical verb occurs to the right of *not*, i.e. no V-to-I movement has taken place, and where *do*-support is lacking:

(22) a. *We have roast meat, dinner and supper, throughout the weeke; and such meate as you know I **not use**$_V$ to care for;*
'We have roast meat, dinner, and supper throughout the week, and such food as you know I usually don't care for.'
(STRYPE-E3-P1,178.29)

b. *R.R. Shall I so breake my braine To dote vpon you, and ye **not loue**$_V$ vs againe?*
'R.R. Shall I rack my brain so to dote upon you, and you don't love us again?'
(UDALL-E1-P2,L1401.610)

Apart from these patterns, the insertion of the auxiliary *do* becomes more and more frequent:

(23) a. *and told her that if she **did**$_{AUX}$ **not take**$_V$ great heed she knew by her Art that some mischance was neere her: which prooued true*
'... and told her that if she didn't take great heed she knew by her art that some mischance was near her: which proved to be true.'
(JOTAYLOR-E2-P1,3,88.C1.367)

b. *It is like to prove a very troublesome busines, if we **doe**$_{AUX}$ **not agree**$_V$ quickly*
It is likely to prove a very troublesome business if we don't agree quickly.'
(KNYVETT-1620-E2-H,58.87)

c. *Maddam, I **doe**$_{AUX}$ **wryte**$_V$ to you praying not your ladyship to be wroth with my husband for the money that he received of my M=rs= your daughter,*
'Madam, I do write to you praying your ladyship not to be angry with my husband for the money that he received of my Miss, your daughter.'
(ABOTT-E1-P1,229.5)

The examples in (23) a. and b. exhibit the insertion of *do* in negative declaratives. The example in c. contains the use of *do* with an **emphatic meaning**. This reading is quite clear in the sentence because the writer urges the reader not to be angry (see the use of the verb *praying*), and this is emphasised by the writer by using *do*. Note, however, that in EModE times there was no strict rule requiring this reading, which means that in these contexts *do* could be present without having the emphatic meaning. Today, this is no longer the case. In affirmative declaratives it can only be used if the speaker/writer wants to emphasise a positive fact as opposed to its negation. In this case, *do* has to be stressed (which is marked by capitals):

(24)   But you DO love him, don't you?
       *But you do love him.

In the course of time, *do* occurs in more and more contexts and thus replaces the old structures where only the lexical verb sufficed. These contexts are 1) affirmative direct questions (25 a.), 2) negative direct questions (25 b.), 3) negative declaratives (25 c.), 4) negative imperatives (25 d.), and 5) affirmative declaratives (25 e.). Below I give one example for each of these contexts, the examples are from Shakespeare's works.

(25)   a. **Did**$_{AUX}$ this in Caesar **seeme**$_V$ Ambitious?
       b. **Didst**$_{AUX}$ thou **not hear**$_V$ a noyse?
       c. You **do**$_{AUX}$ **not giue**$_V$ the Cheere.
       d. **Do**$_{AUX}$ **not muse**$_V$ at me, my most worthy Friends.
       e. You all **did**$_{AUX}$ **loue**$_V$ him once.

As discussed above, in PDE *do* still occurs in these contexts with the exception that in affirmative declaratives it must have an emphatic meaning, otherwise the sentence is ungrammatical.

The system that has developed from ME to EModE has become fixed and established towards PDE. In the contexts we investigated above, lexical verbs no longer occur in a position left of negation, instead auxiliaries including the modals and *do* occupy that same position. For the sake of completeness, I will conclude with some examples from the corpus of Modern British English (from 1710 to 1914) illustrating the use of *do* and modals in the position to the left of negation (or I):

(26)   a. it may, possibly, be dull to you, when every day **does**$_{AUX}$ **not present**$_V$ you with something new;
           (MONTAGU-1718,118.471)
       b. I **could**$_{AUX}$ **not look**$_V$, without horror, on such numbers of mangled human bodies, ...
           (MONTAGU-1718,87.128)
       c. By this means, they **cannot**$_{AUX}$ **fail**$_V$ of learning the Latin Tongue.
           (ANON-1711,5.25)
       d. There has been found several degrees in bigness of these Spiders, and the colours the same; so that they **do**$_{AUX}$ **not alter**$_V$ or change their colours as they grow bigger.
           (ALBIN-1736,6.125)

e. *When the war began there was hardly a man on either side who **did**$_{AUX}$ **not believe**$_V$ that he was fighting in behalf of constitutional monarchy.*
(OMAN-1895,380.9)

f. *The Parliament made one final attempt to negotiate with the king, only to receive the answer, 'I **will**$_{AUX}$ **not part**$_V$ with these three things - the Church, my crown, and my friends'*
(OMAN-1895,392.276)

Tax: 'Luckily for us, we have travelled through time and also through a number of dimensions, so things sounded familiar.'
Syn: 'Yes, that helped a lot, and thus it is not that difficult to do the following exercises: **1)** which properties did the (pre)modals have in OE times? Give relevant examples to illustrate these properties; **2)** how does Lightfoot explain the change of these verbs? What type of movement are they subject to? **3)** analyse the examples below in terms of the presence/absence of V-to-I and I-to-C movement. Explain the conditions that must be met for these movements to occur.'

(27) a. *And he holt   so moche lond that he knoweth not the ende*
and he holds so much land that he knows   not the end
'And he has so much land that he doesn't know where it ends.'
(MANDEV,26.622)

b. *for sche wyst   not what sche seyde as þei   wende.*
for she knows not what she said   as they made-their-way
'for she doesn't know what she said as they made their way.'
(KEMPE,8.132)

c. *Of al þis I conclude þat he com   nevere at Rome;*
of all this I conclude that he came never at Rome
'From all this I conclude that he never arrived in Rome.'
(POLYCH,VI,221.1595)

d. *Ne   wiste ȝe   not þat I muste be in þe nedys of my Fadyr?*
NEG knows you not that I must be in the needs of my Father
'Don't you know that I must be in need of my Father?'
(CMWYCSER,356.2310)

e. *From hence came the first vse of the Ring in Weddings, to represe t this euennes:*
from hence came the first use of the ring in weddings to represent this occasion
'From this point in time the first use of the ring in weddings came to represent this occasion.'
(SMITH-E2-P1,31.227)

f. *for if you make not a Noise, they hardly think you intent on what you are doing.*
for if you make not a noise they hardly think you intent on what you are doing
'for if you don't make a noise they hardly think you are intent on what you are doing.'
(FRYER-E3-P2,1,215.80)

Tax: 'And here's another one: **4)** analyse the status of *do* in the examples and describe the rise of dummy *do* in the history of English.'

(28) a. *Yf Y do not the werkis of my fadir, nyle   ȝe   bileue to me;*
if I do not the works of my father NEG-will you believe in me
'If I don't do the works of my father you won't believe in me.'
(NTEST,10,20J.1037)

b. *In speakynge these wordes, ye   shal vnderstand, that I do not entend to speake agaynste*
in speaking these words you shall understand that I do not intend to speak against
the strengthe, polysye, and prouision of a kyng,
the strength, policy, and provision of a king
'In speaking these words, you should understand that I don't intend to speak against the strength, policy, and provision of a king.'
(LATIMER-E1-H,32L.236)

c. *If thou do not say they eate like the prodigall Childe with thy   fellow hogs, ...*
If you do not say they eat like the prodigal child with your fellow hogs
'If you don't say they eat like the prodigal child with your fellow swine ...'
(DELONEY-E2-P2,52.338)

Tax: 'Before we come to an end we will summarise again what we have learnt in this chapter. First of all, we have seen that the theoretical concept of (verb) movement analyses and explains the observation that lexical verbs occur in different positions in the history of English.

Syn: 'And we have also dealt with two types of movement, V-to-I and V-to-I-to-C movement. V-to-I movement can be identified by assuming that a negation element or VP-adverbs indicate the left edge of the VP. Under this assumption, lexical verbs occurring to the left are outside the VP, and those occurring to the right are inside the VP. In terms of movement, lexical verbs occurring to the left of these elements have moved out of the VP, from the V position to the I position. Lexical verbs that occur to the right of these elements have not undergone such movement. V-to-I-to-C movement, which has been dealt with before under the name of Verb Second, can be identified by assuming that the finite verb inverts with the subject in main declaratives which are introduced either by objects, adverbs and PPs, or *wh*-elements and negation. In this case, the finite lexical verb undergoes movement from the V position inside VP, to the I position and the C position.'

Tax: 'We have further seen that this type of movement is head movement which is subject to the *Head Movement Constraint*. Concerning the development of these two types of movement, it was shown that a number of changes occurred. Lexical verbs lost their ability to move to the I position, and today's modals along with *do* lost their status of lexical verbs resulting in I-insertion. An explanation for these changes could be the loss of inflectional morphology in English. Lexical verbs lost person inflection and therefore could no longer move out of the VP. To support an unsupported tense, modals and *do* which had become auxiliaries, came to be inserted in the I position to mark agreement and tense properties of the sentence. It was said that at the end of the EModE period these changes were completed, and this system was fixed. This explains why in PDE auxiliaries appear in front of negation whereas lexical verbs appear to the right.'

Literature: Lightfoot (1979) discusses the reanalysis of the English modals as auxiliaries in a theoretical (generative) framework for the first time. Roberts (1985) reconsiders Lightfoot's analysis and states that English has lost V-to-I movement. The author further attempts to relate the loss of this movement operation to impoverished verbal morphology. In Lightfoot (1991) and Lightfoot (1999) the topic is taken up again and discussed in terms of acquisition and learnability (especially in the 1999 book). Warner (1993) is a comprehensive and thorough empirical investigation of the history of the

English auxiliaries. It further critically discusses Lightfoot's 1979 assumptions. Denison (1985) deals with the rise of *do* support and claims that the auxiliary developed from an earlier raising/control verb which had a bare infinitive complement. Vikner (1997) states that there is a correlation between V-to-I movement and agreement inflection, and that this correlation only holds in VO languages. In the third part of Roberts (1993) verb movement in the history of English is discussed. The author claims that the changes which can be observed are due to changes in the internal structure of the Infl head. Moreover, the book is very valuable from a comparative perspective because a number of English and French syntactic constructions are compared and analysed in the Principles and Parameters framework.

Epilogue

Syn: 'So is this the end of the story? I actually started to enjoy dealing with, and living in the world of, syntax.'
Tax: 'No, it's just the end of the book! There are many more things that could be said about this topic, don't you think?'
Syn: 'Yeah, you're right. For example, we could take a look into the future and ask ourselves which further developments of English we could expect. The negation *not* springs to mind and the question of whether the reduced form will gradually vanish.'
Tax: 'Yes, and another question could be whether 'residual Verb Second' will eventually disappear.'
Syn: 'Hmm, that's right. Then, if we think about grammatical theory many would want to know if a model like generative syntax or dependency grammar can be used and applied to other fields.'
Tax: 'Good question! And I even have an answer because I have seen corpora with syntactic annotation! So if you're searching for a syntactic pattern like Verb Second you can query the corpus accordingly with a special tool, and the result you get will be presented in trees!'
Syn: 'This is a great example! It shows that other fields like corpus linguistics work with the theoretical models we have come across during our syntactic enterprise. Shall we discuss it?'
Tax: 'No, let's go now. This is an entire new story that will be told elsewhere…'

Bibliography

Abney, S. (1987). *The English Noun Phrase in its Sentential Aspect*. MIT, Ph-Diss. Cambridge, Mass.
Adger, D. and Smith, J. (2010) "Variation in agreement: a lexical feature-based approach". *Lingua*, (120):1109–1134.
Allen, C. L. (1995). *Case marking and reanalysis: grammatical relations from Old to Early Modern English*. Clarendon Press, Oxford.
Allen, C. L. (1997) "Investigating the origins of the 'group genitive' in English". *Transactions of the Philological Society*, 22(2):375–409.
Anderwald, L. (2008). *Negation in non-standard British English: Gaps, Regularizations and Asymmetries*. Routledge Studies in Germanic Linguistics 8. Routledge, London, New York.
Anderwald, L. (2009). *The Morphology of English Dialects: Verb-Formation in Non-Standard English*. Cambridge University Press, Cambridge.
Axel, K. (2007). *Studies on Old High German Syntax: Left Sentence Periphery, Verb Placement and Verb-Second*. Benjamins, Amsterdam/Philadelphia.
Baker, M. (2001). *The atoms of language*. Oxford University Press, Oxford.
Baker, P. S. (2003). *Introduction to Old English*. Blackwell, Oxford.
Barsky, R. F. (1997). *Noam Chomsky. A life of dissent*. MIT Press, Cambridge, Mass.
Baugh, A. C. and Cable, T. (2005). *A History of the English Language*. Routledge, London, 5th edition.
Beal, J. C. (2004). *English in Modern Times. 1700-1945*. Arnold, London.
Beal, J. C. (2006). *Language and Region*. Routledge, London and New York.
Biberauer, T. and Roberts, I. (2008) "Cascading parameter changes: internally driven change in Middle and Early Modern English". In Eythórsson, T., editor, *Grammatical change and linguistic theory: the Rosendal papers*, pages 79–113. Benjamins, Amsterdam/Philadelphia.
Blake, N., editor (1992). *The Cambridge History of the English Language*, volume II. Cambridge University Press, Cambridge.
Bloomfield, L. (1935). *Language*. Holt, Rinehart and Winston, New York.
Bornstein, D. (1976). *Readings in the theory of grammar: From the 17th to the 20th century*. Winthrop, Cambridge, MA.
Bresnan, J. (1978) "A realistic transformational grammar". In Halle, M. et al., editors, *Linguistic theory and psychological reality*, pages 1–58. MIT Press, Cambridge, Mass.
Brown, K. (1991) "Double Modals in Hawick Scots". In P. Trudgill, J. C., editor, *Dialects of English: studies in grammatical variation*, pages 115–165. Longman, London.
Bursill-Hall, G. L. (1971). *Speculative Grammars of the Middle Ages: The Doctrine of Partes Orationis of the Modistae*. Approaches to Semiotics 11. Mouton, The Hague.
Bussmann, H. (1996). *Routledge Dictionary of Language and Linguistics*. Routledge, London.
Campbell, A. (2003). *Old English Grammar*. Clarendon Press, Oxford.
Cardinaletti, A. and Roberts, I. (2002) "Clause structure and X-second". In Cinque, G., editor, *Functional Structure in DP and IP: the Cartography of Syntactic Structures*, volume 1, pages 123–166. Oxford University Press, Oxford.
Carroll, J. B., editor (1956). *Language, thought and reality: selected writings of Benjamin Lee Whorf*. Technology Press of Massachusetts Institute of Technology, Cambridge, MA.
Chambers, J. and Trudgill, P. (1980). *Dialectology*. Cambridge University Press, Cambridge.
Chomsky, N. (1957). *Syntactic Structures*. Mouton, The Hague/Paris.
Chomsky, N. (1965). *Aspects of the Theory of Syntax*. MIT, Cambridge Mass.
Chomsky, N. (1966). *Cartesian Linguistics: A Chapter in the History of Rationalist Thought*. Language Studies. Harper and Row, New York.

Chomsky, N. (1981). *Lectures on Government and Binding. The Pisa Lectures*. Foris, Dordrecht.
Chomsky, N. (1986). *Knowledge of language. Its nature, origin, and use*. Praeger, New York.
Chomsky, N. (1988). *Language and problems of knowledge. The Managua Lectures*. Praeger, New York.
Chomsky, N. (1993) "A Minimalist Program for Linguistic Theory". In Hale, K. and Keyser, S., editors, *The View from Building 20. Essays in Linguistics in Honor of Sylvain Bromberger*. MIT Press, Cambridge Mass.
Chomsky, N. (1995). *The Minimalist Program*. MIT Press, Cambridge, Mass.
Chomsky, N. (2002). *Syntactic Structures*. Mouton, reprint of 1957, The Hague.
Chomsky, N. (2009). *Cartesian Linguistics: A Chapter in the History of Rationalist Thought*. Language Studies. Cambridge University Press, edited with a new introduction by James McGilvray, New York.
Cook, V. and Newson, M. (2007). *Chomsky's Universal Grammar*. Blackwell, Oxford.
Dahl, Ö. (1979) "Typology of Sentence Negation". *Linguistics*, (17):79–106.
den Besten, H. (1983) "On the Interaction of Root Transformation and Lexical Deletive Rules". In Abraham, W., editor, *On the Formal Syntax of the Westgermania*, pages 47–138. Benjamins, Amsterdam/Philadelphia.
den Besten, H. (1985) "The Ergative Hypothesis and Free Word Order in Dutch and German". In Toman, J., editor, *Studies in German grammar*, pages 23–65. Foris, Dordrecht.
Denison, D. (1985) "The origins of periphrastic do: Ellegård and Visser reconsidered". In Eaton, R., Fischer, O., Koopman, W., and v. d. Leek, F., editors, *Papers from the 4th International Conference on English Historical Linguistics*, pages 45–50, Amsterdam/Philadelphia. Benjamins.
Egli, U. (1986) "Stoic Syntax and Semantics". *Historiographia Linguistica: International Journal for the History of the Language Sciences/Revue Internationale pour l'Histoire*, 13(2-3):281–306.
Fillmore, C. (1968) "The Case for Case". In Bach, E. and Harms, R. T., editors, *Universals in Linguistic Theory*, pages 1–90. Holt Linehart Winston, New York.
Fillmore, C. (2003) "Valency and Semantic Roles: the Concept of Deep Structure Case". In Vilmos Ágel, L. M. E. e. a., editor, *Dependenz und Valenz: ein internationales Handbuch der zeitgenössischen Forschung.*, volume I, chapter 36, pages 457–475. Mouton de Gruyter.
Fischer, O., van Kemenade, A., Koopman, W., and van der Wurff, W. (2000). *The syntax of early English*. Cambridge University Press, Cambridge.
Freeborn, D. (2006). *From Old English to Standard English. A Course Book in Language Variation across Time*. Palgrave Macmillan Press, London, 3rd edition.
Fuß, E. and Trips, C. (2002) "Variation and Change in Old and Middle English - on the validity of the Double Base Hypothesis". *Journal of Comparative Germanic Linguistics*, (4):171–224.
Greenbaum, S. and Quirk, R. (1990). *A student's grammar of the English language*. Longman, London.
Grewendorf, G. (2002). *Minimalistische Syntax*. Francke, UTB Sprachwissenschaft 2313, Tübingen.
Grewendorf, G. (2006). *Noam Chomsky*. Beck, Beck'sche Reihe: bsr - Denker; 547, München.
Haeberli, E. (2002) "Inflectional morphology and the loss of verb second in English". In Lightfoot, D., editor, *Syntactic Effects of Morphological Change*, pages 88–106. Oxford University Press, Oxford.
Haeberli, E. and Pintzuk, S. (2006) "Revisiting verb (projection) raising in Old English". *York Papers in Linguistics Series 2*, 2(6):77–94.
Haegeman, L. (2001). *Introduction to government and binding theory*. Blackwell, Oxford.
Haegeman, L. (2006). *Thinking Syntactically. A Guide to Argumentation and Analysis*. Blackwell, Oxford.
Haegeman, L. and Guéron, J. (1999). *English grammar: a generative perspective*. Blackwell, Oxford.
Harris, Z. (1951). *Methods in Structural Linguistics*. Chicago University Press, Chicago.

Hasty, D. (2011) "I Might Not Would Say That: A Sociolinguistic Study of Double Modal Acceptance". *University of Pennsylvania Working Papers in Linguistics*, 17(2):90–98.

Hasty, D. (2012) "We might should oughta take a second look at this: A syntactic re-analysis of double modals in Southern United States English". *Lingua*, (122):1716–1738.

Hawkins, J. A. (1979) "Implicational universals as predictors of word order change". *Language*, (55):618–48.

Hawkins, J. A. (2014). *Cross-Linguistic Variation and Efficiency*. Oxford University Press.

Hickey, R., editor (2010). *The Handbook of Language Contact*. Wiley-Blackwell, Oxford.

Hockett, C. F. (1958). *A course in modern linguistics*. Macmillan Press, New York.

Hogg, R., editor (1992). *The Cambridge History of the English Language*, volume I. Cambridge University Press, Cambridge.

Hogg, R. (2007). *An Introduction to Old English*. Edinburgh University Press, [Edinburgh textbooks on the English language], Edinburgh.

Hogg, R. and Denison, D., editors (2008). *A History of the English Language*. Cambridge University Press, Cambridge.

Horobin, S. and Smith, J. (2003). *An Introduction to Middle English*. Edinburgh University Press, [Edinburgh textbooks on the English language], Edinburgh.

Hunt, R. W. (1980). *The history of grammar in the Middle Ages: Collected papers*. Amsterdam studies in the theory and history of linguistic science : Series III, Studies in the history of the language sciences. Benjamins, Amsterdam.

Iatridou, S. and Kroch, A. (1992) "The Licensing of CP-recursion and its Relevance to the Germanic Verb-Second Phenomenon". *Working Papers in Scandinavian Syntax*, (50):1–24.

Jackendoff, R. (1972). *Semantic Interpretation in Generative Grammar*. MIT, Cambridge, Mass.

Jankowsky, K. R. (1972). *The neogrammarians. A re-evaluation of their place in the development of linguistic science*. Mouton, The Hague, Paris.

Jespersen, O. (1917). *Negation in English and other Languages*. Bianco Lunos Bogtrykkeri, Copenhagen.

Joly, A. and Stefanini, J., editors (1977). *La Grammaire generale: Des modistes aux ideologues*. Publications de l'Université de Lille III, Lille.

Jungen, O. and Lohnstein, H. (2006). *Einführung in die Grammatiktheorie*. Fink, UTB 2676, Sprachwissenschaft, Literaturwissenschaft, München; Paderborn.

Jungen, O. and Lohnstein, H. (2007). *Geschichte der Grammatiktheorie. Von Dionysios Thrax bis Noam Chomsky*. Fink, München.

Kayne, R. (1994). *The Antisymmetry of Syntax*, volume 25 of *Linguistic Inquiry Monograph*. MIT Press, Cambridge, Mass.

Kiparsky, P. (1995) "Indo-European Origins of Germanic Syntax". In Roberts, I. and Battye, A., editors, *Clause Structure and Language Change*, pages 140–167. Oxford University Press, Oxford.

Kloss, H. (1952). *Die Entwicklung neuer germanischer Kultursprachen von 1800-1950*. Pohl, München.

Kortmann, Bernd, E. S. et al. (2005). *A Handbook of Varieties of English: A Multimedia Reference Tool*. Mouton de Gruyter, Berlin.

Kroch, A. (1989) "Reflexes of Grammar in Patterns of language change". *Language Variation and Change*, (1):199–244.

Kroch, A. and Taylor, A. (1997) "Verb movement in Old and Middle English: Dialect variation and language contact". In Kemenade, A. v. and Vincent, N., editors, *Parameters of Morphosyntactic Change*, pages 297–325. Cambridge University Press, Cambridge.

Kroch, A. and Taylor, A. (2000) "Verb-Object Order in Early Middle English". In Kemenade, A. v. and Vincent, N., editors, *Diachronic Syntax. Models and Mechanisms*, pages 132–164. Oxford University Press, Oxford.

Kroch, A., Taylor, A., and Ringe, D. (2000) "The Middle English Verb-second Constraint: A Case Study in Language Contact and Language Change". In Herring, S., Schoesler, L., and van Reenen, P., editors, *Textual Parameters in Older Language*, pages 353–391. Benjamins, Amsterdam/Philadelphia.

König, E. and Gast, V. (2008). *Understanding English-German Contrasts*. Number 29. Erich Schmidt Verlag, Berlin.

Labov, W. (1972a). *Language in the Inner City: Studies in the Black English Vernacular*. University of Pennsylvania Press, Philadelphia.

Labov, W. (1972b). *Sociolinguistic Patterns*. University of Pennsylvania Press, Philadelphia.

Labov, W. (2001). *Principles of Linguistic Change. Social factors*, volume 2. Blackwell, Oxford.

Lamprecht, A. (1986). *Grammatik der englischen Sprache*. Cornelsen, Berlin.

Land, S. K. (1986). *The Philosophy of Language in Britain: Major Theories from Hobbes to Thomas Reid*. AMS Press, New York.

Lass, R., editor (1999). *The Cambridge History of the English Language, Vol. 3: 1476-1776*. Cambridge University Press, Cambridge.

Law, V. (1993). *History of linguistic thought in the early Middle Ages*, volume 71. Benjamins, Amsterdam studies in the theory and history of linguistic science. Series III, Studies in the history of the language sciences, Amsterdam/Philadelphia.

Law, V. (1997). *Grammar and Grammarians in the Early Middle Ages*. Longman, London.

Law, V. (2003). *The History of linguistics in Europe from Plato to 1600*. Cambridge University Press, Cambridge.

Lightfoot, D. (1979). *Principles of Diachronic Syntax*. Cambridge University Press, Cambridge.

Lightfoot, D. (1991). *How to Set Parameters*. MIT Press, Cambridge, Mass.

Lightfoot, D. (1999). *The Development of Language: Acquisition, Change and Evolution*. Blackwell, Oxford.

Lightfoot, D., editor (2002). *Syntactic effects of morphological change*. Oxford University Press, Oxford.

Lowth, R. (1799). *A short introduction to English grammar*. R. Aitken, reprint of 1762, Philadelphia.

Matthews, P. H. (1993). *Grammatical theory in the United States from Bloomfield to Chomsky*. Cambridge University Press, Cambridge.

McMahon, A. (1994). *Understanding Language Change*. Cambridge University Press, Cambridge.

MED online (2001). *Middle English Dictionary online*. Michigan University, Michigan.

Mitchell, B. (1985). *Old English Syntax*. Clarendon, Oxford.

Mitchell, B. (1995). *An Invitation to Old English & Anglo-Saxon England*. Blackwell, Oxford.

Mitchell, B. and Robinson, F. C. (2003). *A guide to Old English*. Blackwell, Oxford, 6th edition.

Mossé, F. (1991). *Handbook of Middle English*. The Johns Hopkins University Press, reprint of 1952, Baltimore and London.

Müller, S. (2013). *Grammatiktheorie*. Stauffenburg Verlag, Stauffenburg Einführungen 20, Tübingen, 2nd edition.

Müller, S. (2014). *Grammatical theory: from transformational grammar to constraint-based approaches*. Language Science Press, Lecture notes in language sciences 1, Berlin.

Nevalainen, T. (1998) "Social mobility and the decline of multiple negation in Early Modern English". In Fisiak, J. and Krygier, M., editors, *advances in english historical linguistics (1996)*, pages 263–291. Mouton de Gruyter, Berlin.

Nevalainen, T. (2006). *An introduction to Early Modern English*. Edinburgh University Press, [Edinburgh textbooks on the English language], Edinburgh.

Newmeyer, F. (1986). *Linguistic Theory in America*. Academic Press, Orlando.

Osborne, T. (2005) "Coherence: A dependency grammar analysis". *SKY Journal of Linguistics*, (18):223–286.

Padley, G. A. (1976). *Grammatical theory in Western Europe 1500-1700. The Latin Tradition*. Cambridge University Press, Cambridge.
Padley, G. A. (1985/1988). *Grammatical theory in Western Europe 1500-1700. Trends in Vernacular Grammar*. Cambridge University Press, Cambridge. two volumes.
Parret, H., editor (1976). *History of Linguistic Thought and Contemporary Linguistics*. Foundations of Communication. de Gruyter, Berlin.
Paul, H. (1990). *Prinzipien der Sprachgeschichte*. Niemeyer, reprint of 1880, Halle.
Pintzuk, S. (1991). *Phrase Structures in Competition: Variation and Change in Old English*. PhD thesis, University of Philadelphia, Philadelphia.
Pintzuk, S. (1999). *Phrase Structures in Competition: Variation and Change in Old English*. Garland, New York.
Pintzuk, S. and Kroch, A. (1989) "The Rightward Movement of Complements and Adjuncts in the Old English Beowulf". *Language Variation and Change*, (1):115–143.
Pintzuk, S. and Taylor, A. (2006) "The Loss of OV Order in the History of English". In van Kemenade, A. and Los, B., editors, *Blackwell Handbook of the history of English*, chapter 11, pages 249–279. Blackwell, Oxford.
Pollock, J.-Y. (1989) "Verb-Movement, Universal Grammar, and the Structure of IP". *Linguistic Inquiry*, 20:365–424.
Quirk, R., Greenbaum, S., et al. (2004). *A Comprehensive Grammar of the English Language*. Longman, London.
Radford, A. (1997). *Syntactic theory and the structure of English*. Cambridge University Press, Cambridge.
Radford, A. et al. (1999). *Linguistics. An introduction*. Cambridge University Press, Cambridge.
Reinhart, T. (1976). *The syntactic domain of anaphora*. PhD thesis, MIT, Cambridge, Mass.
Rizzi, L. (1982). *Issues in Italian Syntax*. Foris, Dordrecht.
Rizzi, L. (1990) "Speculations on verb second". In Mascaró, J. and Nespor, M., editors, *Grammar in Progress: A Festschrift for Henk van Riemsdijk*, pages 375–385. Foris, Dordrecht.
Rizzi, L. (1996) "Residual Verb Second and the Wh-criterion". In Belletti, A. and Rizzi, L., editors, *Parameters and functional heads*, pages 63–90. Oxford University Press, Oxford.
Roberts, I. (1985) "Agreement parameters and the development of English modal auxiliaries.". *Natural Language and Linguistic Theory*, (3):21–58.
Roberts, I. (1993). *Verbs and Diachronic Syntax: A Comparative History of English and French*. Kluwer, Dordrecht.
Roberts, I. (1997) "Directionality and Word Order Change in the History of English". In van Kemenade, A. and Vincent, N., editors, *Parameters of Morphosyntactic Change*, pages 397–426. Cambridge University Press, Cambridge.
Roberts, I. G. (2007). *Diachronic Syntax*. Oxford University Press, Oxford.
Robins, R. H. (1985). *Ancient and Mediaeval Grammatical Theory in Europe: With Particular Reference to Modern Linguistic Doctrine*. University Microfilms International, Ann Arbor and Mich.
Robins, R. H. (1993). *The Byzantine grammarians: Their place in history*. Trends in linguistics : Studies and monographs. Mouton de Gruyter, Berlin and New York.
Robins, R. H. (1994). *A Short History of Linguistics*. Longman, London, 3rd edition.
Ross, J. R. (1967). *Constraints on Variables in Syntax*. PhD thesis, MIT, Cambridge, Mass.
Rowicka, G. J. (2006) "Canada: Language Situation". In Brown, K., editor, *Encyclopedia of Language and Linguistics*. Elsevier Science.
Rögnvaldsson, E. and Thráinsson, H. (1990) "On Icelandic Word Order Once More". In Maling, J. and Zaenen, A., editors, *Modern Icelandic Syntax*, number 24 in Syntax and Semantics, pages 3–40. Academic Press, New York.

Santorini, B. (1995) "Two Types of Verb Second in the History of Yiddish". In Andrew Battye, I. R., editor, *Clause Structure and Language Change*, pages 53–79. Oxford University Press, Oxford.
Sapir, E. (1970). *Language. An introduction to the study of speech*. Rupert Hart-Davis, reprint of [1921], London.
Saussure, F. d. (1969). *Cours de linguistique générale*. publié par Charles Bally et Albert Sechehaye avec la collaboration de Albert Riedlinger. Payot, Paris, 5 edition.
Smith, J. (1991). *Essentials of Early English*. Routledge, London.
Sobin, N. (2011). *Syntactic analysis. The basics*. Wiley-Blackwell, Oxford.
Stein, A. (2010). *Einführung in die französische Sprachwissenschaft*. Sammlung Metzler; 307. Metzler, Stuttgart, 3rd edition.
Sturtevant, E. H. (1947). *An Introduction to Linguistic Science*. Yale University Press, New Haven.
Swiggers, P. (2002). *Grammatical Theory and Philosophy of Language in Antiquity*, volume 19 of *Orbis Supplementa*. Peeters, Leuven.
Taylor, D. J., editor (1987). *The history of linguistics in the classical period*. Benjamins, Amsterdam/Philadelphia.
Tesnière, L. (1965). *Éléments de syntaxe structurale*. Klincksieck, Paris, 2nd edition.
Tesnière, L. (2015). *Elements of Structural Syntax*. Benjamins, Amsterdam/Philadelphia, translated by timothy osborne and sylvain kahane edition.
Thiersch, C. (1978). *Topics in German Syntax*. PhD thesis, MIT, Cambridge, Mass.
Thomason, S. G. and Kaufman, T. (1988). *Language contact, creolization and genetic linguistics*. University of California Press, Berkeley.
Tieken-Boon van Ostade, I., editor (2008). *Grammars, Grammarians and Grammar-Writing in Eighteenth Century England*. Mouton de Gruyter, Topics in English Linguistics 59, Berlin, New York.
Travis, L. (1984). *Parameters and effects of word order variation*. PhD thesis, MIT, Cambridge, Mass.
Trips, C. (2002). *From OV to VO in Early Middle English*. Benjamins, Amsterdam/Philadelphia.
Trips, C. and Fuss, E. (2009) "The syntax and semantics of the temporal anaphor "then" in Old and Middle English". In Alexiadou, A., Hankamer, J., McFadden, T., Nuger, J., and Schäfer, F., editors, *Advances in Comparative Germanic Syntax*, number 141 in Linguistik Aktuell, pages 171–195. John Benjamins, Amsterdam/Philadelphia.
Trudgill, P. (1974). *The Social Differentiation of English in Norwich*. Cambridge University Press, London.
Trudgill, P. and Chambers, J. K., editors (1991). *Dialects of English: Studies in Grammatical Variation*. Longman, London.
van Kemenade, A. (1987). *Syntactic case and morphological case in the history of English*. Foris, Dordrecht.
van Valin, R. (2001). *An introduction to syntax*. Cambridge University Press, Cambridge.
Vikner, S. (1995). *Verb Movement and expletive subjects in the Germanic Languages*. Oxford University Press, Oxford.
Vikner, S. (1997) "V-to-I movement and Inflection for Person in all Tenses". In *The new comparative syntax*, pages 189–213. Longman, London.
Visser, F. T. (1963-1973). *An Historical Syntax of the English Language*. E. J. Brill, Leiden.
von Humboldt, W. (1960). *Über die Verschiedenheit des menschlichen Sprachbaues und ihren Einfluß auf die geistige Entwickelung des Menschengeschlechts*. Dümmlerbuch. Dümmler, reprint of 1836, Bonn; Hannover; Hamburg; München.
Wagner, S. (2005) "English dialects in the Southwest: morphology and syntax". In Kortmann, B., Burridge, K., Mesthrie, R., Schneider, E. W., and Upton, C., editors, *A Handbook of Varieties of English: A Multimedia Reference Tool*, volume II, pages 154–175. Mouton de Gruyter.
Warner, A. (1993). *English Auxiliaries: Structure and History*. Cambridge University Press, Cambridge.

Weinreich, U., Labov, W., and Herzog, M. I. (1968) "Empirical Foundations for a Theory of Language Change". In Lehmann, W. P. and Malkiel, Y., editors, *Directions for Historical Linguistics. A Symposium*, pages 95–195. University of Texas Press, Austin/London.

Index

A
abstract case 83
academy 31
acceptance 30
actant 87
adjunct 77, 88
affix hopping 118, 211
Age 99
agglutinating 36
agreement 18, 20, 81, 83, 85, 114, 118, 155
allophone 44
analogical levelling 160
analogy 11, 41
analytic 36
anomaly 11
arbitrariness 11, 43
argument 77, 86, 88, 113
argument structure 87
Aristotle 6
ars grammatica 9
Aspects model 59
asymmetric Verb Second 193

B
basic word order 173
Behagel, Otto 39
behaviorism 49, 54
Bilaterality 43
binary parameter 173
Bloomfield, Leonard 45
Boas, Franz 45
Bopp, Franz 35
bridge verb 107, 194
Brugmann, Karl 39
Bullokar, William 28

C
Case Grammar 87, 89
Case Theory 58
c-command 83, 153
Cicero 27
circumstant 87
classification 46
clause 68
codification 31, 32

cognate 40
Colet, John 28
comparative linguistics 29, 35
competence 30, 54
complement 57
complementiser 120
complex sentence 69
compound sentence 69
concord 81
congruency 81
congruitas 18, 20
constituency model 13
constituent 47, 51, 71–74, 136, 189, 196
constituent negation 78, 142
constructional homonymity 51, 52
coordination 69, 74
corpus 50
correlative 17

D
Danish 102
Dante 26
declension 160
deep level 117
deep structure 51, 53, 59
deletion 74
dependency 21
dependency grammar 4, 47
dependency model 13
dependency relation 21, 81, 85
dependent 47
dependent clause 69
descriptive 3, 33
descriptive adequacy 55
descriptive grammars 18
diachrony 4, 40, 43, 44
diffusion 31
diglossia 27
discontinuous 166
discovery procedures 46, 51
distributionalism 45, 46, 49, 54
ditransitive 87
dominance 120
Donatus, Aelius 12
do-support 138, 217, 220

Double Base Hypothesis 177
double modal 96, 99
DP-Hypothesis 86
D-structure 55, 117, 209
Dutch 102

E
E(xternalised)-language 54
Education 99
elaboration of function 31
emphatic meaning 220
empiricism 26, 29, 38
enérgeia 39, 42
epistemic value 98
ergon 39, 42
explanatory adequacy 55
expletive pro-drop 130
external change 184
extraposition 177

F
family tree theory 35
female teacher grammarians 33
Firbas, Jan 45
First Germanic Consonant Shift 39
Fisher, Ann 33
foregrounding 74
French 103
fronting 73
functional grammar 4
functional phonetics 44
functional sentence perspective 45

G
Gender 99
General grammar 30
Generative Grammar 4, 30
Generative Semantics 60
generative transformational grammar 53
glossematics 45
governee 82, 84
government 13, 81, 83, 85, 88, 153, 155
governor 47, 82, 84, 85, 153
grammar 3
grammars in competition 180, 182
grammatical (structural) borrowing 182
grammatical subject 71
grammatical theory 3
grammaticality 50

Grimm, Jakob 35, 39
Grimm's Law 39, 40
group genitive 166

H
Harris, Zellig 45, 46, 49
head 57, 153
head movement 210
Head Movement Constraint 213
head parameter 57
Head-driven Phrase Structure Grammar 62
head-final 156, 173
head-initial 173
historical linguistics 35
Hjelmslev, Louis 45
Humanists 26
Humboldt, Wilhelm von 36, 38, 46, 50

I
I(nternalised)-language 54
Icelandic 102
identity 100
I-insertion 216
immediate constituent analysis 47
i-mutation 41
incorporating 37
Indo-European 35, 36, 39
Infl 114, 115, 174
inflectional 36
inherent case 158
inner organ 38
innere Sprachform 39
internal change 184
Interpretive Semantics 89
intransitive 87
introspection 46
isolating 36
isomorphism 12
I-to-C movement 121, 213, 214

J
Jakobson, Roman 44
Jespersen's cycle 147
Johnson, Samuel 32
Jones, Sir William 35

L
langage 42
language acquisition 26, 54, 55, 90, 91

language acquisition device 54
language contact 79, 182, 203
language diversity 29
language typology 36
langue 30, 42
left-adjoined 116
leftward movement 173
Lexical Functional Grammar 60, 89
lexis 9
Lily, William 28
linear precedence 120
Linearity 44
linguistic sign 43
local operation 213
Locality Principle 56
locative inversion 204
logic 8
Logical Form 60
logical problem of language change 184
logical subject 71
lógos 7, 9
lowering 118
Lowth, Robert 32

M
main clause 69
maintenance 31
marked 73
Martin of Dacia 23
Mathesius, Villém 44
m-command 153
merge 113
Minimalist Program 60
modal 96, 215–217, 219
Modists 22
modus significandi 22
movement 56, 112, 117, 207

N
naturalist-conventionalist debate 7
negative concord 95, 142, 146
negative concord languages 79
Neogrammarians 39, 42
neutralisation 85, 159
nominal agreement 81, 151
Nominalists 24
non-agreement 97
non-negative concord languages 79
notational subject 71

null subject 59, 71, 93, 130
null subject parameter 92, 93

O
observational adequacy 55
ónoma 7
OV approach 173

P
Palsgrave, John 27
paradigmatic 43
parameters 55, 90
parametric variation 99, 100
parole 30, 42, 45
particular grammar 30
passivisation 85, 159
Paul, Hermann 39
performance 30, 54
phōnē 9, 44
phoneme 44, 46
Phonetic Form 60
phonological attrition 160
phrase marker 52
phrase structure rules 51, 53, 59
Plato 6
Plato's problem 54
polysynthetic 37
positive attitude 100
poverty of the stimulus 54
practical grammar 19, 33
Prague School 44
predicatum 21
premodal 216
prescription 31, 32
prescriptive 3
prestige 99
preterite-present verb 216
primary linguistic data 54, 90
principle of linguistic relativity 38, 46
principles 55, 90
Priscian 13
Projection Principle 58
pronoun exchange 97

Q
question formation 73
Quintillian, Marcus Fabius 10

R
raising 118

rationalism 29, 38
reanalysis 216
recategorisation 216
rection 82
regimen 20
regulae 11, 15
Regularity Hypothesis 40
residual Verb Second 106, 109
response 46
resumptive pronoun 104
rewrite rules 52
rhéma 7
rheme 45
rhetoric 4
rightward movement 173
root sense 98

S

Sanctius 29
Sapir, Edward 45
Sapir-Whorf hypothesis 38, 46
Satzperspektive 45
Saussure, Ferdinand de 4, 42, 43
Schlegel, August Wilhelm 35
Schleicher, August 35
Scholastic 15
School of Port-Royal 30
Schulgrammatik 11, 12, 15
scrambling 175
segmentation 46
selection 30
semantic equivalence 98
semantic role 87
sentence negation 78, 95, 142
sentence-medial 171
Seven Liberal Arts 16
signified 43
signifier 43
simple sentence 68
Skinner, Burrhus Frederic 46
sociolinguistic variable 97
Socrates 6
Sophists 6
sound change 39, 41
specifier-head relation 86, 153
speculative 19
Sprachform 39
S-structure 55, 117, 209
standard 96

Stiernhielm, Georg 28
stimulus 46
Stoics 8
strong inflection 120
strong verbs 152
structural case 157
structuralism 42
Sturtevant's Paradox 41
subiectum 21
subject-auxiliary inversion 56, 77
subject-drop 71, 130
subject-verb agreement 81, 151
subject-verb inversion 77, 106, 189, 201, 208, 214
subordination 69
substitution 72
surface level 117
surface structure 53, 59
Swedish 102
symmetric Verb Second 193
synchronic variation 198
synchrony 4, 43, 44
syncretism 151
syntactic variation 95, 97, 98, 177, 180, 185
syntagmatic 42
syntax 4, 32
synthetic 36
system 42, 44

T

T(ense) 174
taxonomic structuralism 45
tekhnē grammatikē 9
Tesnière, Lucien 47
thematic roles 87
thematic subject 71
theme 45
Theory of Government & Binding 57, 82, 209
Theory of Principles & Parameters 55, 90, 102
Theta Criterion 58, 87
Theta Theory 58
Thrax, Dionysius 9
T-model 60
transformation 117, 209
transformational derivations 51
transformational rules 53
transitive 21, 81, 83, 87, 102, 113
transitivity 13, 20
Tree Adjoining Grammar 62

tres linguae sacrae 26
Trubetzkoy, Nikolaj 44

U
Unification Grammar 62
universal 19, 29, 39, 54, 56
Universal Grammar 23, 30, 54, 55
universals 29
unmarked 73

V
Vachek, Josef 44
valence 87
valency 87
valency grammar 4
valeur 43
variable rules 98
variationist sociolinguistics 97
variety 27, 30, 78, 96, 127, 142, 161
Varro, Marcus Terentius 10
verb (projection) raising 176
verb movement 121, 203, 209, 212, 214, 216
verb raising 176
Verb Second 102, 188
Verb Third 104, 195, 198

vernacular 27–29
Verner, Karl 39
Verner's Law 40
verse grammar 15
VO approach 173
VP-adverb-verb inversion 209
VP-internal subject hypothesis 113
V-to-I movement 213, 217, 219
V-to-I-to-C movement 121, 217

W
wave model 36
weak inflection 120
weak verbs 152
William of Ockham 24

X
X-bar Theory 57, 60, 82

Y
Yiddish 108

Z
Zeno of Citium 8

www.ingramcontent.com/pod-product-compliance
Lightning Source LLC
Chambersburg PA
CBHW030618230426
43661CB00053B/2054